Standing Ovations for *Rock the World Rehab*

"We all know that getting these beautiful temples of ours cleansed & shining is super important. But every time I read another diet or detox book? I fall asleep. And I totally think the authors who write them are marathon-running, celery-stick-adoring, lycra-swaddled machines. Not at all like this rainbow-wrapped-happy-hippy who prefers meandering to sprinting & the peanut butter ON the celery stick. At last, beautiful Denise has chirped the song to my heart & made a detox plan that's actually delicious & divine. If you are a hankering to be a Radiant Goddess, *Rock the World Rehab* is your soul's sister."

~Goddess Leonie Dawson, author of *73 Lessons Every Goddess Must Know*, retreat leader, visual artist, mama, and vessel of wild creativity & cosmic prosperity for the 20,000+ Goddess-sisters who orbit around this virtual altar each month

✫ ✫ ✫ ✫

"*Rock the World Rehab* is a *magnifique* must-read for women from all walks of life in search of self-acceptance, self-respect, balance, and *joie de vivre*...all packaged in an entertaining and effective program. Denise keeps it real with her genuine voice. This chick's message must be heard!"

~Edwige Gilbert, Wellness/Life Coach and author of *The Fresh Start Promise: 28 Days to Total Mind, Body, Spirit Transformation*

"*Rock the World Rehab* will rock your world! If you're in search of your authentic self, she can be found between the covers of this super-fun, highly creative, all-encompassing book. Denise delivers a much-needed message in a conversational style and playful format. But don't let her tone fool you. This is downright serious stuff. Your life on every level will never be the same after experiencing this adventure. Let the Concert Chick revolution begin!"

~Kristin McGee, yoga/Pilates teacher, celebrity trainer, host, writer, TV personality, a Contributing Editor for *Health* magazine and star of over 15 fitness DVDs, cover girl, avid spokesperson for companies and causes that promote health and wellness, and a Fila Yoga Ambassador

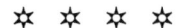

✯ ✯ ✯ ✯

"This book rocks! If you want to lighten your load and brighten your life, a detox with Rox is awesome!"

~David "Yeah Dave" Romanelli, author of *Yeah Dave's Guide to Livin' the Moment: Getting to Ecstasy Through Wine, Chocolate and Your iPod Playlist,* which hit #1 on Amazon's Self-Help Bestseller List

CONCERT CHICK PRODUCTIONS PRESENTS

Rock the World Rehab

✭ ✭ ✭ ✭

A 4-STEP "GET RED CARPET READY" BODY+MIND+HEART+SOUL DETOX ADVENTURE
STARRING YOU!

✭ ✭ ✭ ✭

by Rox, the Original Concert Chick, as chirped

to

Denise Marie Nieman, Ph.D.

Copyright © 2012 by Denise Marie Nieman

All rights reserved. This book or any portion thereof may not be reproduced or used in any manner whatsoever without the express written permission of the author except for the use of brief quotations with credit to source. The scanning, uploading and distribution of this book via the Internet or any other means without permission of the author is illegal and punishable by law. Please purchase only authorized electronic editions, and do not participate in or encourage electronic piracy of copyrighted materials. Your support of the author's rights is appreciated.

Author photo credit: Susie Bowman

✽ ✽ ✽ ✽

All inquiries are to be sent to:

Concert Chick Productions, LLC
P.O. Box 504
Palm Beach, FL 33480
or
roxdetox@concertchick.com

✽ ✽ ✽ ✽

Printed in the United States of America
First Printing, 2012

ISBN: 1461063647
ISBN-13: 978-1461063643

Library of Congress Control Number: 2011905599
CreateSpace, North Charleston, SC

Must-Read Legal C.R.A.P.
(**c**ertain **r**eminders **a**bout **p**rinciples, a.k.a. the fine print)
complete c.r.a.p. is on following page

Must-Read Legal C.R.A.P.
(certain reminders about principles, a.k.a. the fine print)

Imagine a world where there is no need to post disclaimers. Outside of fantasyland, I know of no such place, but have my fingers crossed that the day will come before I move onto my next life. In the meantime, read and heed this c.r.a.p. so we can truly be BFFs.

If you are pregnant, bulimic, anorexic, diabetic, breast-feeding, malnourished, significantly overweight or underweight, or have any other emotional, mental, or physical condition or issue that may prevent you from safely enjoying and benefitting from *Rock the World Rehab*, please check with your health care provider before you embark on this detox adventure. This is very important! No two people are alike and you could subject your body to harm if there is anything about you that shouldn't check into rehab. In fact, even if you are a healthy chick, ask your doc if it's cool for you to go on this journey. Nothing herein is a substitute for professional consultation, diagnosis, and/or treatment of any kind. Nothing! Not. One. Single. Thing.

On that note, the tone of this book is light, conversational and fun, and "rehab," "detox," and other related terms are used playfully but certainly with respectful recognition and no downplaying of the fact that there are people with life-threatening addictions and conditions that require detoxification and treatment in a rehabilitation center under the guidance of trained professionals.

Rox, Denise, and/or Concert Chick Productions, LLC, are not liable to you in relation to the contents of this book or anything or anyone connected thereto. Don't even think about asking your lawyer to contact our lawyer about damages of any kind including, but not limited to, direct, indirect, special, or consequential loss or loss of consciousness or your conscience. No one—at least on our end—is forcing you to read and/or check into *Rock the World Rehab* though we are so happy that you are here. Anything you may or may not do as suggested in this book is your sole decision. Self-responsibility is where it's at, sweetie, which we're guessing you already embrace by the very fact that you are reading this book—you want to take control of your life, knowing that you are the only one who can and ultimately are the one responsible for same. This is exactly what an original Concert Chick would do. Kudos to you!

While every effort was made by Denise to verify the accuracy of what Rox chirped to her, some tweets may have been lost in the translation since they were proffered in rapid-fire French and Denise is only halfway through Intermediate French and is not as far along as she had hoped to be. Internet addresses that were correct and products mentioned in the Swag Lounge that were available at the time of publication may have changed or may otherwise be no more. Bear in mind that not only do Rox, Denise, and Concert Chick Productions, LLC, have zero control over these shifts and/or disappearing acts, they also assume no responsibility for third-party products or Web sites or their content. It's impossible to swear on a stack of Bibles, pancakes or anything else for that matter that the info you find cited from other sources and in the Swag Lounge is accurate, true, complete, and/or even safe (though every single item was tested, read, consumed, worn, and more as the case may be by us).

Should you see yourself in any of the chapters, know that any likeness to a real person, whether dead or alive, is purely coincidental. Sorry. Your fifteen minutes of fame will come soon enough from elsewhere. In no way, shape, or form is the reference to pole dancers and Playboy bunnies herein intended to endorse, encourage, or otherwise suggest certain activities, aspirations, avocations, and/or gyrations. This book was created to deliver a much-needed, meaningful message. Let it reveal itself to you through an open mind and a sense of humor. There are plenty of other crusades if you're up for a fight, like the abuse of poultry raised for food. For obvious reasons, this is very troubling for a Concert Chick. On that note, be advised that no animals have been harmed in any way in the creation of this book, though much human sleep was skipped and Rox lost a few feathers testing bikini wax strips. Further, the use of sweatshops is not part of our creative process, unless you consider proofing drafts poolside in the hot South Florida sun such a use. Last but not least, please do not read this book while operating a motor vehicle or any heavy equipment. And you'll have to provide your own batteries.

Now that the legal c.r.a.p. is out of the way—HOORAY!—let the life-changing trip begin!

✫ ✫ ✫ ✫

This book is dedicated to my heaven angel and to my earth angel, both guardians in their own special way.

To my brother Dennis, who shines his light on me from above with the occasional wing whack to the back of my head to keep me on track.
✢
To my husband Joe, who loves me unconditionally and supports my dreams, even when I am and they are a bit wacky.

You both have permanent residence in my heart no matter where you are, up there or down here. I am truly grateful and abundantly blessed.

✫ ✫ ✫ ✫

Table of Contents

Meet + Greet
    What is a Concert Chick?   xxii
    Meet Your Inner Concert Chick   xxv

Chapter 1: The "Rock The World Rehab" Tour   1
    Why a Stint in Rehab is Cool + What's in it for You   3
        It Ain't Just About the Junk in Your Trunk   4
        You'll Flush Out the Crap Trap
            So the Rock 'n' Roll Can Flow   5
        You'll Lose Tons of Weight   6
    The Program in an Eggshell (Nothing Nuts Here!)   7
    Holy Wow, You Are Absolutely Perfect Right Now!   8

Chapter 2: Get Your Attitude Adjustment Here   11
    Key 1:   Be Yourself—Find Your Light   13
    Key 2:   Follow Your Bliss—Be Your Light   24
    Key 3:   Do What's Right—Shine Your Light On Others   31

Chapter 3: It's Time To Rock 'n' Roll!   37
    Step 1:   Intervention: You Do Need This!   37
        True Confessions + Genuine Expressions   37
        Intake Assessment   38
        Book 'em, Chick-Ohhhhh!   43
    Step 2:   Preparation: Get Ready to Do It!   48
        Bag + Snag Swag   49
        Fluffing Your Nest for Detox + Rest   50
        Let's Go Shopping!   52
        The Numbers Game   54
        Smile + Say "Chick"!   56
        "Rock 'n' Roll Rehab Eve" Ritual   57
        Get Swagged!   60

Step 3: Detoxification: You're Doing It!	60
Rehab Menu	60
What to Expect	62
How to Avoid a Relapse	64
Step 4: Celebration: You Did It!	67
Chapter 4: Feeding Your Body+Mind+Heart+Soul	**69**
Prep Days 1+ 2: Yeehaw, It's a Free For All!	70
Days 1 + 2: Bottoms Up!	70
Days 3 + 4: Get Juiced + Juicy!	72
Days 5 + 6: Solid Wine with a Splash!	73
Days 7 + 8: Be Fruit Loopy!	74
Days 9 + 10: Veg Out + About!	76
Days 11 + 12: Still Vegging + Fruity!	78
Days 13 + 14: Souper You!	79
The "Rehab Red Carpet Concert Chick Bar"	80
Sipping + Supping Tips	82
Bites for Your Mind+Heart+Soul	83
Chapter 5: You Gotta Move It, Move It To Lose It, Lose It!	**85**
Let's Play!	86
Who?	86
You!	86
What?	86
Cardiooooooooooohhhhh, Yeah!	86
Strut Your Stuff	87
Shake Your Booty For Inner + Outer Beauty	88
Top Secret Weapon of Ass Destruction	
Just Beat It!	91
Chick Power!	91
Moves for Your Wings + Other Upper Body Things	93

Get Down, Get Down Junky	
Booty + Bird Legs Ban	95
Be Flexible!	98
Bendy Chick Basics	98
Yoga: How to Get Ahead by	
Lying on Your Back	100
Where?	101
Anywhere + Everywhere, In +/Or Out	
When?	102
Morning, Noon, or Night—Anytime is Right!	
How?	103
Get Hot! Be Cool!	103
Security Check	104
Cop an Attitude + Then a Buzz	105
Don't Hold Your Breath	106
Pleasure Yourself	106
Going Undercover	107
Why?	111
The Perks of Playing Around	
There's No Question About It!	112
All Excuses Are Lame	

Chapter 6: Sparkles In: That Inner Bling Thing — 117

Sparkle Therapy: A Dozen Eggs to Put In One Basket	118
The Bane of A-Drama-Me Strain	119
Nuclear Reactivity	121
Soulitude™:	122
Egg #1: Pray	123
Egg #2: Meditate	125
Egg #3: Be Present	129
Egg #4: Speak Up + Be Heard	131
Egg #5: Create	134
Egg #6: Seek Wisdom From Others	135
Egg #7: Light One Up + Inhale	136
Egg #8: Pop Natural Sedatives	139

Egg #9: Give Yourself a Break   139
Egg #10: Hallucinate to Illuminate   140
Egg #11: Make Some Noise!   142
Egg #12: Wear a Tiara   144

Chapter 7: Sparkles Out: That Outer Bling Thing   **147**
Enough With The Stuff Already!   148
Wardrobe Call!   152
  Say Hello to Your Stylist   153
  Register Your Trademark   154
  Gift Wrap   155
  Outer Bling Things to Be to Jazz It Up a Bit 156
    Be a Flasher   157
    Be a Shady Character   157
    Be a *Bijoux* Babe   157
    Be a Bag Lady   158
    Be a Hip-Hot Wrap Star   158
    Be a Shoe Slut   158
    Be an Undercover Agent   159
The Lowdown On Makeup   159
  Let's Face It   160
  Window Dressing   160
  Mwaaaah!   161
  Body Bare + Care   161
The Mane Attraction   161
  Quickies   162
    Get Banged   162
    Be a Tease   162
    Be Not Afraid of The Braid + Hail to
      the Ponytail   163
    Clip-Ons + Extenders   163
    The Ultimate Headdress   164
    When All Else Fails…Be a Head Case! 164

The Red Carpet Ooh La La Spaaaaahhhhh, a.k.a.
Chez Moi Spa ... 164
    It's a Wrap! ... 165
    Get Stoked with a Soak ... 166
    Shower Power ... 168
    Spaaaaahhhhh'ing with Wine is Divine ... 169
    Polish it Off ... 169
    Give 'em the Ol' Brush Off ... 170
    Face the Music ... 170
    Get Nailed! ... 171
        Facts for Fancy Fingers + Tips Toward
            Twinkly Toes ... 171
        "*Chez Moi Spa*" Get Nailed Menu ... 172
        Grab a Roadie ... 173
        Sweet 'n' Glow ... 173
        Teabag Debag ... 173
        Leftover Makeover ... 173
        Make It Yours ... 173

Chapter 8: How To Cope With The Dope + The Mope ... **175**
    You First ... 177
    Now Others ... 178
    The Dopes + Mopes, a.k.a. The "Tools" ... 179
        The One-Upper/Party Scooper/Rain On
            Your Parader/All About Themster ... 180
        The Whiner/The Party Pooper/The Crybaby ... 181
        The Drama Queen + King ... 181
        The Grand Opposition ... 181
        The Know-It-All ... 182
        The Holier-Than-Thou ... 183
        The Saboteur/The Heckler ... 183
        The Mean, The Catty, The Drunk, The Green ... 184
        The Back Yakker + Stabber ... 185
        The Simple Yakker ... 186
        The Users + The Takers ... 187
        The Yes-Actor No-Acter ... 187

It's Time to Name Names...If You Want to
    End the Games   187
Disconnect: What To Do With The "Tool"
    The Detox "Tool" Box   190
        Tool #1: Non-Reactivity   191
        Tool #2: A Red Velvet Rope   191
        Tool #3: Circumcision   192
        Tool #4: Exorcism   195
        Tool #5: Flip 'em a Wing, Flash 'em
            a Smile   196
    Sparkly Chicks' Tips + Tricks   196
Connect: What To Do With The True + Cool   204
    Cyberspace Can Be a Heart-Sharing +
        Warming Place   205
    Write, Make Rite + Simply Right Expressions   205

Chapter 9: Celebrate Yourself!   209

    Chick Caveat   210
    Show Day Survey   212
    Go Glam + Get Glow for Your Show   213
    Things To Do To Celebrate You   214
        Be a Lush + Get Bombed   215
        Be a Roadie   215
        Pack It, Park It   216
        From "C" to Shining + Tasty "C"   216
        Biker Chic Chick   216
        Create Some Ooh La La   217
        Chic Chickulture   217
        Be a Bird Brain   218
        Pitch a Tent, Not a Fit   218
        Mermaid Madness   218
    Sparkles for Bubbly You!   219

Chapter 10: After-Party Afterthoughts   221

    Post Debut Interview of You by You   222
    What's Next?   223

Keeping the Light Switch On	224
Write Your Own Script + Song	226

Chapter 11: Your All-Access VIP Pass to Magic Red Carpet Rides — 229
Be a Sparkle Junkie	229
Concert Chick Credo	231

VIP (Very Important Peep) Swag Lounge — 237
Rock The World Rehab Commitment	238
Your Daily Prescriptions	240
Cool Stuff for Hot Chicks	265

La Gratitude — *293*

About the Author — 299

Meet + Greet

Be who you are and say what you feel. Because those who mind don't matter, and those who matter don't mind.
~Dr. Seuss

Bonjour! Welcome to our little nest. We embrace you with open arms and wings. Please do make yourself comfortable. Would you like a flute of champagne? *Oui? Très bien!* We are going to get along just fine.

There's a good chance that you are a chick who has had enough of the fluff, puff, and stuff or else we wouldn't be meeting this way. So let's get this party started.

I, Denise, am a dreamer, doer, just be-er, writer, yogini, globetrotter, reader, entrepreneur, lawyer, creative old soul, Natural Health Ph.D.'er, and ex-ballerina who still loves (and wears, mum's the word) tiaras and tutus. I'm a right-brained chick who dreams of Left Bank bistros. I've never tasted coffee. Ever. But I have tasted Twizzlers. Many. *J'adore* the beach, the moon+stars+sun, pink flamingos, anything and everything French, the word "sparkle,"[1] my amazing husband, Joe, and our adorable "kids," Oliver and Roxi. Champagne, anything sprinkled with glitter, bubble baths, blowing bubbles, and dark chocolate-covered caramels with a dust of sea salt bring on fits of joy.

H&M, Target, Chanel (Coco has been my muse since I was eight years old), Tiffany's, Sephora, and Dairy Queen for Butterfinger Blizzards send chills up my spine. I have an obscene collection of costume jewelry housed in an old pine armoire-turned-jewelry-box.

---

[1] Be forewarned. This word and variations thereof are generously sprinkled throughout the pages of this book. You will either love the word, too, or eventually gag every time you see it. While I hope the former, I apologize in advance in case of the latter.

Yes. *That* obscene. I inherited this addiction from my beloved Nana who still guides any expansion thereof from above. If you're sending me flowers, lilacs, lilies of the valley, and pink roses make a sensational bouquet. Airplane tickets and salon blow-dries are my crack. I'm also Rox's (who you will soon meet) manager/agent/handler/chief wineglass washer/chirp interpreter. The fact that I am also her creator keeps her in line, as much as a chick can be so kept.

Notwithstanding the fact that I survived earlier life experiences from which scary movies are made, I believe that everyone is inherently good and genuinely honest. I also believe in Santa Claus and have sent him a letter every year since I was a little girl. (I'm not mocking my first statement with the second—I really do believe in both.) The only difference between then and now is that the notes are written in *la francaise* and I add peppermint schnapps to the hot chocolate that is a must during this ritual. This annual event is the equivalent of a big ol' honkin' prayer, energized by the season of giving and getting. (For the record, I do get most of what I ask for, so hold your chortles, though lots of good hard honest work is involved, too.)

I'm described as Pollyannaish (Santa! People are good!), which sadly is viewed as a liability in some of my circles. I simply can't help but see the beauty in everything and everyone. Which is a good thing because if I meet you when you're having a horrific day and you show me your fangs, I'll think things are just a little off for you at the moment and not that you're some scary psycho nut job. When you tell me something, I believe that you're telling me the truth. Silly me, but that's how I roll. And you know what? This is how I want to show up so spare me the "people are shit" lecture (unless you're my friend Jackie from Dallas whose mother created this expression). Cynicism just ain't me. I tried it on for size once and, thank God, it didn't fit. I chucked it after the longest thirty-two minutes of my life. It was so flippin' constraining that my circulation cut off. Now, that *is* some shit.

My day job as a government lawyer can be a shade stressy at times. Add to the mix my right brain's constant knocking at the door, which causes tremendous headaches if not opened (not cool for me as an attic drop years ago left my head a tad vulnerable). Truth be told—always—the past four years have sorta sucked. Even excessive shoe, handbag, and accessory shopping couldn't take the edge off. Red velvet, cream-cheese frosted cupcakes with sprinkles on top washed down with Cupcake Vineyards Pinot Noir chasers didn't do the trick either, though I must admit, they were quite yummy and buzzy. My tried-and-true arsenal of yoga, meditation, deep breaths, brisk walks, and long baths were useless weapons in the combat zone I was in. I felt stressed, depressed, suppressed, essentially a freakin' mess! I wasn't supposed to be feeling like this. After all, I'm perky and life loving and balanced and positive. WTF?

I allowed my inner peace to be shattered, which made me feel even worse because my trademark is calm. You can always count on me to flash a smile and enthusiastically let you know that "everything is wonderful!" Call me chipper chick! But circumstances were chipping away at that chipper and I had no clue how to deal with this foreign feeling. When I tried to share how I felt with others, people didn't want to hear it because I'm the strong one that just handles things, so gosh golly, if I'm having problems, we're all doomed.

So yes, even as my friend plucked 274 blond hairs off my black jacket one morning before a meeting, I smiled and shrugged it off to a new shampoo. Yeah, right, the kind that adds a shiny finish to the strands right before they jump follicle. I was losing my mind one strand at a time. And then I started to feel grumpy inside, yet still sporting that big ol' friggin' grin on my face. I wasn't being sincere for the first time ever as far as I could recall, fronting the pillar-of-strength image. Let me add right here that I am no drama queen, so don't even go there.

Then came the lumpy on the outside. Ugh. That, too. My fabulous wardrobe shrunk overnight. What was a stressed-to-the-max (in maxi cover-up dresses, a.k.a. muumuus) chick to do? I was being clobbered every which way, and something had to give.

And then it dawned on me. The something that had to give was me, and not to others anymore, but to myself, another first. I finally decided that I'd had enough. Enough of trying to resolve everyone else's problems. Enough of taking on responsibilities that belonged to others. Enough of ignoring my creative soul. Enough of allowing other mortals to squeeze the last drop out of me. Enough of the guilt I felt when I asked for what I needed because I didn't want to be a burden. And enough snacking, sipping, and shopping for stuff I didn't need/want/even like. Sauvignon blanc and Cheez-Its have their place at happy hour among dear friends, right, Karen? But really. A box and a bottle for dinner? And how many black shoes does a chick need? Never mind. Bad example. Need many.

The beauty in all this (See? There's always an upside) is that I was practically forced to step back and not only say WTF? but to actually answer the question. I made a list of the people, places, and things in my life that drained my energy, and checked it twice (Santa!). It was time to let go of everyone and everything that dimmed my light and weighed me down. I craved genuine relationships with likeminded souls who I knew cared about me just as much as I cared about them. I was jonesing for glitter glue sticks, scissors, and empty journals. I had to fit into that hot Derek Lam corset dress hanging in my closet, dammit! Most of all, I yearned for me.

Every time I said no to something or someone on *the* list I said yes to myself. I welcomed back my bliss-inducing arsenal and even added new ammunition. Slowly but surely I released all that weighed me down. Over time, I purged every bit of what blocked my body+mind+heart+soul from shining their brightest. And my clothes miraculously unshrunk! I felt so light and free. And then the universe's gifts came pouring in (*Merci, Père Noël*). From the chaos emerged Concert Chick Productions. I designed a tee, launched a Web site, welcomed Rox into the world, and learned to blog. I created the perfect escape hatch. At the end of the day, I'm a chick just like you: wanting to be the best I can be, to embrace *joie de vivre*, the carefree heart-filled enjoyment of life.

Everything in this book has gone through a series of trial runs by *moi*. I know firsthand that your life will change dramatically when you bid farewell to the drama of toxic anything and anyone. And the focus here isn't only on the physical body pounds and poisons that most detox plans emphasize. I want you to have a brilliant mind, a joyful heart, a sparkly soul, *and* a red carpet body. No longer will you be the one who is dumped on. It's time for you to do the dumping, sister! It's time to hold life by the ankles and shake, shake, shake until all the negative thoughts are out of your head, the toxic people (and your reactivity to them) out of your life, the walls around your heart dismantled, and the extra padding on your gut and butt deflated.

On that high note, it's time to meet Rox.[2]

Rox is Concert Chick Productions' mascot. She was born from my overactive imagination in a seaside village in the South of France. (Her image was sketched in the Bellini Bar at Hotel du Cap Eden-Roc in Cap d'Antibes—amazing what a few *très* expensive bellinis can cause one to scribble on a cocktail napkin that, as I recall, wasn't paper. My sincere apologies to the hotel management.) Rox loved music and dreamed of hanging out backstage and on the tour bus with her fave band. She thought she had to be like all the other chicks if her dreams were to come true. Just when she was ready to give up because who they were was so not her, she decided to just be herself and *voilà*! She found herself—and then found her way backstage, on the bus, and everywhere else she wanted to be. Chick chick hooray! Rox represents the free spirit that resides in each of us, the chick who desires to show up authentically, free, and sparkly. She lives in harmony with the rhythm of her body+mind+heart+soul. That's what Concert Chicks do. And we want the same for you.

---

2 For the complete story of Rox, the Original Concert Chick, please visit www.concertchick.com

WHAT IS A CONCERT CHICK?

Great question. Glad you asked.

At first, it was nothing more than a couple of words that popped into my head as I was being entertained by a gaggle of chicks trying to make their way past security at a Green Day concert, as in "Wow, those concert chicks must *really* want to get back there to do *that* to the guy at the gate." (For the record, they were not admitted...at least that time). So, "Concert Chick" became nothing more, nothing less than a term of endearment for girls flipping their hair and wriggling their butts to party with a rock star. Cute. Harmless. Meaningless really.

And then everything changed during a four-hour silent meditation hike in a desert in Arizona. Blame it on the 100° plus temperature (whoever made up that "yes, but it's dry heat" should stick their head in an oven and then see if they want to retract their statement). There I was, minding my own business, being all mindful (nothing like the threat of rattlesnakes, scorpions, and tarantulas to keep you in the moment) and quiet—no one to talk with other than me to me in my head, and girl, did we have a conversation![3] As I was reflecting on how thankful I was to be out of Dodge for a few days and how nice it would be to do this every week yet recognizing that my desire wasn't possible (reason rears its ugly head even on vacation), my thought train sped out of the station and went something like this: *I really need to find a creative outlet...I'm so relieved that I haven't seen any snakes yet...I wonder what's for lunch...I want to design a Web site...I'm looking forward to my hot stone massage... OMG did that person just pee on that cactus?...Hey, maybe I'll create a right-brain venture using Concert Chick somehow...Oh, I do hope they're serving brownies for dessert...Holy crap! There's a snake!*

As soon as I was back in the van (*sans* snakebite but with some cactus stickers) where the silence officially ended, the only words I could muster were, "Who has a pen?" I scribbled all my Concert

---

3 Come on, you know it happens to you, too. You start with one thought and it takes on a life of its own.

Chick ideas on the brown bag containing my lunch (dang, no brownie). I'd set up a Web site to sell "cool stuff for hot chicks," starting with T-shirts. And this I did. Naturally, when people saw the name of the brand they automatically thought, "Far out, a chick who can hook us up with the latest concert news and great tix." My husband is in the music business, after all. But that wasn't what it was intended to be. Nope, not about the music we hear but about the music we are.

> *Mind, body, and spirit act in concert to determine health and well-being.*
> ~Dr. Carl Thoresen

As with everything in life, Concert Chick evolved and has a much deeper meaning today.

The word "concert" used here is more in line with the French origin of the word, *concerter*, which means to bring into agreement. A "concert" is generally defined as a harmony of sounds, things, or persons. So as much as we love other folks' music, the focus here is on our internal melody—the *magnifique* harmony created when one's body+mind+heart+soul are in agreement. Each of us has a unique song that longs to—*needs* to—be expressed, and *out loud*!

> *We are all, in a sense, music.*
> ~Don Campbell

As for "chick," the word is slang for a girl or young woman, especially an attractive one, or a young child. It's also used as a term of endearment. "Chick" in our context is your inner, playful child. We all have one and she is forever young, attractive, and attracting on all levels no matter how many years she has been alive.

Merge the two and *voilà!*

A Concert Chick is someone who lives in harmony with the rhythm of her body+mind+heart+soul resplendently working in tune with each other. She sings her own song. She dances to her own music. She marches to her own drummer. On her stage. Essentially and gracefully rockin' her world, thus the entire planet. *She is you.*

A Concert Chick is beautiful inside and out, fearless, compassionate, generous, sparkly, creative, confident, and life loving. She's intelligent but even more than that: she's brilliant. And even more than that: she's authentic. She's not just a girl who wants to have fun (though that is a very good thing to want—just ask my "great minds think alike" friend and partner in "crime," Tammy). A Concert Chick embraces who she truly is—an original masterpiece—and not just some *cheep*[4] imitation of someone else. *Rare art, just like you.*

A Concert Chick taking center stage in her life is not only about getting all glamorous (though there's nothing wrong with going glam—a day without glitter is glum!) and strutting her stuff (but surely, if you've got it, work it, girl!). And she's not someone who needs the spotlight, making sure all eyes are focused on her. It's not all about her. And it's not all about her age, clothes, job, IQ, weight, home, education, bank account, car, shoes (though Concert Chicks *love* shoes), height, hair, skin, or eye color. A Concert Chick knows that being her is pretty damn cool and hot at the same time. And she's right. Because from the depths of her heart, she knows this to be true. Hearts never lie. *Listen to yours.*

A Concert Chick cherishes her body+mind+heart+soul. She practices moderation in all things, avoiding excess of any kind. Well, most of the time, because she is not perfect, nor would she want to be even if it were possible. The time *un verre du vin* turns into *deux* and then into *cinq*—*ouf*! But we fluff our tail feathers and carry on, right, Catherine? (But girl, did we have fun!) A Concert Chick is aware of who and what energizes her light, enhances her glow, and fuels her soar. She's also well aware of who and what dims her light, makes her feel low, and what she needs in her life no more. She's able to let go of what holds her back. And nothing ever truly does. *You are unstoppable.*

---

4 *Oui,* it should be "cheap," but Concert Chicks have their own language and "should" doesn't exist in our playbook. Thus, "cheep" it is. It's clearly in the spirit of all things chick, *non?*

MEET YOUR INNER CONCERT CHICK

There is no question in my mind, even though we just met, that you are a Concert Chick. But because our essence is easily clouded through exposure to toxic people, places, and things, we sometimes lose sight of our sparkly standing. Let's see how close you are to getting your sparkle on. Circle the music note in front of the statements below that ring true for you.

♫ I go with the flow. Music inspires, motivates + moves me.

♫ I believe that dreams come true. Mine do.

♫ I am enough + I have enough, right at this very moment.

♫ I have worn a tiara.

♫ I usually wear a tiara + a feather boa.

♫ I am an original me, not some cheep imitation of some other chick.

♫ I rock the world with my upbeat energy + good vibrations.

♫ I let others be, recognizing that the world would be quite boring if we were all the same. I embrace differences.

♫ I march to my own drummer, enjoying life one step at a time.

♫ I wear fabulous shoes + am not afraid of heights.

♫ I sing my own song. I am not afraid to speak up + be heard. I swipe on sparkly lip gloss regularly.

♫ I flash smiles all day long. I laugh with others + at myself.

♫ I know when to shut up + listen.

> ♪ I honor + respect myself, all peeps + nature.
>
> ♪ I don't chirp about others. I ignore the cluckers. I know that what goes around comes around.
>
> ♪ I honor + respect myself, all peeps + nature.
>
> ♪ I believe that everything should be enjoyed in moderation, with the exception of shoes.
>
> ♪ I mean what I say + say what I mean. I am never, ever a mean chick + I keep my promises.
>
> ♪ I dance to my own music. I keep moving, evolving growing. Slow but sure dancing is OK.
>
> ♪ I wear sparkles during the day. I share my brilliance with the world in all ways.
>
> ♪ I show up my best self, do what's right + follow my bliss.
>
> ♪ I stand tall with confidence, front + center, no matter what others think of my stance, physically or otherwise.
>
> ♪ I live my life as an exclamation! not an explanation. I never make excuses for who, what, where I am. *Joie de vivre* rocks.

The more notes you circle, the closer you are to being your authentic self—a Concert Chick, whose body+mind+heart+soul harmonize splendiferously. As Otter said in *Animal House*, "Damn glad to meet you!"

Now that we're new BFFs, without further ado, let's join hands and skip into the next chapter, where you'll receive a strong dose of what's in store for you, oh fabulous you, and learn all the top (and bottom) secret bits and sound bites of detox glory! The magic potions, elixirs, fairy dust, and transformative powers required are already within you. The Rox Detox will help you access this natural wellspring of sparkly energy. We're here to support you as you embark on this amazing journey. *Merci beaucoup* for allowing us this honor to share this adventure with you every step of the way.

Go ahead and lace up those awesome Beverly Feldman cheetah print with crystals booties. It's time to take a tour of *Rock the World Rehab*. Hold on!

Chapter 1

The "Rock the World Rehab" Tour

*Life's journey is not to arrive safely at the grave in a
well-preserved body, but rather to skid in sideways,
totally worn out, shouting, "holy shit...what a ride!"*

~Unknown

Have you been playing too hard, exercising hardly, working too much, taking care of yourself too little, or saying yes too often and no not enough? Are know-it-alls, mean chicks, that jerk of a boss, or your so-not-deserving-you boyfriend testing your last nerve? Are your closets crammed, yet you have nothing to wear? Do you show up filled with fear and worry about the small stuff, including the size of your rear? Do you question why you are here? If you answered yes to even one question, then you have come to the right place, dear heart. People, places, and things can really weigh you down. But no worries, because *Rock the World Rehab* can really lighten you up—all of you—body+mind+heart+soul. Let's go!

I wish I could convince you—heck, what am I talking about? I'd love to convince myself!—to buy only organic produce and to never ever allow sugar, saturated fat, white flour, alcohol, and animal products to pass through your M·A·C high-glossed lips, but for the occasional La Crema Pinot Noir and *chou à la crème*. And how sweet would life be if we had only peaceful thoughts and spoke only pleasant words. What if our minds could stay in the present moment and not constantly flit to and fro to what has already been or to what may come (or not)? What if no one could push our buttons? What if we knew what our purpose was from the day we were born and allowed that divine plan to unfold painlessly and perfectly? What if we always had good hair days?

You can put yourself in the best position to come close and closer to the "what ifs" mentioned above. You do this by purging all the people, places, and things in your life that no longer resonate with who you are today. The *Rock the World Rehab* adventure is just what the rock doc ordered to show you how.

We're more aware than ever before of what we need to do to take care of ourselves—eat less, move more, declutter constantly, love and accept all, live purposefully, think positively, talk less, listen more, say "please" and "thank you", and wear sensible shoes. But there are so many parties to attend with buckets of bubbles and buffets bursting with bacon-wrapped bay scallops on sticks. And how about those total suck days from hell when the only heavenly solace is to wrap yourself in those adorable tattered flannel duckie jammies and cannonball into bed, armed with a bag of Kettle Chips in one hand and a pint of Cherry Garcia in the other, ready to get lost in chick flick space?

Oh yeah, and what's up with that psycho mean girl parked in a nearby cubicle who spreads vicious rumors about you when she isn't focused on sticking pins into a voodoo doll's eyes while chanting your name? Of course, at least you know where she's coming from. Worse are the chicks that won't stick pins in your eyes but have no problem stabbing a cleaver in your back. Uncorking a bottle of Smoking Loon chardonnay to take the hurt away may seem OK. But there are much healthier ways to handle what's dumped on you. It ain't easy being you or anyone else in the world we live in now. And I'm sorry—sometimes (often) nothing else but stilettos will do, so screw that sensible shoes thing. Well, *mon petit chou*, Rox to the rescue!

You've most likely heard of the 12-step program used by Alcoholics Anonymous and other structured support groups. They work. But since we're Concert Chicks, we're hardwired to do things differently and prefer to play by our own rules...our own steps (in amazing shoes).

> *It ain't no sin if you crack a few laws now and then,*
> *just so long as you don't break any.*
> ~Mae West

Rock the World Rehab, commonly known and hereinafter referred to as the "Rox Detox," works a 4-step process: intervention (you *do* need this!), preparation (get ready to do it!), detoxification (you're doing it!), and celebration (hooray—you did it!). You'll go from feat to *fête* (with awesome shoes on your feet) in just two weeks!

Most detox programs focus on juicing, herbal concoctions, and a colonic or two to downsize and cleanse your butt and gut. And because the mind-body connection has gone mainstream, you may see some oomph in the form of oms and downward dogs. But none promotes a complete release of all that physically and energetically weighs you down the way the Rox Detox does. You are about to embark on a total body+mind+heart+soul purge. Brace yourself and be brave! This is going to be one wild, daring ride.

WHY A STINT IN REHAB IS COOL + WHAT'S IN IT FOR YOU

Don't let the *r* word scare you. Red carpet celebrities do rehab all the time, and since your birthright is to be on that red carpet, get used to it. What should scare the hell out of you is all the toxic crap in, on, and around you and your life that keeps you from being and doing your best. Rehab is nothing more than a chance to restore your body+mind+heart+soul to harmonious health. And then you'll be working that red carpet for life in rhythm with all that makes you a finely, divinely tuned goddess. How *magnifique* is that? *Très*.

You may be thinking, "Yeah, so, what's in it for me, really? My name isn't Lindsay." Ah, there are many bennies that will perk you up. Here are a few to wet your whistle:

1. It ain't just about the junk in your trunk.

We're constantly consuming and being consumed by toxins. And not just in the form of sugar, trans fats, food additives, hormones, pesticides, mercury, lead, and other poisons. Toxicity also lurks in our thoughts, beliefs, behaviors, and relationships. We can find the big *t* hanging out with the people we hang out with, in the noise around us, in our office or home environment, in our closets, even under our bed, chillin' with the boogeyman. There are a lot of psychic and physical toxins out there that clutter, clog, and congest our lives. It's no wonder that our bodies+minds+hearts+souls are seriously polluted. The Rox Detox is tonic for the toxic.

You can't do something that helps your body without impacting your mind, your heart, and your soul. All aspects of you are deeply connected, so it's only natural that what benefits or upsets one, benefits or upsets all, as the case may be. For example, you get a call that terribly disturbs you. Your heart is heavy with sadness and you're also pissed off. You have at least two ways to deal—allow your feelings to surface and process them, or go numb through "treat therapy."

The latter is what many administer, believing that inhaling a package of Oreos will transform bitterness into sweetness. And it works. For a moment. With all that sugar, how could you not be buzzing like a bumble bee—or in this case, a numbly bee? You may experience a couple of temporary highs, but also bigger thighs, a soul that no longer flies, and a mind filled with "I'm such a loser" lies. Ouch—that stings! Now you're in a worse position and may feel even more bummed than right after the call. Think of any scenario and play out the domino effect. This is why all aspects of you deserve equal billing. The Rox Detox embraces every bit of you with tender loving care.

In rehab, you'll have the chance to explore, experiment, experience, and enjoy various ways to energize your body+mind+heart+soul as a team. And you do this by clearing the junk in your trunk on your body, as well as the trunks in the form of closets, boxes, bags, and drawers filled with material goods, and the imaginary trunks in the attic in your head that store limiting thoughts and feelings and replay the past over and over again. In rehab, you'll dump the funk from your trunks.

2. You'll flush out the crap trap so the rock 'n' roll can flow.

Have you ever felt trapped? Not every relationship—be it work, intimate, friendship, business, whatever—is right for you where you are on your journey today. As soon as you unblock the trap, you'll start to go with the flow and attract people and situations that resonate with and support you and your dreams. You'll have room to breathe wholly and bloom fully, something you really can't do in the midst of weeds.

The primary purpose and focus of the Rox Detox is to let go, let go, let go! And then let go some more. Perk one, described above, addresses the junk attached to your body, on your mind, and in your physical space. If your body+mind+heart+soul is filled to capacity with *caca*—a toxic wasteland—there's nowhere for the superior substance to go. We now move into releasing toxic people and situations outside your home—your external trap. You have to clean the external crap out, too, to be completely free.

3. You'll lose tons of weight.

You can expect to lose up to ten body pounds. Some chicks have lost more, some less. It all depends on how much extra padding you have when you check into rehab and whether you partake in all detox activities. So, *oui,* you'll lose weight. But mo' bigger and better than that, you have the potential to drop thousands of pounds in the form of people, places, and things that add nothing positive to your life. By working the first two perks, you'll drop weight where it really matters. It's time to lose what you don't use and what uses you.

So you see, sweetie, it isn't all about your ass and thighs. When you Rox Detox, you'll shed *all* that weighs you down—people, places, things, thoughts, worries, fears, stuff, blubber—anything and everything that blocks your natural light. The Rox Detox is like a light switch that you flip on to get out of and rid of the dark. When you lighten your load and lighten up, every part of you becomes brilliant, radiant, and twinkly. Think gazillions of sequins!

And think about rehab as going back into the egg from whence you came. You settle into your comfy nest and allow the magic to happen. When your two-week incubation is up, you'll move into a vastly different world, braver, stronger, more confident, and with fewer feathers. You'll break through your shell, slip on a pair of fancy shoes, and strut your stuff and not stuff your face, your calendar, your relationships, your closet, your briefcase, and anything else you over-cram. No more stuffing of any kind except for charity invitation envelopes, Thanksgiving birds, and Christmas stockings. You will create space for the miracles that will take place. Pinkie swear promise.

The time is now to release, clean out, finish up, get rid of, resolve, come to terms with, purge, toss, trash, donate, consign, accept, and surrender to make room for the many gifts waiting for you in the wings—a rockin' body, a joyful heart, a brilliant mind, and a sparkly soul. What are you waiting for?

THE PROGRAM IN AN EGGSHELL
(NOTHING NUTS HERE!)

Now that you're familiar with the basic works and perks of rehab, let's take a quick lap around the chapters.

Chapter 2 is all about you you you and an attitude adjustment. Chapter 3 walks you through the details of all four steps of the Rox Detox adventure. Next up, catering. Chapter 4 dishes out your rehab menu. You'll meet what you'll eat and, for dessert, learn how to nourish other parts of your divine essence, too. Lots of juicy bits there. Then you'll flip to Chapter 5 where you'll be coached on how you're gonna move it, move it to lose it, lose it. The top (and bottom) secret weapon of ass destruction will be revealed along with some other physical treats that will have you rockin' your Rock + Republic skinny straight legs straightaway.

Chapter 6 flashes the inner bling thing. We'll explore ways to stay calm in the middle of chaos, to shine from your center, and to create a buildup of internal sparkles so powerful that you will set the world on fire. Which brings us right to Chapter 7's outer bling thing *boudoir*, where we'll chat about ways to really sparkle, glisten, and glow on the outside. Think scrubs, rubs, tubs, and more! Can you say spaaaaaaahhhhhh? We'll also tackle tossing stuff that is no longer who you are. You'll hang out in wardrobe with your stylist, who will show you how to adorn your blingy body with clothes, accessories, makeup, and more glamazon galore. Repeat after me: Shoooooooooooooooes + sparkles.

And. Then. There. Is. Chapter. 8. A very important chapter! For it is here that you will pick up the extra-strength prescription to help you cope with all sorts of dope and mope. The downers that tarnish your twinkle, stain your sparkle, glum your glitter, and otherwise weigh you down, dim your light, drain your energy, and burn you out. With the "Detox 'Tool' Box" you'll find here, you'll be able to repel even the most toxic peeps (a.k.a. "tools"). And like a crescendo reaching its climax, the red carpet rolls out in Chapter

9. After your Rox Detox, you'll be a brand-new you for your debut. A *très* cool celebration of *vous*!

After your *fête*, we'll reconvene the next day in Chapter 10 for a little after-party. We'll gab about your rehab and debut experiences. You'll decide what to keep, to toss, to do next. The last chapter—11—is your gateway to a life on the red carpet. Always and forever. And just like most super *soirées*, there's a goodie bag for you to take home after the tour wraps up. Swag, *bébé*! You have an exclusive invitation to visit the VIP (Very Important Peep) Swag Lounge and help yourself 24/7 to the goodies in this treasure chest of a place to enjoy in rehab and beyond.

Are you excited or what? Me too. But there's one very important fact that you must acknowledge and accept before we move ahead:

HOLY WOW, YOU ARE ABSOLUTELY PERFECT RIGHT NOW!

Yes, right now. You are gorgeous and alive and breathing and have much to offer this universe as you sit there on your perch at this very moment, even if you think you have big roaster thighs, a plump rump, and flappy wings. Even if your life is overextended and overstuffed in all ways. Even if your BFF isn't. From this day forward, there will be no more chickenshit thinking! It's time for a "this chick is it!" mindset. Because knowing that no matter what—no matter how big your body, how mumbled your mind, how heavy your heart, how sullied your soul—your birthright is beauty, bliss, brilliance, health, happiness, and joy—all of which adds up to the red carpet. At this very moment, you are divine and perfect by design (hereinafter "i rock").

Yeah, there's some tough love in rehab, but it's unconditional and doled out with great respect. It's absolutely essential for your happiness and health to unequivocally believe what I'm telling you. Rehab is the place to face the truth—the good, the bad, and the ugly. The one truth that is being revealed to you at this time is absolute. *You are amazing!*

So say "i rock!" three times as if you really mean it. Better yet, sing it at the top of your lungs while shaking your tail feathers a bit (OK, a lot!), and then come back and autograph this pledge, inserting today's date:

---

i rock as i am right now!

_____   _____
     date   concert chick extraordinaire

Oh. Yes. You. Do! Copy this declaration many times and place it where you'll see it often—in your office, home, closet, car, wallet, handbag, locker, everywhere and anywhere to remind yourself that you really are beyond fabulous even if you throw this book away without turning to the next page. (But really, why would you want to toss the book? It was written just for you!)

Now that the tour of what's in store is officially over, it's time for an attitude adjustment. Shall we? I promise that it won't hurt—much.

Chapter 2

Get Your Attitude Adjustment Here

Outer changes always begin with an inner change of attitude.
~Albert Einstein

In earlier drafts of this book, this chapter appeared somewhere in the middle. As time went by, it found itself in the starting lineup because the message really is the foundation from which all Concert Chick happiness hatches. If you accept and practice the wisdom of this chapter, you'll be in the best position to repel a relapse while in rehab or beyond. That's why an attitude adjustment at the get-go makes perfect sense. By the time you reach the gateway unlocked in Chapter 11, you'll return to where you began, only better, with the "this chick is it" mindset permanently installed.

Let's get one thing clear. This adjustment doesn't create an *attitude* in the common negative connotation of the word. It's not about "being all that." The attitude here isn't copped, it's embraced. It's a way of showing up *à la* Concert Chick. It's more of an aura of authenticity. Let's call it "chickatude." The concept came to me over a pile of cheese. Huh?

·

Some years ago, I was asked to speak at a ceremony for college students graduating with honors. The gist of what was to be presented was given to me beforehand; all I had to do was run with it. And run with it I did—far away from it, actually. My husband, Joe, and I stopped at a Waffle House on our way to the ceremony (quit chuckling, it was close and convenient). It was here that I was served up an "aha! moment" along with my "smothered and covered (cheese!)" hash browns (sometimes you just gotta go there!). I decided to scrap the original text of my "speech" for something *really* original. I decided to hand back the expected and hand over the keys to being happy that have been on my key ring for a very long time (though I do admit to misplacing them during *that* period mentioned during our meet + greet).

Four and a half paper napkins filled with scribble later, I had *the* message. The one that would speak to the essence of who the students were and not to what they "should be" according to others. I knew I was onto something when a few stoic professors each gave me a thumbs-up as I returned to my seat on the stage and later when students and their parents thanked me during the reception that followed. Being real rocks!

And so do you! I now hand over these three sacred keys that will open the chest containing your body+mind+heart+soul treasures:

BE YOURSELF.
FOLLOW YOUR BLISS.
DO WHAT'S RIGHT.

You may be thinking, "whoop-de-doo, heard those clichés before, tell me no more." But have you ever given any real thought to the meaning behind each? Let's look at "be yourself." You'd think that being you is a no-brainer, because who else could you be? Truth is, most of us are or were what everyone else wanted or expected us to be.

> *To know what you prefer instead of humbly saying "amen"
> to what the world tells you you ought to prefer is to keep
> your soul alive.*[5]
> ~Robert Louis Stevenson

And forget about our dreams, if we even dare have them. How selfish and trivial when there are bills to pay and so many to-dos on our lists. Piss on bliss! And then we have to do what's right while we're being stabbed in the back by a "friend" or otherwise so stretched to the max that even if you did want to help someone else, there's no time or room on your plate? Screw that. Besides, isn't it each man for himself anyway in this dog-eat-dog world we live in? Yikes. One attitude adjustment coming up!

KEY 1: BE YOURSELF
FIND YOUR LIGHT

> *Be yourself. Everyone else is already taken.*
> ~Oscar Wilde

Your light is always present, although it's prone to dimming and burnout. Confidence is your best defense. Do you believe you matter? Do you believe that you are enough? Do you believe that you make a difference? Do you believe that because of you, the world is a better place? If you answered yes to all these questions, you are one confident chick and I'm applauding you wholeheartedly. If you're like most of us at one time or another and thought, "yeah, right," read on.

---

[5] I know that my words rock, but I'd be a fool to think that I'm the only one with something of value to express. In this spirit, I've sprinkled the pages of this book with others' wise words, with extra splashes in this chapter, to be used as reflection prompts. You'll see that some quote authors' names are in bold print along with a mini-bio. These are my personal friends that stand out in my life, so I wanted them to stand out here, too. Spend some time with each quote and see if it speaks to your body+mind+heart+soul. If it does, grab your journal and explore the feelings that bubble up.

> *He who trims himself to suit everyone will soon
> whittle himself away.*
> ~ Raymond Hull

> *Whatever you are, be a good one.*
> ~Abe Lincoln

Even if you're squeezing into 14s while all those beautiful 10s hang in your closet tormenting you; even if you seek solace in sweets when things don't work out as you planned; even if you still have thoughts of revenge when Ms. Venom casts her web (again!); and, yes, even if you have no idea what you what to do when you grow up, show up as if you're already a size-10-wearing, healthy nonreactor able to fend off toxic everything with a single glance, knowing that you are here to do something gloriously significant with your unique talents. Walk tall, on purpose, with chickatude and a twinkle in your eye. "Act as if" and your light will be glowing brightly in a jiff.

Aspire to show up the same no matter where you are. Your authentic self doesn't wear different masks, summon other personalities, or change voices depending on the audience. I know someone who alternates between being a total bitch and a sweet chick. I never knew which one was going to show up for dinner. So today I opt to not sit at the same table, if you know what I mean. Sure, our moods can change depending on the circumstances, and we play many roles that require minor tweaks, such as not letting our hair down at a client meeting in the same manner we would if we were in a local pub with our pals pounding pints. What I'm getting at is complete personality conversions to and fro. Some people you simply must let go of before they go off on you yet again.

> *Always be a first-rate version of yourself, instead of a
> second-rate version of somebody else.*
> ~Judy Garland

> *Remember always that you not only have the right to be an individual, you also have an obligation to be one.*
> ~Eleanor Roosevelt

As human beings, we innately desire, whether we admit it or not, to be appreciated, loved, and respected. We want people to like us, to have them see the good in us. But we must do and see it first. The official stamp of approval ultimately can come only from you. If you seek validation from the outside, you will singlehandedly drain your life force quicker than any of the mopes and dopes you'll meet (though I suspect that you already know most of them) in Chapter 8. First and foremost, you must believe that you matter. That you are enough. That you don't have anything to prove to anyone. You must master self-approval, because in the end, frankly chicklet, those people do not give a damn about you. OK, that was harsh, but many folks are only out for themselves. Even if all loved all unconditionally and every beauty pageant contestant's wish for world peace came true, you still must know deep down inside that you are an amazing person.

Here's an experience I had when *Rock the World Rehab* was going to press that the "be yourself" key fit into nicely. And it just so happened to unlock a bit more for me on this topic. Geez, just when you think you have it all figured out. Anyhow, someone I hold in high regard suggested that people would think I'm a flake in the context of my day job after they read this book. When I asked him what a flake meant to him, he gestured with a fluttering movement like a butterfly, "you know, out there." Another friend heard this and fine-tuned it to mean "free spirited". That's me for sure. But being the word freak that I am, I had to know exactly how the experts defined a flake to make an educated decision on whether to accept or reject it. Here's the gist of the word as it applies to name-calling: a flake is a person with an odd personality; an unusual person; a whimsically eccentric person[6].

---

[6] Courtesy of www.freeonlinedictionary.com. I intentionally omitted "fruitcake," "crackpot," "nut case," "screwball," "whacko," and "nutter," as I don't readily accept what's flung my way unless it holds true for me, which these terms do not, except for how I can turn into a complete nut case when someone finds the shoe I was looking for at a drastically reduced priced.

Okay, so I did admit in our meet + greet to wearing tutus and tiaras and to not only believing in Santa Claus but to actually sending a "Dear Santa" letter every year for most of my 50 years. And yes, I use the word sparkle. A lot. And I smile. A lot. And I can't imagine life without glitter. Not even for one day. And don't get me started on my obsession with the search for the perfect shade of red nail lacquer. It must be out there somewhere.

But just because I'm all of the above plus have been blessed with an overactive creative imagination that needs more than the thrill of contract and ordinance drafting, and just because I wear metallic trimmed sweater sets and chandelier earrings to—shudder—the office[7], doesn't mean that my left brain hibernates while my right brain creates. *Au contraire.* Some of us (like you I suspect) do have it all going on, which I suppose does make us unusual and odd, eccentric even.

So it turns out that I am indeed a flake, and a fabulous one at that. I mean, come on. Who wants to be usual these days? What is normal? I don't fit into the classic stereotype of the person one would think should hold my job[8]. *Whew.* And I don't do a darn thing to change that perception. I suppose I could cut my hair into a professional bob or at least twist it into a tight bun. I could smile less and snarl more. I could trade my fabulous Jimmy Choo wedges for some (no offense, just not me) Naturalizers. I'd rather poke my eyes out with pencils. Okay, not really because my eyesight is very important to me—how else am I to spot a shoe sale a mile away? See? I just can't help myself.

I should be bragging about how I graduated from high school on my 16th birthday and how I entered college shortly thereafter while working almost full-time and taking care of my father and four younger brothers. I could boast about making mostly

---

7   I concede that a tutu and a tiara would be a bit much for my day job gig unless it's dress-down Friday or a holiday.

8   I write this with all due respect to my colleagues that I consider pals. But I hate to be the one to break it to y'all; you don't quite fit the mold either.

straight A's and being disruptively bored out of my mind in middle school, so much so that I had a "use anytime" art pass that I flashed to my teachers to get me out of class and into the closet the art instructor allowed me to convert into my own little studio where I created coverings for every bulletin board in the building. I also worked full-time while going to law school contrary to the strong suggestion that students not work at least during their first year. Another thing that comes to mind is my fearless business acumen. Every morning before school my mother would drop me off to open our family business, a laundromat. I had no idea where she was off to at the time, and even though I do now, I'll leave that story for another day. What's pertinent is that I was there, setting up shop, washing, drying, folding, and wrapping the drop off service, running the dry cleaner machines, removing the change, readying the bank deposit, filling the vending machines, and dealing with customers—many pleasant, some not. After school I did the same thing, at times closing the joint. Did I mention that I did this while I was in middle school? Yep, I'm a flake.

With me, what you see is what you get. I suppose I could play the part and look smart though I prefer to play real me and just be smart. In other words, I'll take flake over fake any day!

The person who is never criticized is not breathing.
~VERN McLELLAN

Some folks will love the watercolor abstract you created; others will hate it. All that matters is that you believe your work is a masterpiece. You can't go from "wow, I'm great!" when someone tells you your painting is brilliant to "geez, I suck" when someone two minutes later takes a peek and slams your art. It's the old love vanilla, hate vanilla, gimme chocolate thing. Tastes differ. Simply shrug your shoulders and smile, knowing that you've got talent and everyone has an opinion.

I tell myself to "make today my masterpiece!" Whether I am in a personal interaction or project or at work, I always ask—is this the absolute best I can do?
~ Marcelle Miller, Acupuncture Physician

But what about stage fright? It isn't always easy to stand up and show 'em what you got. Be fearless! Don't be afraid of what others think or say about you. Shoo off the hecklers. They secretly wish they had the courage to get up on the stage like you did, and they struggle with that internally. Rather than address their failings and fears, they take the easy route and ridicule you instead. Pay no attention. It's possible that you will inspire them to move forward and the world will be all the better for it thanks to your bravery.

As for worrying about what other people might think— forget it. They aren't concerned about you. They're too busy worrying about what you and other people think of them.
~Michael LeBoeuf

What you think of yourself is much more important than what others think of you.
~ Seneca

Don't worry about what other people think…they don't do it very often.
~Seen on a Bumper Sticker

So, get up there and shine. Sure, your audience may "boo" you, but they could also "woohoo" you. You'll never know until you get out there. As much as you desire a glowing review, most often it will have to come from you to you. No matter where you stand on the stage—front and center or in the back row where you can hardly be seen—there's a reason for you to be there. Without your contribution—big or small—the show would not be the same without you. *You matter.*

> *If you think you're too small to have an impact, try going to bed with a mosquito.*
> ~Anna Roddick, founder, The Body Shop

> *If you can't be a good example, then you'll just have to be a horrible warning.*
> ~Catherine Aird, crime novelist

Put this book down, give yourself a round of applause, and then take a bow. If you're really talented—and I know you are—do both at the same time. And repeat often.

> *The person who seeks all their applause from outside has their happiness in another's keeping.*
> ~Claudius Claudianus

Here's an excellent example of what I'm talking about. It's a good thing that Elvis Presley didn't listen to one guy's opinion. After he finished a performance at the Grand Ole Opry, his manager fired him, telling him that he may as well go back to driving a truck because he just didn't have what it took. I bet Elvis was happy that he carried on despite that moron's "expert" evaluation. Double or nothing that manager spent many a day and night kicking himself. Where it hurts. *Really* hurts.

> *Why try to be someone you're not? Life is hard enough without adding impersonation to the skills required.*
> ~Robert Brault

While we're on the subject of icons, Lady Gaga gets it. This Concert Chick is seriously multi-talented and could be an egomaniacal mean chick, and maybe she is, but when I saw her perform she either pulled a fast one on the thousands of her "little monsters," as she calls her fans, that packed the arena or she genuinely embraced her message. I like to believe the latter. She constantly reminded the audience that they had to be themselves. She lives authentically and wants her fans to do the same. So with Lady Gaga as my backup (I'm cracking up as I'm typing this—imagine that!): *Be yourself!* Authenticity rocks!

Before we move to the second key, I want to share responses I received from friends of mine, all male, to the question: "what makes a chick sparkle?" The point isn't to tell you what you have to do to get some guy's attention or approval, but rather, to bolster the importance of just being yourself. Most chicks think they know what will make them rock in others' eyes, especially the guys, but I want to let you in on a little secret. What you think it is, it ain't. It isn't about having the perfect figure or the best moves. What you'll learn may be surprisingly helpful as you embrace your fabulous self.

This scenario backs up what the boys have to say. Have you ever seen a sorta chunky chick wearing a kinda "out" outfit with a sorta poor fit enter the room and all the guys' heads spin around to check her not once, but twice? You may wonder how someone like her can make such an impression on all those boys that you think should be drooling over you. (I know you'd never wonder such a thing because being judgmental is so unattractive and mean and not Concert Chickish at all, so this statement is for illustration purposes only). It's really about what can't be seen, only sensed—her energy. She's confidence in action, letting the world know that she is awesome no matter what you may think. She's simply being herself. And there's no question that she's a girlie girl. The guys aren't flocking because she's an ESPN junkie or can belch, fart, and scratch with the best of 'em. She just is. No pressure, no drama, she's fun to hang out with. She's comfortable in her own skin. Period. End of story.

Now for the wise guys. First off, these aren't the words of nerds. No boys with slide rules poking out of top pockets and chess club meeting schedules crumpled in back pockets. Not that there's anything wrong with geeks. It's just that our panel is comprised of very hot, cool "guy" guys, some in the entertainment business, others simply entertaining. The kind you'd like to hang out with ranging from a bizman in cowboy boots to a retired network executive, with music industry guys (a couple rockin' the wine, too!) rolled in to keep with the Concert Chick theme. Mainly what you'll see—and why I put this info here—is that these men, while they don't dismiss looks, admire and want more. Check out for yourself what the sparkly-chick experts have to say:

A chick loaded with sparkle is one who has a great smile, and who has intelligence and lots of personality along with a humble attitude!
~BYRON RUSSELL, CHAIRMAN & CEO, CHENEY BROTHERS, INC., ISLAND HOPPER, AVID BOATER, ALL-AROUND FUN GUY

A big smile makes a chick sparkle…a smile that includes her eyes. And flirtation sure doesn't hurt! I love them all.
~DREW MCMAHON, ATTORNEY, WINE CONNOISSEUR, CROSS-COUNTRY TRAVELER, ASPIRING COLUMNIST

Confidence, humor, openness—for me that's the triumvirate of feminine sparkletude.
~GREG ROACH, SPIRITUAL TRAVEL GURU AND FOUNDER OF SPIRIT QUEST WORLD

A happy chick is a SPARKLY CHICK! She's a lady who can really touch you, and I'm not talking sex here, but rather, with the confidence she has that she shares with others. You can look into her eyes and see her soul and the magic takes over and all you will do is give in to her every want and need.
~JOHN "THE BIG DOG" ANDERSON A.K.A. "BODYGUARD TO THE STARS," REGIONAL VP, CONTEMPORARY SERVICES COMPANY, NATIONALLY RECOGNIZED WOMEN'S SOFTBALL COACH, NICEST GUY EVER

Sparkly chicks look pretty and feel pretty inside and out. They are interesting, but also interested in the world and the people around them— you can't be one without the other. They care about themselves honestly enough to be able to care about others. And they look great naked, at least in a dim light!
~LENNY BERGER, ATTORNEY, GUITAR PLAYER, FUTURE BARBER, BIG EGGROLL ROLLER

Being sparkly has to do with a chick's demeanor when she does something sporty, whether it be winning a major race or simply accomplishing something like finishing a first race, etc. Guys are either beating their chests or perhaps the opposite—just trying to act cool. Chicks sparkle when they're confident and just do it!

~ROD STEELE, ESQ., DUANE MORRIS,
INTELLECTUAL PROPERTY ATTORNEY EXTRAORDINAIRE,
TRIATHLETE, PUBLISHED AUTHOR, CHAIRMAN OF
SPARKING LIFE, INC.

I would say a sense of humor is my #1, followed by poise. Humility is good, but not to the point of being second class. Just not arrogant or pushy. Witty and smart are good. Someone who carries herself well. Maybe that is confidence expressed physically. AND, another favorite, ya gotta smell good.

~HERB THIELE, LEON COUNTY ATTORNEY, FUNNIEST
GUY ON THE PLANET, FORMER FIGHTING IRISH BAND
MEMBER (TRUMPET!), FATHER OF SIX, GOOD-SMELLING
OLFACTORIST

So you want to know what attributes make a chick sparkle to me? Besides being physically hot? I like self-confidence combined with a bit of self-deprecating wit and humor. Nothing says cool, confident chick more than a funny girl who is not afraid to make fun of herself.

~CHRIS HAMMOND, ROCK 'N ROLL WINE,
CERTIFIED AND CERTIFIABLE CHICKOLOGIST,
RESIDENT CORK ROCKER

What makes a chick sparkle? Confidence and drive. There's nothing more attractive than a confident woman. Someone who looks you in the eye when she speaks to you and knows where she's going in life. Regardless of whether she's just pulling onto her street of dreams or is cruising on the autobahn of accomplishment, she has a purpose for getting out of bed each morning and LIVING her life to the fullest!

~SONNY BARTON, ROCK 'N ROLL WINE,
INTERNATIONAL MAN OF LEISURE

A sparkly chick always wakes with the optimism of the opportunities that each new day brings. She sees the best in people and you need only look into her eyes to see the dreams and excitement that fuel her enthusiasm. Simply stated, she is the girl that makes you be more than you ever thought you could be!

~JIMMY MARTZ, CIRCUIT COURT JUDGE,
CUPID SHUFFLER

There are three things a girl must possess to hold the cherished title "sparkly chick": confidence, intelligence, and an ability to flirt. When I see all three, I am more than willing to leave the safety of the shallow end of the pool and jump in deep with both feet, even if I am in over my head.

~JOE NIEMAN, LIVE NATION, SR. VP/VENUES
– FLORIDA MUSIC + GENERAL MANAGER/
CRUZAN AMPHITHEATRE, FOOTBALL STAR STILL WAITING
FOR THAT DRAFT DAY CALL, BASKETBALLER, TIKI BAR-ER,
CRACKBERRY JUNKIE, LONG DISTANCE RUNNER

My perspective is a result of my total global experiences! A "Sparkly Chick" must have sensuality, appeal and intrigue, style, sophistication, substance, humility, be smart with a serious intellectual foundation and curiosity, have wit and a clever sense of fun and humor, be worldly, and have a sense of independence and confidence. Work and a career are a plus since that negates needy and dependent relationships, which lose their luster after a short while.

~AAVO KOIV, RETIRED NETWORK TV PRODUCER/
PRODUCTION EXECUTIVE, NEW YORK/ HOLLYWOOD,
WORLD TRAVELER-CITIZEN-SOUL

The End. (I hope they take note of the fact that they're being given the last word here. Who said it never happens?)

KEY 2: FOLLOW YOUR BLISS
BE YOUR LIGHT

Follow your bliss.
If you do follow your bliss,
you put yourself on a kind of track
that has been there all the while waiting for you,
and the life you ought to be living
is the one you are living.
When you can see that,
you begin to meet people
who are in the field of your bliss,
and they open the doors for you.
I say, follow your bliss and don't be afraid,
and doors will open
where you didn't know they were going to be.
If you follow your bliss,
doors will open for you that wouldn't have opened
for anyone else.
~Joseph Campbell

"Bliss" has always been one of my favorite words, next to "sparkle," "shoe," and "sale," especially when all appear in the same sentence. Seriously, "bliss" is simply a beautiful word in and of itself. The gist of "bliss" is: ecstasy, extreme and perfect happiness, cloud nine, heaven, walking on air, serene joy, paradise. Don't you feel tingly all over just reading these words? Imagine the power of living them! To me, it means doing what you love, something you are passionate about, what you were put on this earth to do and would be doing all day long for no pay if you didn't have that pesky mortgage payment to make. (Eventually, doing what you're passionate about can pay your bills, but that's a subject for another book).

Concert Chicks are leaders, not followers, except when it comes to their bliss. This they pursue zealously. So many people focus on what's going on in others' lives, personally known or not. This is being a busybody, not a body busy discovering what makes her tick. What will you follow to the end of the earth? What is your bliss?

People go gaga over movie stars (Bradley Cooper!), rock stars (Chad!), bizstars (Jessica Simpson!), and other notables (Oprah!). Just think of all those celebrity magazines out there. I can think of two off the top of my head: *Life & Style*, which I subscribe to (mum's the word) and *US Weekly*, which I pick up at the airport when I'm traveling, along with a bag of raw almonds and the occasional package of pretzel M&Ms (double mum's the word). They provide quick page-flipping entertainment and are awesome sources of the latest hot products and cool beauty tips. But if I ever became obsessed with these magazines, then I would not be following my bliss, unless I truly believed that I was created to flip the beads on the Brad and Angelina child count abacus and monitor what and whom Snooki was doing today. There isn't an *L* branded on my forehead, and there isn't one on yours either. So enjoy the magazines, TV, and movies (and the M&Ms), but for their intended entertainment value only (and in moderation). Make sure you spend more time reviewing and creating your very own star-filled, red carpet life.

> *Is not life a thousand times too short for*
> *us to bore ourselves?*
> ~Friedrich Nietzsche

> *You live but once, you might as well be amusing.*
> ~Coco Chanel

We're all entertainers, playing various roles every day. Be as enthusiastic about your life as you are about the lives of others. Live your life as a creator—not a mere spectator. Pay attention to yourself for at least two hours for every hour you spend watching or reading about some other celebrity. You not only write the script, you produce, create, and direct most acts and scenes (with the universe playing a major supporting role). What is your movie about? A mystery? An adventure? A comedy? A drama? One of those silent flicks? Or will a blank screen appear because you never got around to having a life? That would be a real tearjerker! Don't settle for a flash of "The End" on your final screen. That's what will happen if you watch other folks' flicks. Sure, "The End" will come for all of us sooner or later, and oftentimes unexpectedly, but it doesn't have to be a dull "lights off, curtains down" thud and cut! Lights on, curtains up, and a joyous celebration of a life well lived and loved is the way to go.

> *You were born an original. Do not die a copy.*
> ~JOHN MASON

When you sit transfixed on or try to ride in on the credits of someone else's existence, the film ends and all you're left with is that annoying static. You're too good for that. Create your own list of credits—a life that inspires and motivates others. Who are you, really? What is your role(s) besides *the* star? What message do you want to send out to the world when you perform on your stage?

> *We have always lived by these three sayings: "Plan as though you will live forever, live as though you will die tomorrow," "Love the life you live... live the life you love," and "Be kinder than usual for everyone you meet is fighting some sort of battle."*
> ~JENNIFER SUSKO, NAIL TECHNICIAN, TOMMY'S MOMMY, ENJOYER OF LIVING THE SIMPLE LIFE

> *An unfulfilled vocation drains the color from a man's entire existence.*
> ~HONORÉ DE BALZAC, "SCENES DE LA VIE PARISIENNE," LA MAISON NUCINGEN, 1838

> *This is the true joy in life, the being used for a purpose recognized by yourself as a mighty one; the being thoroughly worn out before you are thrown on the scrap heap; the being a force of nature instead of a feverish, selfish little clod of ailments and grievances complaining that the world will not devote itself to making you happy.*
> ~GEORGE BERNARD SHAW

> *Alice laughed. "There's no use in trying," she said. "One can't believe impossible things." "I daresay you haven't had much practice," said the Queen. "When I was your age, I always did it for half an hour a day. Why, sometimes, I've believed as many as six impossible things before breakfast."*
> ~LEWIS CARROLL, THROUGH THE LOOKING GLASS

What do you think is impossible? Is it really? Or is it simply something that requires some elbow grease to achieve? Have fun dreaming the impossible dream, but relish more in the knowing that all of those supposed crazy ideas can come to life through belief, faith, commitment, and action. This alone is why life is so awesome! Your bigger concern should be in getting what you ask for. The universe *is* listening to what you put out there.

> *It all started with a dream and a mouse.*
> ~WALT DISNEY

What are your dreams? Big as a moose or small as a mouse, all answer your call.

> *Every single forward step in history has been taken over the bodies of empty-headed fools who giggled and snickered.*
> ~UNKNOWN

Bliss is also activated by another *b* word, "brilliance," which, in my opinion, is superior to intelligence. Your brain on sparkles creates a smart *and* a spectacular life. While book smarts can be impressive for people who like big words and complex theories, why use valuable storage space on stuff that can easily be Googled on your smartphone? Opt for sparks of genius that naturally occur when both your right and left brains are activated.

When I visited Bali, I had the pleasure of meeting Ketut Leyur, the healer who played a starring role in Liz Gilbert's runaway bestseller *Eat, Pray, Love*. Ketut told me that I had two kinds of smarts—head and heart. I graciously accepted his observation. You have the same, too, if you'll recognize, accept, and cultivate this gift. Sparkly smarts with heart is where it's at, *dahling*. You'll discover your bliss when you engage both. In fact, it will find you as long as you keep your light on.

If you think it's too late to do something you've always wanted to do, be inspired by these amazing peeps who accomplished the most the more they lived:

- ◆ Andrés Segovia, at 82, taking bows after a concert, was besieged for encore after encore. He finally said, "I could play for you all night because I am young and vigorous. But the guitar is a fragile instrument and needs its rest."
- ◆ Grandma Moses was a farmer's wife who did needlework until arthritis forced her to quit. She took up painting instead, was discovered in her seventies, and painted 600 canvases before she died at 100.
- ◆ Colonel Sanders founded Kentucky Fried Chicken with his first Social Security check.
- ◆ Dom Pérignon was sixty years old when he first produced champagne. *Merci*, Dom!
- ◆ Michelangelo was 72 years old when he designed the dome of St. Peter's Basilica in Rome.
- ◆ Benjamin Franklin was 79 when he invented bifocals.
- ◆ Frank Lloyd Wright was 91 when he completed his work on the Guggenheim Museum.
- ◆ Dimitrion Yordanidis was 98 when he ran a marathon in seven hours and 33 minutes in Athens, Greece.
- ◆ Ichijirou Araya was 100 when he climbed Mount Fuji.
- ◆ Theodor Seuss Geisel began writing Dr. Seuss stories when he was 53, he wrote *You're Only Old Once* at 70, and was awarded a Pulitzer Prize for his wit and wisdom at 80.

> *I've missed more than 9,000 shots in my career. I've lost more than 300 games, and 26 times I've been trusted to take the game-winning shot and missed. Throughout my life and career I've failed, and failed, and failed again. And that's why I succeed.*
> ~Michael Jordan

> *If you have anything really valuable to contribute to the world, it will come through the expression of your own personality—that single spark of divinity that sets you off and makes you different from every other living creature.*
> ~Unknown

> *No bird soars too high if he soars with his own wings.*
> ~William Blake

> *One can never consent to creep when one feels an impulse to soar.*
> ~Helen Keller

> *Nobody grows old merely by living a number of years. We grow old by deserting our ideals. Years may wrinkle the skin, but to give up enthusiasm wrinkles the soul.*
> ~Samuel Ullma

> *Though my muscles may stiffen, though my skin may wrinkle, may I never find myself yawning at life.*
> ~Toyohiko Kagawa

So what do you get all hot and bothered about? It's never too late to do what you were born to do. It's only too late when you die. And that could happen at any time. What are you waiting for? What is your bliss?

Rehab is the place to break out of your comfort zone. Make sure you do at least one brave act while in detox. Bungee jumping, walking through fire, speaking in front of an audience that includes real people and not just your household pets, or getting a Brazilian bikini wax are some ideas. Or try an alternative treatment such as reiki, acupuncture, cupping, or ear candling. Explore your destiny and essence through a psychic, a tarot card reader, an astrologer, a handwriting analyst, or a palm reader. How about some karaoke? Or learn to express yourself in a different language. You're a Concert Chick, not a chicken! Concert Chicks are courageous beings. Be outrageously courageous! Kick limitations out and kiss your bliss in. I double dare you!

> *Take chances, break barriers, fight for what you believe, and destroy all obstacles placed in your path.*
> ~ANNA HERNANDEZ, WISE-BEYOND-HER-YEARS COLLEGE AND LIFE STUDENT, ARTIST, MUSICIAN, ANGELIC VOICE SINGER, CREATIVE WRITER

That Anna is a smart chick. In other words, be a Concert Chick warrior not a worrier. Put your energy into making things happen for you on your way to the state of blissfulness, the ultimate destination where you will take up permanent residence after you move out of your old way of showing up.

> *Our deepest fear is not that we are inadequate.*
> *Our deepest fear is that we are powerful beyond measure.*
> *It is our light, not our darkness, that most frightens us.*
> *We ask ourselves: "Who am I to be brilliant, gorgeous, talented, and fabulous?"*
> *Actually, who are you not to be?*
> *You are a child of God.*
> *Your playing small does not serve the world.*
> *There is nothing enlightened about shrinking so that other people won't feel insecure around you.*

> *We were born to make manifest the glory of
> God that is within us.
> It is not just in some of us; it is in everyone!
> And as we let our own light shine, we unconsciously
> give other people permission to do the same.
> As we are liberated from our own fears, our presence
> automatically liberates others.*
> ~Marianne Williamson, A Return to Love:
> Reflections on the Principles of
> A Course in Miracles

KEY 3: DO WHAT'S RIGHT
SHINE YOUR LIGHT ON OTHERS

> *To laugh often and much; to win the respect of intelligent people and the affection of children; to earn the appreciation of honest critics and endure the betrayal of false friends; to appreciate beauty; to find the best in others; to leave the world a bit better, whether by a healthy child, a garden patch, or a redeemed social condition; to know even one life has breathed easier because you have lived.
> This is to have succeeded.*
> ~Ralph Waldo Emerson

The first key helps you find your light. The second key is about being that light. And now, with the third key, you shine your light on others. You do this by being grateful for all the abundance in your life and then sharing your gifts with the world. Key 3 opens not only doors but, more important, hearts.

Gratitude is the foundation of doing what's right. When you do what's right for you, you're doing what's right for others by showing up as a bright spot in their lives. Your heart-filled actions will inspire and motivate others to be themselves and to follow their bliss. This is the natural rhythm of living, receiving, and giving. This cycle is the vehicle that leads to your genuine happiness, illuminating not only your path, but the path of others as well. You'll bring light to darkness wherever you go. Sparkles for everyone!

There are so many reasons to be thankful. Think of how many miracles happen every brand new day beginning when your alarm goes off (actually, they're constantly occurring whether you're awake or not, but let's use this as our starting point). Let the *beep, beep, beep* be a real wake-up call, and not just some noisy nudge for you to get your tush out of bed. As in *"Wake up!* You are—hooray!—still breathing." And you heard the buzz of the alarm—ears working, check! And how about giving yourself a hand for that hand you have at the end of your arm, complete with fingers no less, to shut the alarm off or to press the snooze button if you want a few more winks. And speaking of winks, when you open your eyes, you can still—yippee!—see. Notice that you're in a bed in a room with a roof, your head is on a pillow, and a warm blanket is hugging you. Or maybe it's that special someone snuggled next to you who loves you deeply. You have a reason to get up, somewhere to go—perhaps to a job (paycheck!) or a doctor's appointment (insurance/health!). All this before your feet even hit the floor! You have many reasons to wake up happy, not crappy.

> *Let us rise up and be thankful, for if we didn't learn a lot today, at least we learned a little, and if we didn't learn a little, at least we didn't get sick, and if we got sick, at least we didn't die; so, let us all be thankful.*
> ~BUDDHA

Make it your personal mission to thank everyone who does something that makes your life easier, sweeter, kinder, or just because. There are as many opportunities to say thanks as there are stars in the sky. Don't be shy. To the guy who let me in the left lane during rush hour: "Thanks!" To the lady who served my lunch: "Thank you!" To the person who dumps the trash in my office: "Thank you so much!" All. Day. Long. Give. Thanks.

Do you feel your attitude adjusting yet? Being filled with gratitude helps with the attitude. Step outside one clear night and look up and at the twinkling stars. These twinkles are reminders of all the blessings you have in your life. If you're grateful for what you already have, the universe delights in this and showers you with even more. We're talking deluges here! If you don't acknowledge your gifts or if you take them for granted or if you're simply aware that they have arrived and blow them off, the universe shrugs and thinks, "why bother? This one is an ingrate so let's redirect our gifts to someone who appreciates them," and it may even send you a shit shower. Not very refreshing and I imagine quite stinky. [9]

My father taught me early on that what goes around comes around. There are many ways you can share your light with others. The only requirement is that it must be genuine generosity, meaning you are giving from your heart. Altruism is more than a tax write-off, a photo op, or a resume builder. If you can donate dollars, do it. If you have time to volunteer to answer phones, deliver turkeys during the holidays, or stuff envelopes for a fundraiser invitation, do it. If you want to donate clothing to Goodwill or some other organization, do it. Just do something! And please don't forget the intangibles such as a smile, a listening ear, a kind word, a hug. I know some people who are generous with their dollars or time, but don't give others the time of day. Being kind, nice, thoughtful, compassionate, attentive, respectful, and appreciative are priceless gifts we can and must give to others. These intangibles don't cost you a dime, only a few moments of your time. Invest wisely in yourself and others and the returns are outstandingly off the charts.

> *Example is not the main thing that influences others, it's the only thing.*
> ~ALBERT SCHWEITZER

Most of all, become a massive giver—*I try to help at least one person a month that has less than I do and could use a little sparkle of their own in their lives. Who doesn't like to put a smile on someone's face when they*

---

[9] OK, so I doubt the universe through angels would ever use such rough language and take such gross action, but still. Anything is possible. Keep in mind that angels fly and wear shiny halos. I wouldn't want to piss them off.

are down, or help them get that bounce back in their step again? "Pay it Forward" is my mantra!
~**Denise Distel**, young soul still in training

No man becomes rich unless he enriches others along the way.
~ Andrew Carnegie

The highest destiny of the individual is to serve rather than rule.
~Albert Einstein

You can do things I can't do, and I can do things you can't do, but together we can do great things.
~Mother Teresa

If you still aren't convinced that you can make a difference or maybe you're stuck in the "each man for himself" mindset, you might be interested to know that it has been scientifically proven that "...a strong direct correlation...exists between well-being, happiness, health, and longevity in people who are kind and compassionate in their charitable helping activities...Love...makes the way easier and healthier for both those who give and for those who receive."[10]

One of my favorite books is *The Little Engine That Could* by Watty Piper. All it takes is the belief that you can do something and you'll be well on your way. Believe you can make it in rehab, that you can let go of all that weighs you down, that you can be yourself, follow your bliss, and do what's right. That you can and will leave trails of glitter in your wake and not debris that dims others' light as long as you live with enthusiasm and wonder and in turn inspire others to do the same. Sparkles are abundant and sparkly is contagious!

---

10 S. Pang, "Is Altruism Good for the Altruistic Giver?" *Dartmouth Undergraduate Journal of Science*, Spring 2009.

So there you have it. Put these keys on your key ring and use them often. They are guaranteed to unlock and open the real you that may have been smothered and stuck by all that body+mind+heart+soul weight. Go ahead and share your passion, your pocketbook, your day planner, and that beautiful smile of yours. Shine on!

And now, it's time to unlock the doors to rehab. Rox is ready to rock 'n' roll with you!

Chapter 3

It's Time to Rock 'n' Roll!

Life is one grand, sweet song, so start the music.
~RONALD REAGAN

*O*ui, it's time to rock 'n' roll in rehab! By now you should be ready to jump right in with both Moschino'd feet, so let's two-step through the four steps to give you an idea of how your total transformation will come about. After the captivating introduction in Chapter 1 and the empowerment of Chapter 2, intervention should be a breeze. So let's cross the threshold, shall we?

STEP 1: INTERVENTION
YOU DO NEED THIS!

TRUE CONFESSIONS + GENUINE EXPRESSIONS

The first step is to admit that you have issues. Hey, we all do, so don't feel bad. No judgment here. We already told you that you're perfect as you are today and nothing you tell us can change that fact. So, fess up! OK, so you self-medicate with merlot and muffins, you're addicted to silver shoes,[11] you regularly overdose on people who are downers, you inhale every negative vibe and make it your own, you're dependent on the approval of others for your happiness, and you find yourself jonesing for your acrylic paints but opt for a TV fix instead. It takes a strong chick to admit that she needs some body+mind+heart+soul detoxing. Good for you!

Throughout this book, there will be a lot of Q&As. If you have a blank journal and a special pen, please go get them now. If you don't, add these must-haves to your shopping list (check out the Swag Lounge for awesome journal resources) and grab something to write with and on and pull up a chair. We need to go over a few things.

INTAKE ASSESSMENT

Getting to know yourself inside and out is something to be celebrated. Find a quiet space, pour yourself a flute of Veuve Clicquot, a goblet of Perrier with lime, a cup of chamomile tea, or any other beverage that feels festive to you. Light an energizing soy candle, turn on whatever tunes set the tone for some word dancing, open your journal, put pen in hand, and enjoy meeting you!

Visualize your life as you want it to be. Dream big! No desires are too far-fetched. Use a separate page in your journal for each question. Take your time with this. What do you see? What does your perfect day look like? What does your best self look like? How do you act? What do you love to do? What do you not like to do at all? What do you do when no one is watching? Who supports, encourages, inspires, and loves you unconditionally? Feel free to jump ahead to Chapter 8 journaling prompts to access your relationships. Who, what, where is toxic to you? What habits no longer serve you?

On another page, draw an outline of your body as you see it now, leaving space around your image to jot notes. In this exercise,

---

[11] For the record, one can never have too many silver shoes, but we promised not to judge. Consider this simply an important public service announcement.

you'll go from head to toe, inside and out, to identify parts of yourself you love and parts you'd like to change. Start at the top of your head and think external and internal—is it time for a new color, a new 'do? Or do you just need a good deep conditioner? And then move *into* your head. Are you always worrying or thinking the worst? Constant chatter? Next up, your peepers. How about playing up your gorgeous eyes with a smudge of taupe shimmer on your lids and lushing up your lashes with falsies or triple swipes of dramatic mascara? And then ponder what you tend to see *through* your eyes. Do you wear rose-colored glasses? Or are you looking through dirty windowpanes? Do you see the good in yourself and others or only notice flaws?

Here are some random word prompts and queries to kick off this head-to-toe exploration of your body+mind+heart+soul. Engage all your senses on this journey. For extra guidance, fast forward to Chapters 6 and 7 for inspiration on how to add some oomph and *ooh la la* to your inner and outer worlds.

Don't overthink this assessment. Scribble the first thoughts that pop up.

Mind:

    Half full, half empty?
    How do you express your brilliance?
    What do you want to learn? A new language, how to be patient?
    How can you challenge yourself?
    New York Times crossword puzzle, meditation?
    Do you mind your own business?
    Are you losing your mind?

Hair:

    Is it time for a new style, color, or cut?
    Is it falling out? Stressed?
    Do you twirl it because you're anxious?
    Frames your face?
    Brings out your best features?

Do you hide your face behind your tresses?
Is it shiny? Healthy?
What's the long and short of it?

Eyes:

See the good or only the bad? Or just what is?
Play with shadows in full range of colors?
Does your shadow self need light?
Denial, eyes closed to obvious?
Windows of your soul, how are they framed?
See beauty? Rose-colored glasses?
Make eye contact?
Glare or stare?
Twinkle?
Hide behind sunglasses?

Mouth:

Do you speak up in your unique voice?
Or do you squeak? Timid as a mouse?
Are you heard?
How do you express yourself best? Spoken or written words?
Frame your smile with sparkly lip gloss or siren red lipstick?
Is it open more than your ears?
What goes in? Nutritious? Junk?
What comes out? Nurturing? Junk?

Nose:

Do you stop and smell the roses?
Do you have a signature scent?
What is your favorite aroma and why?
Do you always smell a rat (cynicism)?
Is your nose in other people's business?
Snotty?

Ears:
> Listen *and* hear?
> Open more than your mouth?
> Clogged?
> Adorned? Chandelier earrings, big hoops, or sparkly studs?

Skin:
> Are you comfortable in your own skin?
> Do you love the skin you're in?
> Do you moisturize more than you criticize?
> Any rough patches in your life?
> Hairy? Sunscreen protected?
> Show too much skin?
> Too covered up? Hiding from anything?
> Covering something up?

Neck:
> Do you stick it out often? Too much? Not enough?
> Look straight ahead or down? Or backward, rubbernecking at your past or overstretching into your future?

Arms:
> Hugs? Give and receive?
> Strong? Embrace?
> Arm-in-arm?
> Decorated with wing bling?

Shoulders:
> Do you carry the weight of the world on them?
> Posture, shoulders back? Slouched?
> Stand tall or act small or not at all?

Hands:
> Pat yourself on your back? Pat others on theirs?
> Applaud yourself and others?

Manicured, adorned with chicktail rings?
Bite nails? Chew cuticles?
Grasp dreams or slap them down?
Greet others firmly or limply?
Walk hand-in-hand with loved one?

Belly:

Take deep breaths? Shallow breathing?
Fearless belly flops in the deep end of the pool or
bobbing in the safety of the shallow end?
Belly laughs?
Digest good food and well? Or stuffed with junk and gunk?
Is there a fire in your belly?
What are your core values?
Do you follow your gut instincts?

Butt:

Do you sit around and watch the world pass you by?
Do you say "yeah, but...," always ready with an excuse why
something can't be done?
Perky? Pancake? Lumpy?
Constipated? Full of shit or honest?

Heart:

Beating, loving, fluttering, soaring?
Open or closed? Made of stone?
Full? Empty?

Soul:

Shimmery?
Fed soul food?
Untethered?
Wonder or wander? Or both?

Legs:

    Support you, take you places?
    Where are you going? Running from anything?
    Stand tall, firm in your convictions?

Feet:

    Pedicured, embellished with fabulous shoes?
    Are you a doormat? Do you step on others?
    Any rough spots to deal with?
    Calloused view of life?
    Good on your feet?
    How do you pace yourself?
    Are you a pacer?
    Slow, shuffle, run, glide, fly?

Review your assessment and journal entries. Place stars next to the areas you'd like to focus on in rehab. These can be your intentions that fuel your detox.

BOOK 'EM, CHICK-OHHHHH!

When people say to me: "How do you do so many things," I often answer them, without meaning to be cruel: "How do you do so little?" It seems to me that people have vast potential. Most people can do extraordinary things if they have the confidence or take risks. Yet most people don't. They sit in front of the telly and treat life as if it goes on forever.
                                                ~Philip Adams

Before I ask you to pull out your calendar, let's address the big *t* word and nip *that* in the bud pronto. And I'm not talking about television, though that could certainly be a huge part of it. Stay tuned for more on that later. For now, it's about "time," or the perceived lack of it. Yeah, that *t* word, the one that ticks most people off when I talk about it.

"You will never *find* time for anything. If you want time you must make it": so said Charles Buxton. I don't know who Mr. Buxton is other than an English author, but I tip my silver sequined beret to him and say, "Right on and *merci*, Chuckie." We all get the same 1,440 minutes a day. How many of them belong to you? You have more control over what you do and don't do than you realize. I hope by the end of rehab you'll be able to say "yes" to what you truly want and "no" to what you don't. We'll explore this in another chapter. All you need to know at this point is that to say "I have no time" is a load of *caca*. It's really just a lame excuse for "don't wanna." You do have time. And you know you wanna.

First, you need to identify what and who devours your day. Keep a list of everything you do tomorrow from the time you wake up until the moment you climb back into bed. Every. Single. Thing. You. Do. Note how much time you spend on each activity. Review your list the following day. Are you shocked? How much time did you spend gabbing with your co-workers when you could be getting your work done so you would not have to bring files home at night? How about vegging in front of the TV? (You knew I'd get here eventually). The average American spends more than thirty hours a week in front of the boob tube. That's almost another full-time job! This is one boob job that will not enhance your life—not saying that the other one necessarily does, but at least you have something (really, a couple of things) to show for it. What can you eliminate? The time you blow off in "idle" is the time you could be in "drive" for *you*, to make your dreams come true.

I don't have any children but before you say, "Aha! You have no clue!" let me share with you that I raised four brothers from the time I was very young. I was definitely clueless then, but I did what I had to do. I worked almost full-time and took care of the household—I cooked (if you can call it that), cleaned (Did I mention I had four brothers? Love them, but boys will be boys.), shopped (and not for Miu Miu mules, mostly milk and meatballs—my spaghetti was edible—barely), did the laundry (remember, four boys—that's a lot of underwear and socks), and performed other tasks that you may be all too familiar with. I started college full-time when I was sixteen, so add studying to the mix. Yet I still found time to go to the beach, take ballet classes, read, paint, and do other things that I enjoyed. No, I'm not all holier than thou, but I knew that if I didn't escape once in a while to take care of myself, I'd jump off the side of a building and then who would take care of everything in my absence? Besides, I'm afraid of heights (except when it comes to shoes) and I don't like making a mess.

I'm constantly asked how I had the time to write this book since I have a very full-time day job. It's all about priorities and circumstances. My husband works concerts many nights, so instead of being out and about while he's working, I write. I get up at 5:00 a.m. and write. I don't watch any TV at all; instead, I write. I decline social invitations so I can write. And I've pulled many all-nighters through the weekends so I can write. If you're passionate about something, you will always find the time to—thank you Nike!—just do it.

Back to your calendar. I'm talking seventeen days—two free-for-alls, fourteen in detox mode, and one for a party—out of 365 days. Surely you're worth it. Trust me—the world will not stop spinning just because you're stopping your whirlwind activities. Movie stars, rock stars, and other celebrities take downtime between gigs to refresh and renew. And since you are red carpet material, so must you.

I recommend clearing your calendar as much as you can to fully immerse yourself in rehab. Lock yourself in your nest as often as possible for two weeks to give yourself the best shot at total detox bliss. Only do the absolutely necessary, like your day job for gas money. Enjoy the rare retreat to hibernate and create—space, a new you, a new life.

I completely understand that there are circumstances that prevent you from blocking two weeks off to focus on you. Being flexible is also a Concert Chick trait, so if you really, truly are "no way, no how" now, cut the time in half—one prep day followed by seven days of detox and a party. Or, cherry-pick the program—maybe you're not interested in detoxing your body right now because tis the season, but you want to focus on calming, clearing, and centering your mind and will commit to meditating and journaling every day to avoid getting your tinsel in a tangle. Perhaps you want to open your heart. Can you commit to treating yourself and others with kindness, gratitude, and appreciation? Could it be that you want to clean out your body as well as your garage? Maybe it's your soul that intrigues you. You can spend two weeks in rehab exploring what you are here to do. What is your life purpose?

Whatever you do, acknowledge the treasure called your life, something that can be taken from you at any moment without warning. Go for "good enough," not "perfect," and I don't mean satisfied with a half-ass job. I mean not making yourself nuts trying to color inside the lines when there's so much out there in this wonderful world of ours to experience, discover, and explore. Don't spin your wheels on stuff that doesn't matter in the big picture, such as alphabetizing your spices or ironing your boyshorts, unless expending your energy in such a way somehow makes your life easier and you happier and healthier.

Now that you've been stripped bare of any excuses, it's time to open your calendar, day planner, smartphone, or whatever/wherever you can find a consecutive Friday and Saturday where you eat like a pig, followed by a Sunday-to-Saturday two-week period where you eat like a bird, followed by a red carpet debut where you party like a rock star. But as every good Concert Chick knows, rules (not laws, ever!) are meant to be broken or at least twisted and/or tweaked or interpreted in a new and exciting way, so if Friday isn't your preferred start date, no biggie. Pick any day and start from there. It's just that TGIF energy is always positively charged! And who doesn't want permission, if not an outright order, to eat and drink whatever they fancy over the weekend? Monday is the typical get back on track day. People pig out all weekend or really any day before the new weight loss program starts (again). So, why not acknowledge this, and officially start on a Friday, so by the time Monday rolls around, you're already on day four. The Rox Detox is also unique in that you are commanded to buy shoes! You read right. There is a mandatory food and beverage consumption of whatever your body+mind+heart+soul wants and a field trip to Nordstrom's infamous shoe department.

Once you've figured out what works best for you, claim this time by blocking off the days you selected. And not in pencil if you use a paper calendar like I still do. Surely you deserve to commit to yourself in ink. Jazz the pages up a bit with stickers and sparkles. I color in my chosen days with a bright yellow highlighter to symbolize my "light" time no matter what. And I am seriously addicted to glitter glue sticks. Little dots and swirls of sparkles make me smile. Show the universe colorfully loud and clear with sprinkles and a cherry on top that you are worth taking care of, that you deserve to treat yourself to this time, and that you matter at least as much (more!) as anything or anyone on your calendar.

YOUR DATE TO CELEBRATE

And now, for the ultimate calendar entry—open to your debut day and sketch and color in a red carpet, add some red glitter for extra appeal, and affix gold stars all over. Your celebration of you is detailed in Chapter 9, but now is the time to start thinking about where you want to roll out the red carpet. Once you decide the location, make reservations if necessary and tend to other to-dos to make it happen (new outfit, new hairdo, another pair of shoes!). You'll then be able to focus on your detox, with the light at the end-of-the-red-carpet-paved tunnel ready to illuminate so brightly that you are compelled to add Jackie O sunglasses to your shopping list if you don't already own a pair. Every chick should.

My fave celebration is brunch since debut day is on a Sunday and there are so many wonderful places to linger over a meal whether I'm in the mood for a beachside diner, a tiki bar deck, or a fancy-schmancy restaurant. Besides, brunch fits beautifully with my usual celebration theme—things that start with the letter "b": bubbles (as in bath and champagne), beach, and book. Salmon Eggs Benedict washed down with Bloody Marys, anyone? Your day, your way! Yay!

And remember, birds of a feather flock together, especially Concert Chicks. Recruit a rehab pal if this will make it more fun for you. This is your adventure whether you fly solo or in a flock.

Now that we have a date, and you probably know more about yourself than you did before, it's time to get familiar with the Rox Detox. But there's one last bit of business to wrap up before we climb to step 2. Pen your autograph on the *Rock the World Rehab* agreement that can be found in the Swag Lounge. Signing on the dotted line solidifies your commitment. Signed? Congratulations on your "commit to it" move. After you take a celebration break, I shall see you in "preparation." A cheerful cheers toast to you, chickie!

And now, without further ado, step *deux*...

STEP 2: PREPARATION
GET READY TO DO IT!

Welcome back! I hope you're still in a celebratory mood because step 2 is all about celebrating awesome you.

These first two days are very important. Prep isn't a pass to gorge yourself silly, but rather, it's a mandate to celebrate yourself fully (you will be doing much of this throughout the Rox Detox adventure). This step prepares you mentally, physically, emotionally, and spiritually for rehab, to put in action what you read and hopefully realized in Chapter 2. Go ahead and peruse what's in store for you and then return to Step 2 on the Friday you calendared to get things ready for the big purge.

Prepping for rehab is easy as pie—in fact, any pie you want. I'm deliciously serious, cupcake. One slice of key lime with thick graham cracker crust for *moi, s'il vous plaît*. On these two magical, transformative days, you can eat whatever you want. You can enjoy happy hour chicktails[12] and bar snacks with your peeps. You don't have to eat like a bird. The main theme of preparation is awareness. Pay attention to what you're eating, drinking, doing, saying, buying—basically how you're showing up—and whether what you witness is truly an expression of your best self. Are you walking the Chapter 2 talk (and in fabulous shoes)?

So, when you have that baker's dozen, ask yourself if you could've been satisfied with just one or two Krispy Kremes. When that guy cut you off on the highway and you flipped him a wing, did you really need to go there? Or could you fathom that the cutoff might not have been intentional, but that he lost his job ten minutes ago or worse, someone he loved dearly? We don't know what's going on in another's head or life. Nothing is to be gained by having your default set on "what a jerk!" mode. What else is your body+mind+heart+soul teaching you? Do you eat too fast? Talk too much? Feel guilty? Are you happy at work? Pay attention.

Prep days are also about wrapping up little projects (and swag!), running errands, anything you need to do to clear the decks for some detoxing. Now about that swag...

BAG + SNAG SWAG

Celebrities know all about swag, and since you're one, too, you must acquaint yourself with this fabulous word if you haven't met it yet. Swag is your reward for an excellent performance. Your swag doesn't have to be the $38,429 basket holding a 5G iPhone (plus the pad and pod), a Cartier tank watch, Prada pumps, an Hermés scarf, and other treats celebrities walk away with. I'm guessing that a huge difference between them and us is that we'll be gifting ourselves, and not counting on Prada execs to put this season's ultimate pump in our Grammy presenter gift basket. I don't know about you, but the last time Prada dropped off the latest "it" strappy

---
12 You just know we had to change "cock" to "chick."

sandal to my nest was…like…never. Not even in my dreams, and I dream large (a 39, to be exact, just in case said Prada rep is reading). Seriously, Concert Chicks are celebrities who like to take care of themselves anyway, *thankyouverymuch*.

Your swag is any treats that make you smile, keep you motivated and looking forward to another day of rehab, be it a bottle of drugstore fluorescent pink nail polish or a Tiffany Celebration Ring.

And because Concert Chicks are their own breed of celebrity, we appreciate intangible swag most of all in the form of ideas, thoughts, quotes, and other takeaways that you can't buckle down, zipper up, or strap on. These treats and tips have value because they come from the heart. Your daily prescription includes a Rox "rah-rah + hurrah" Box where you will find inspirational, motivational, practical words complete with pompom energy. In other words, you won't find a coupon for a chinchilla stole to wrap around your perfect shoulders, but rather, thoughtful tidbits to wrap your mind and heart around. Priceless!

FLUFFING YOUR NEST FOR DETOX + REST

If your home isn't already your sanctuary, you must sprinkle some glitter around your space, even if you have a minivan full of kids finger-painting your walls. It's essential to find one little spot under your roof that you can call your own. Where is your cozy cocoon? Hang a "do not disturb or else" sign on your bedroom, bathroom, attic, or even a closet doorknob. Or stake out a comfy chair tucked away in a nook, with a cozy throw on its arm that you can hug yourself with. Remember the forts you'd create with chairs and sheets when you were a kid? How about that? Or perhaps a tent in your backyard. Be playfully resourceful.

While it's nice to have a designated cocoon, perhaps what your body+mind+heart+soul desires is not to be tied down anymore, and you could support that feeling of moving a bit by assembling a rehab basket filled with essentials to enjoy during portable pauses. Line a fairly large basket, picnic or otherwise as long as it has a handle, with a piece of cloth (a few napkins do the trick) and add a candle, matches, some healing crystals such as rose quartz, colored pens, your journal, an iPod loaded with relaxing, energizing, make you want to dance playlists and ear buds, books (one nonfiction, one chick lit), a blanket, a pashmina (perfect for cocooning and it also makes a handy Wonder Woman cape if you're so inclined), and whatever else says "me time!" You can then flit around like a butterfly, to the beach, a mountaintop, up or under a tree, even park yourself in your car. You're limited only by your imagination.

After you've claimed some space, drop by your kitchen for a "pitchin' + ditchin'" party of one. Go through your fridge, pantry, and kitchen cabinets and toss old, expired, empty, moldy foods, and other "nutrients" that really aren't. And since you're in Step 2 prep mode and can eat and drink anything your sweet body+mind+heart+soul desires, feel free—guilt-free!—to sip that sauvignon blanc and savor those gingersnaps you discovered. It's your party.

You'll be tossing more than kitchen stuff while in rehab. In the previous section, a "daily prescription" was mentioned. To take the thinking and remembering out of the mix—you have plenty to do as it is—a daily "prescription", a.k.a. your "daily script", was created to guide you through all four steps of rehab, including a daily dump. Yep, a dump—of everyone and everything that weighs you down and dims your light.

While you're prepping your nest, get ready to make this dump by placing shopping bags and boxes near your closet and drawers, anywhere you stash stuff.

Let's practice the purge, shall we? Put this book down and go to any closet, drawer, floor, place you have stuff and pull one thing out that is no longer you due to fit, color, stain, tear, style. Anything that doesn't have a place in your world as you are at this very moment. Something you've been holding on to for years "just in case." A thing you may have no idea how it even found its way into your closet or, worse yet, you don't even know what the heck it is (a turkey baster or the part of Aunt Tildo's enema system that went missing during her visit last summer?). And then toss, donate, or consign (or return to your aunt). Do whatever must be done—just get it out of your life and then join me back on this page. What did you dump and why? How did it feel? Liberating? Debilitating? Did you pick up a few items before settling on one, telling a story about each, not being able to let it go because of some sentimental value? Get used to these feelings, as much time in rehab will be spent tossing useless space annihilators. You'll be showing the world who's the boss of *your* world with each and every toss!

Both the instructions and daily scripts can be picked up in the Swag Lounge. Now is a great time to go there, get that to review and fill so you'll be ready to roll as soon as you check into rehab.

Embrace *happinest*, as in "I am happiest when in my nest!" You may never want to leave.

LET'S GO SHOPPING!

But leave you must. It's time to shop for swag, sustenance, shoes, and stuff to make your rehab experience special.

Ideally, you'll be going to the grocery store every other day for your chick chow. You may be used to going once a week or so, but the Rox Detox focus is on freshness and mindfulness. Carry a canvas shopping bag or a *très chic* Parisian market basket and pretend you're in the South of France, Rox's birthplace, strolling an outdoor farmer's market, picking up ingredients for tomorrow's chicktails—lemons, water, cayenne pepper, cinnamon, and maple syrup. You'll be sipping nothing but these delish libations for the first two detox days. Also, make sure you stock up on the pills and drinks listed in your daily script instructions.

Treat yourself to new bed linens and towels, soy candles, and other things to spruce up your nest. A lush terry robe and a pair of satin kitten heel slippers with marabou trim make for a glamorous rehab uniform. How about a new place setting of dishes, glassware, and utensils? T.J. Maxx, Marshall's, HomeGoods, and Target are excellent "make your nest the best for rest" sources. How about your very own red carpet and red velvet rope? Browse the aisles of the Chapter 8 section in the Swag Lounge for all this and more.

You can buy all your swag at once before checking into rehab or shop as you detox. If you want to get it all at the mall or by logging on to your best-loved cyber shop pre-rehab, buy sixteen treats—one reward for committing to the Rox Detox adventure, one for each day you're detoxing, and one grand prize to accept on the red carpet. Another option is to visit the Swag Lounge in the back of this book at the end of every detox day and buy something that interests you. After you've had fun shopping, assemble all your goodies in an area where they won't be disturbed. *Voilà!* Your very own Swag Lounge.

I wasn't joshing in my galoshes when I told you that you must buy shoes. Two pairs actually! One to wear as you walk into rehab and another to step onto that red carpet on debut day. Keep your eyes out for shoes in a style that you normally wouldn't wear but would love to. Christian Louboutins are wonderful reminders of the red carpet mindset commitment, what with those dashing red soles and all. But if $1,000ish shoes are ridiculous in your book (pocket or otherwise), grab a pair in any stress-free price range. You can always paint your soles red or insert red insoles. Slide into the Swag Lounge for the 411. How many "diet"[13] programs have commanded shoe acquisitions?

FRIDAY

It's fun Friday! The day you officially embark on your Rox Detox adventure. Yeehaw!

---

[13] I despise this word and this is the last time you'll see it in this book. Originally, it meant "a way of life," but now it's simply a common four-letter word similar to "dull," "drab," and "dodo," and it is not a part of the Concert Chick vocabulary. We prefer to "get light," just as we know that we "glisten," not sweat.

The first order of business requires a scale, a tape measure, and a camera. I know, I know. We're off to a yucky start, but the sooner we get this out of the way, the sooner we can play.

THE NUMBERS GAME

Hop on the scale first thing in the morning after you've pooped and peed and are completely bare-ass naked. Make sure there isn't even one bobby pin in your hair, no rings on your fingers or toes, and off with the jammies, tiara, last night's ball gown, glass slippers, everything until there is nothing. Whatever the number is, do not freak out. Record your "start" weight in your journal and be done with it.

There are a couple of reasons for doing this now. First, knowing that your conditioned mind still judges itself through inches and pounds, if you wait for Sunday, day one of detox, you may see the effects of your free-for-all prep days and get discouraged.

Second, you get it out of the way. Numbers are merely a baseline from which you can measure your success in the traditional manner (five pounds lost—three inches gone—I'm the bomb!). I believe that numbers are bullshit because it truly boils down to how you feel, how healthy you are, and what kind of energy level you have and radiate. Scale readings have been forever the gauge of hot or not, and I'm afraid that there's no end to this silliness in sight. *Big sigh.* Weight fluctuates naturally whether you're packing pasta or crunching carrots. Don't ever get hung up on the numbers. The only reason you're being asked to get on that damn scale is for awareness purposes. The bottom line is that your worth is not measured and found in numbers.

Take age, for instance. Why people lie about their age is a mystery to me. Get into the habit of becoming a better person every single day, so when all those days add up to years, you'll be happy to announce how many years you have been *alive*, as in Q: "How old are you?" and A: "I've been ALIVE for fifty years!" Feel the difference when you put it this way? Besides, Concert Chicks also like to be technically correct, open, and honest.

Just *know* (no thinking about it) that you are so much more than your physical body. Sure, health is of the utmost importance because your body is the temple for your mind, heart, and soul, and without it functioning well, your soul's work isn't given the best chance for success in this lifetime. But you have to look at yourself holistically, and that means you don't focus on the size of your thighs. I hope you caught an upfront and personal glimpse of this as you conducted your own head to toe assessment in Step 1.

My guide is my wardrobe. How my clothes fit tells me all I need to know. If I can't zip up those True Religions, it's a little clue that I need to get down on my knees and confess and pray to Jesus for going to cannoli hell and back, which seemed so heavenly at the time. I either packed on a few pounds or my beloved did the laundry again, bless his heart. For crissakes, the truth of the matter is that I need to cut back on those Nilla Wafers and wine coolers. In any event, you won't weigh yourself again until debut morning. Amen!

While you're still naked, grab a tape measure and wrap it around yourself as described below, recording inches as you go:

- Bust (wrap the tape around your chest, across your nipples): ___"
- Waist (the thinnest part, of course): ___"
- Hips (the widest part, sorry): ___"
- Thighs (once again, the widest part near the top): ___" right ___" left
- Calves (you guessed it, the widest part): ___" right ___" left

Like your closet indicator, measurements provide you with telling information more valuable than numbers on a scale. A pound is a pound is a pound, whether we're talking blubber or brawn, but if you've ever seen a true-to-life model of what a pound of fat looks like versus a pound of lean tissue, you'll know that one chunk is larger and lumpier than the other. Two chicks can each weigh 150 pounds, yet one wears a size 8 and the other a 14. Just remember, numbers are nonsense unless they are found on the winning lottery ticket you have in your hand.

IT'S TIME FOR SOME CLICK, CLICK ACTION
SMILE + SAY "CHICK"

Put the tape measure away and pull out your camera and a red pen. It's before and after photo time! Where's the paparazzi when you need them? Ideally, you're wearing your bathing or birthday suit. This depends on who's doing the photo snapping (and no Photoshopping, girls!) If you must be dressed, wear something body-hugging. This isn't for publication, unless you are the most fearless Concert Chick of all and decide to upload the photo to your Facebook page. Take a full body shot—front and back and from the side, one set in heels and another barefoot, so you can see how your body aligns both ways and how awesome your legs look in those super high and fly Steve Madden wedges. *Ooh la la.*

Sure, you could spin around in front of a mirror and observe your body, but there's something about an objective out-of-body peek at how you're showing up in the world that makes a big difference. Take a headshot, too, and make sure you have a huge smile on your beautiful face when the flash goes off. You have much to be happy about, *bonbon*. Your size, your posture, your stance, your smile—everything speaks volumes about the image and energy you project. It's true that a photo speaks a thousand words, at least.

Now that you've weighed, measured, posed, and put your clothes back on (optional), open your journal and answer these questions. Are you happy with your current weight? Are you satisfied with how your body looks? What are your photos telling you? What would you like to change about your body? Is your smile sincere? How's your posture? Do you come across confident or self-conscious?

Review your entries and make a list of the things that you love about your body and the things you don't. Use that red pen to cross off facts on your list that you can't change, such as your height, the length of your legs, the size of your feet. Keep it real. I wish I had small tootsies, but you know, I can walk and that's a damn good reason to be happy with what I've got. No matter how hard I wish my feet were petite, I'll never be able to click the size 6 box on the www.Zappos.com order screen. In rehab and beyond, concentrate only on what you can do something about. With this in mind, look at your list again and scratch through more if you missed anything during the first round. What remains is your rehab wish list for your body. Whenever your thoughts turn to emptying the cookie jar, refer back to your photos and your journal entries. But remember, *s'il vous plaît*, as we've discussed before, there's no such thing as perfection. Actually, let me take that back. There is. Perfection resides in your best self, as defined by you. A body+mind+heart+soul in harmony is perfect plus.

Spend the rest of the day fluffing your nest, mindfully enjoying meals and happy hour, shopping, relaxing, living as if all you desire already exists. And don't forget to journal between bites, sips, and signing purchase slips. Be *aware* while you rock your frolicking Friday!

SATURDAY

After you've wrapped up whatever you didn't get around to on Friday, and after you've slurped your last appletini and savored that strudel, it's time for a very groovy to get you in the groove ritual.

"ROCK 'N' ROLL REHAB EVE" RITUAL

The "Rock 'n' Roll" ritual solidifies your commitment to roll with the punches of detox. "Rock" is all about being solid in who you are—firm in your convictions, values, beliefs, and your inner knowing of what you desire and what you need to get there. "Roll" is all about going with the flow. You're cool, calm, collected, and connected! Letting go of people, places, and things that no longer shine light on your path isn't easy, but it's necessary. Are you ready for some silly powerful fun?

Gather the following bits and pieces:

- 7 medium-size rocks that you can write on
- 1 big rock (not as in "boulder," but if you have one handy, it would make quite the statement)
- A little roll (but not with the word "sweet" in front of it—7 Ping-Pong balls will do)
- 1 Sharpie pen
- 1 superhero cape
- 1 pair of awesome shoes (the ones you bought to cross over the "new you" threshold)
- 1 tube or pot of glitter lip gloss
- 1 very sparkly tiara
- 2 wide bangle or cuff bracelets, a matching set or not, Wonder Womanish
- 1 invincible attitude

And you are invincible! Tie on your superhero cape, slip on your sassy shoes, top your crown chakra with a sparkly tiara, swipe on glittery lip gloss in the wildest "watch out world!" hue, and slide a bracelet onto each wrist. Then grab your balls, rocks, and Sharpie and find a special place to reflect, write, and rock 'n' roll.

Let's rock on first. During days 1 through 7, the focus will be on *rock*—laying the foundation for your rehab experience and your life. You want to be as solid as a rock, grounded, standing firm in your center. It's important to know who you are and what you want. What works for you and what doesn't? What's nonnegotiable? You may not know the answers at this point, but surely something drew you to rehab, so start there. Write down what you desire on each of the seven rocks. One word or as many as you can fit on the stone. You'll be using these rocks as a daily focus during rehab. At the top of your daily script, you'll see the word "rock" to remind you to grab a rock to focus on that day. If you can't think of seven now, it's OK to leave the stones undeclared. I'm sure something will come to mind as you purge. Put all the rocks, plain and committed, into a basket.

Now it's time to roll out. During days 8 through 14, the focus is on *roll*—going with the flow, moving toward your best self, still being grounded but starting to go places. This time you'll write on each Ping-Pong ball the name of a person, place, behavior, and/or thing you need to let go. You'll roll one out every day (the word "roll" on your script is a prompt for you to grab a ball), or all on one day if you're ready. Ready? Place a marked ball on the floor and kick it. After it stops rolling, stomp it flat with your awesome shoes. Place the crushed ball in the trash. Buh-bye dark. *Bonjour* light!

On your red carpet debut day you'll bring it all together—*rock + roll*—you're whole! We'll do something special that day with the big rock. Keep it in sight as a reminder of your solid commitment to take care of your body+mind+heart+soul.

The grand finale of this ritual involves some bling. Stand tall in your super chick gear, part those sparkly glossed lips and declare, while holding up your arms in V-for-victory style, flashing those bracelets:

> *I am a rock! I stand firm in my light in my awesome shoes! I'm ready to roll and let go of all that blocks my ability to grow and glow! I'm an ass-kickin' sparkly work in progress. Do not mess with me, for I am a Concert Chick! I rock!*

Now that you have everyone's attention, enthusiastically embrace your detox with both wings and get ready to soar higher than ever before!

> *Enthusiasm is the yeast that makes your hope rise to the stars. Enthusiasm is the sparkle in your eyes, the swing in your gait, the grip of your hand, the irresistible surge of will and energy to execute your ideas. Enthusiasts are fighters. They have fortitude. They have staying qualities. Enthusiasm is at the bottom of all progress. With it, there is accomplishment. Without, there are only alibis.*
> ~Henry Ford

GET SWAGGED!

Stop by your Swag Lounge to pick up your Step 2 success prize before you go to bed. You are embarking on something special. *Bonne nuit, chère* chickie. Sweet detoxifying and "you rock and roll" dreams.

STEP 3: DETOXIFICATION
YOU ARE DOING IT!

It's time to officially check out of toxic town and into rehab. You've cleared the decks, made a commitment, assessed where you're at, and where you want to be. Sunday is a wonderful day to begin. See and feel the *Sun* in Sunday: light, radiant, brilliant energy. Be prepared to throw back the heavy curtains to let the sunshine in by removing whatever is blocking your body+mind+heart+soul's felicity. Sense the sun in you.

Chapter 4 explains in depth your detox sustenance, but here's a peek at the menu so you'll have a general idea of what will be on your plate, in your glass, in your gut, and out your butt.

DAYS 1 + 2 (SUNDAY + MONDAY): BOTTOMS UP!

> *Fasting will bring spiritual rebirth...the light of the world will illuminate within you when you fast and purify yourself.*
> ~Gandhi

Depending on how you spent your two prep days, you'll either jump out of bed ready to go or crawl out with a whopping head and tummy ache, feeling and looking a little fuzzy, hung over, sugar buzzed, bloated, with indigestion, heartburn, and more. Jot a few notes in your rehab journal about how you feel. It's all good no matter how awful, because you *will* learn from the experience in one way or another.

Pull out your prescriptions for days 1 and 2 and fill in the blanks. Setting your intentions helps you focus and fuels awareness, even if you don't follow through with everything. This adventure is designed to lighten your load, not weigh you down with more stuff to do.

As for body fuel, you'll be sipping Concert Chick Chicktails. All. Day. Long. For two days.

DAYS 3 + 4 (TUESDAY + WEDNESDAY): GET JUICED + JUICY!

Enjoy veggie + fruit juice each day for two days.

DAYS 5 + 6 (THURSDAY + FRIDAY): SOLID WINE WITH A SPLASH!

Yep, grapes. Nothing but delicious, nutritious, cleansing grapes. These are your solid wine days. Knowing that this reframe could be viewed as more torture than treat, you can sip and savor a 4-ounce glass of "good cheer" wine of your choice each day.

DAYS 7 + 8 (SATURDAY + SUNDAY):
BE FRUIT LOOPY!

Get loopy on two days with as much fruit as you can handle.

DAYS 9 + 10 (MONDAY + TUESDAY):
VEG OUT + ABOUT!

Enjoy any kind of veggies, all day long times two.

DAYS 11 + 12 (WEDNESDAY + THURSDAY):
STILL VEGGING + FRUITY

Yummo-combo days—same drill: crunch, crunch, munch, munch a bunch of veggies and fruit.

DAYS 13 + 14 (FRIDAY + SATURDAY):
SOUPER YOU!

Sip and/or slurp super satisfying super-you soup! (Say that three times fast!)

WHAT TO EXPECT

Honesty is the best policy, so here's the scoop: This is very hard work! But since when is a Concert Chick afraid of a challenge? There's a new you waiting to be hatched that happens when you bid *adieu* to all that dims you. Parting ain't easy, whether it's people, places, things, or behaviors. It *is* sweet sorrow, as the saying goes. Your body+mind+heart+soul craves this well-deserved break, but I wouldn't say it's a walk in the park. There will be much going on, in, and around you. Your digestive system will be decongesting as it's resting. Leftover waste will be dumped into your bloodstream for elimination through your skin, lungs, colon, liver, and kidneys.

You'll be breaking up mucus, purifying blood, reducing gas (after the initial adjustment), stimulating and strengthening organs (especially your heart and liver), calming the nervous system, and resetting those appetite buttons.

While you're letting the not-so-good go, you may experience some not-so-good such as body odor, rashes, bad breath, constipation, extra pee-pee breaks, light-headedness, excess gas, a little fur coat on your tongue, headaches, muscle aches, dizziness, diarrhea (a.k.a. "*le* crack attack"), and/or fatigue.

But please hang in there. The downside is short term, depending on—once again—how toxic you were when you started this adventure. Think of it this way—you're feeling like crap because of crap. Imagine that the toxins in your body are nothing more than little thugs, sitting on stools, calculating their next move with the ultimate goal being a complete takeover of your healthy state. The gangs of gook are using your body as a toxic war zone, trying to protect their turf. If you don't eradicate these gross gremlins, they'll multiply, slowly building, building every day until *bam*! Be prepared for quite an explosion if you don't eliminate these goons! Since we don't get a do-over when our time is up, it's better to stop the takeover with a makeover.

Pay attention to any resistance you may feel. Don't forget that your body isn't the only participant here. Your mind, heart, and soul also have a starring role. Your cellular memory bank has stored everything that has happened to you since birth and when it's recalled, all that open space you create when you deep sweep physical and emotional closets may be uncomfortable. You could cry, and I hope you do. Tears wash away more than just your mascara. You may feel things you've never felt before once you open that door. But keep it open. Trust that it's worth it. And then wait for the miracles to pop up in your life.

Emotions such as anger, sadness, resentment, shame, guilt, and grief can be more toxic to your body+mind+heart+soul than the food you eat. You may have medicated or numbed yourself with food, drink, people, and material things, and in rehab this isn't an option. You're left raw and vulnerable. Stay with it. Write what you're experiencing in your journal. Soon the heavy dark feelings will depart, making room for the light, leaving you joyful, strong, clear, and in tune with your real essence which will be revealed once the sludge is out. Eventually, your skin will be clear and glow, you'll have lots of energy, you'll sleep peacefully, and be less saggy and baggy, if at all. You'll see, feel, be total health in action.

HOW TO AVOID A RELAPSE

Don't blame anyone or anything if you relapse. You have to take responsibility for your health and what you put into your mouth—your life—is totally up to you, unless you're tied down and force-fed, in which case, dial 911 immediately after your next meal is over, if you can't get to a phone beforehand. Don't blame your pushy though well-intentioned family, your possibly jealous friend, your demanding insane boss, the juicy menu at the corner diner, your friend for getting married during rehab, or 2-for-1s at your favorite watering hole. You're in charge of you.

Constantly ask yourself: Is this worth it? Is it worthy of me? Is this the best use of my time? Does what I am about to do support my life goals? Does it resonate with who I am today and who I want to be? Does it move me from the dark to the light? Write these questions on an index card that you can carry around with you as a reminder of your desire to be conscious in your actions. Even if the answer is no to every query but you go ahead anyway, being aware and making a conscious decision will start moving things around so that eventually "no" means "no" all the way around.

Remind yourself often why you're doing this. To lose weight, to recharge your batteries, to fit into clothes you haven't worn in a long time, to stop body jiggle, to reduce stress, to declutter, to lower your blood pressure, to lower cholesterol, to reduce the number of meds you take, to sleep better, to get sick less, to focus more, to strengthen your bones and muscles, to enjoy a longer life. Do you want a better self-image, increased self-esteem, a sense of achievement, space for miracles? How does all of the above sound? Now is the time to say *au revoir* to the energy drainers, smothering stuff, and stifling fluff. Sweetheart, be tough! Haven't you had enough? I thought so.

If you receive gifts of food, bring the stash to your office, a nursing home, or a homeless shelter. Another surefire solution is to simply toss it. This may seem wasteful at the time, but what a waste to use your body as a human garbage disposal.

If people pressure you to relapse, ask too many questions, or make comments about what you're eating or not eating, go ahead and tell them that you're allergic to the specific food or beverage they're pushing. If they are persistent, insistent, and basically annoying, explain in great detail what could happen if you eat/drink what they're pushing, including full body rashes and projectile vomiting. OK, not really, because Concert Chicks don't tell tales. Simply say *"Je suis au régime"*[14] to the inquiring mind who wants to know (even though it's none of his or her beeswax), while flashing your pearly whites once and clicking your Giuseppe Zanottis twice.

One of the most obvious ways to keep food out of your mouth is to stop bringing it there, which means keeping your hands busy or clasped in your lap and your mouth otherwise engaged or shut. Any of these will do the trick:

- ♦ Knit one, purl two, and you'll have a poncho before you're through.
- ♦ Walk. Run. Skip. Do a cartwheel or a backward flip.
- ♦ Surf the net. Surf the sea. Collect shells. Glue shells to frames.
- ♦ Mani or pedi or both. Or neither.
- ♦ Lace on boxing gloves and punch a bag, spar the air.

---

14 This is French for "I'm on a diet." And no, I haven't broken my promise to not put the "d" word in this book again. It's merely a French lesson.

- Try on outrageous shoes.
- Call a friend. Be a friend. Make a new friend. Release an old one.
- Write a thank-you note. Pen a good-bye. Doodle.
- Send sparkly cards to your peeps. Fill with confetti, little fridge magnets, other envelope compatible surprises. Sign with "xx" (double air kisses but with meaning).
- Play an instrument or learn to play one. Play with Play-Doh. Just play.
- Brush your teeth. Whiten your teeth. Brighten your smile. SMILE.
- Chew sugarless bubblegum. Blow bubbles. With each snap, crackle, and pop think of how you're rising to the top. Take a bubble bath.
- Give yourself a facial. Make funny faces in a mirror. Experiment with makeup.
- Needlepoint (but never needle and do not point). Crochet a beret. Bedazzle everything.
- String beads. Sew buttons. Search www.etsy.com to be inspired by other souls' creations and while you're there, order some swag.
- Meditate. Pray. Bask in moonshine. Take in sunshine. Count stars and clouds. Howl at the moon.
- Count blessings. Create a gratitude list. Write "thank you God" one hundred times.
- Collage journal pages, posters, walls, your car.
- Garden. Weed, seed, water, hug a tree. Sit under a tree. Climb a tree. Stand in tree pose. Plant a rose garden. Stop and smell the roses.

- Read a book, simply sit and look. Write a book. Blog about your rehab experience.
- Assemble a 2,000-piece jigsaw puzzle. Celebrate life with a jig. Puzzle others by doing said jig in a packed elevator or in the middle of the street.
- Get your blankie and take a nappy. Dream.
- Scream! Watch a scary movie. Sing the "Monster Mash."
- Wear a mask (boo!) or a masque (another facial!)

OK, so you have completed steps 1, 2, and 3—you are now free to be—YOU—authentically! Yippee! It's time to party!

STEP 4: CELEBRATION
YOU DID IT!

Really, finally, whew, and woohoo!

Today is all about you and your red carpet debut.

You did it! You detoxed your body+mind+heart+soul. You've rocked, you've rolled, and now you rock *and* roll! It's time for the new you to walk that red carpet leading to your stage, where you'll make your debut. Chapter 9 provides you with all the glorious details on how to celebrate your superstar self.

It. Truly. Is. All. About. You.

You've now walked the 4-step path of fame. It's time to dish on some specifics. First stop: catering, for the yummy scoop on your detox menu.

Chapter 4

Feeding Your Body+Mind+Heart+Soul

If it shits, I don't eat it.

~Madonna

Madonna, an über Concert Chick if we ever saw one, will be thrilled to know that nothing on the rehab menu poops.[15] The Rox Detox is actually a shit shift, as in moving the garbage we feed our body+mind+heart+soul out while moving true nourishment on all levels in. While the primary takeaway from this chapter is the food and drink you'll be feeding your body, we'll also touch upon what to feed your mind, heart, and soul, too. The Rox Detox sustenance is nutritious and delicious, because not only will your body sing a new song, your mind, heart, and soul will jump on the bandwagon as well, creating healthy harmony.

The menu is purposely simple yet powerful so you can pay attention to what really weighs you down. It's quite common to gobble not only food, but negative and uncomfortable feelings such as fear, worry, sadness, guilt, shame, resentment, hatred, and other emotions that go bump in the night of your psyche, which oftentimes results in the administration of a snack salve and the

---

15 Though you will be if all goes as planned, so stay close to *la toilette* whilst detoxing.

elimination of the ability to slink around in that darling Rag & Bone jumpsuit.

What we eat is very important to our overall physical and mental health and general well-being. You know this. But what you might not know is how equally important it is to not become obsessive about what you're eating or not eating. Worry, guilt, reactivity, or any other negative garbage can be just as toxic to your body as junk food. Perhaps more so. That's why the rehab menu is a snap to follow. You won't have to think much about the nourishment you're getting; just know that you are getting plenty of it—enough to fuel your rehab activities and more. The ultimate goal is to eat to fuel, nourish, nurture, love, and respect your body, and not for any other reason, such as emotional comfort or stress busting, unless you want to burst out of your J Brand's, which I suspect you do not.

Tie on a bib and grab a spoon and a swizzle stick. It's time to meet what you'll drink and eat. The delicious details (some sizzling!) are dished out here, served up on the most fabulous platters, spinning and twirling no less! Let's dig in!

PREP DAYS 1 + 2: YEEHAW, IT'S A FREE-FOR-ALL!

Anything your body+mind+heart+soul desires. Really.

DAYS 1 + 2 (SUNDAY + MONDAY): BOTTOMS UP!

Rox Detox Chicktails! All. Day. Long. What could possibly go wrong? Enjoy sipping these deep-cleansing libations during your first two days in rehab. Sunday and Monday could very well be the hardest days, but on the heels of the two easiest days, perhaps not so hard. Everything in balance, right? Right! Your body will welcome the rest. Look to other detox activities to sate your appetite.

> ## ROX DETOX CHICKTAILS
>
> fill a gorgeous goblet with:
> 8 oz. room-temperature filtered or bottled no-gas water
> 2 tbsp. of freshly squeezed lemon juice
> 2 tbsp. of Grade B maple syrup
> top with a 1 tsp. sprinkle of cayenne pepper + a dash of cinnamon
> swizzle stick stir
> insert little paper chicktail umbrella
> open beak + sip + savor
> cheers!

This chicktail rocks the big one. The ingredients are healthy powerhouses that do your body good. Maple syrup is an excellent source of manganese and zinc, which are awesome antioxidants. Lemons show your liver love through a stimulating cleanse that knocks out toxins. They are packed with vitamin C, low in calories, and high in potassium. That's nothing to pucker about, tartlet.

Cayenne pepper works its magic on the circulatory system through warming and dilating and can actually equalize blood pressure instantly. It improves digestion and brings blood to the surface, allowing toxins to be taken away. This hot stuff also gives you more pep and energy, which adds more hotness to your already smokin' self.

Cinnamon is a wonderful source of manganese, fiber, iron, and calcium. Studies have shown that just one-half a teaspoon of cinnamon a day can lower LDL cholesterol (the bad one) and aid digestion.

Enjoy at least six chicktails a day, no more than ten.

DAYS 3 + 4 (TUESDAY + WEDNESDAY): GET JUICED + JUICY!

The internal shower continues with another couple of days of liquids only. You're in super-saturation mode now. Sip 64-ounces of veggie/fruit juice a day for two days. Nurse your beverage to allow your brain to register "not hungry." If you chug your juice, you might feel deprived, which could turn into depraved and possibly raving mad, at which time you might raid the pantry. Go slow, not bonkers.

The very best source of juice is from your own kitchen. If you own a juicer, it's time to dust it off if you haven't used it in awhile (or ever) and turn it on. If you've never juiced before and are now the proud owner of a new juicer, unpack it and whir away. There are many excellent juicing books out there. Check out the Swag Lounge for our favorites as well as some info about juicers.

The next best is to have someone else make your juice with their equipment. Many health food grocers and joints have juice bars. But beware! Make sure only fruit and veggies go into the mix, and not yogurt, ice cream, and other additives that some shops use.

The next, next best is to buy bottled juice from your grocery/health food store. This is the option I usually favor, as the last thing I want to do on a workday (or any day for that matter) is peel, chop, blend, puree, and/or squeeze the juice out of apples and carrots, *and* then clean out the juicer (not to mention the dusting I had to perform at the onset). There are loads of amazing products on the market that only require you to buy, open, sip, and enjoy. Pick up eight bottles each containing about 15-16ish ounces of fresh juice (300ish calories max a bottle is a good guideline). Read the labels carefully to avoid bringing home some simulated concoction. Sip four bottles each day for two days. *J'adore* Naked and Bolthouse Farms juice in the two-serving bottles. My favorite Naked juices are Berry Blast, Orange Mango Motion, and Gold Machine. The top Bolthouse Farms juices in my fridge are Açai Berry with Mangosteen, Green Goodness, Berry Boost fruit smoothie, Strawberry Banana fruit smoothie, and Pear Merlot Take Heart.

No matter what juicy road you take, you'll get juiced. And that's all that matters!

DAYS 5 + 6 (THURSDAY + FRIDAY): SOLID WINE WITH A SPLASH!

Be forewarned! These days bite! Well, actually, you'll do the biting, as you are entering solid food days. Hooray! Two days of solid wine! Yay! Grape days are upon us! Yippee! And the splash is one 4-ounce glass of your favorite wine on these two days (and these days only). *Oui*, wine in rehab. Wowee! We told you the Rox Detox is unlike any other.

Let's jaw about the grapes first. Grapes cleanse and harmonize the body. They are an excellent lung and large intestine tonic. Red grapes are preferable because they contain resveratrol (more on this below), but the green ones work, too, if you insist. All you have to do is rinse, eat, and repeat all day long, but pop no more than three standard size bags per day. You can also create refreshing mini popsicles by freezing a bunch. *Délicieux!*

As for the splash, many will balk that alcohol is allowed in a detox program. But screw that because living isn't about deprivation. If *vous aimez le vin rouge* like *moi*, there's no reason to run from this urge while in rehab.[16] Wine pours good stuff on the state of your health. Studies show resveratrol, found in the skin and seeds of grapes used to make red wine, may help reduce the risk of blood clots and plaque formation in arteries, reduce bad cholesterol, prevent damage to blood vessels in the heart, and help maintain a healthy blood pressure.

Red wine also contains flavonoids, an antioxidant that has been shown to increase HDL (the good cholesterol), decrease the risk of clogged arteries, and lower blood pressure. In small amounts, the alcoholic properties of wine could reduce the risk of heart disease, diabetes, strokes, gallstones, and heart attacks. Red wine also contains polyphenols, which have anti-inflammatory and antitumor activities and prevent heart disease. *A votre santé!*

You are almost halfway through rehab. Cheers to you!

---

16 Of course, the splash isn't mandatory, so if you think a splash will morph into a splurge, skip it. Your debut will be here soon enough.

DAYS 7 + 8 (SATURDAY + SUNDAY): BE FRUIT LOOPY!

Enjoy as much fruit as you desire over the next two days. Fruit is filled with vitamins and minerals and satisfies your sweet tooth. Don't fret over the sugar content. It's God's candy and not some manufactured garbage, so it's all good. Fruit is also full of fiber and water, so it's really beyond good.

Fresh is best. Your produce department will have presliced, cubed bits and pieces if it's more convenient for you and/or if you're klutzy with sharp objects. Fruit found in the freezer section is fine if fresh isn't available. Just make sure the bag contains only fruit. Be leery of the jars of fruit you see in the produce cooler. Check the labels very carefully, as there are usually extras that aren't detox friendly. Absolutely no canned fruit, no matter how healthy the label tells you it is. The soggy fruit is usually swimming in heavy syrup that completely negates the benefits.

Here's a list of fruit that is especially detox supportive:

- Apple: Great source of fiber (eat the skin!) and a lovely liver supporter, blood purifier, and kidney tonic. High in potassium, with oodles of Vitamin C in the skin.

- Banana: Don't be afraid of this perfectly gift-wrapped fruit! Gives you quick, excellent energy.

- Blueberries: Fiber and a major antioxidant that fights free radicals, helps prevent cardiovascular disease, and possibly senility.

- Cantaloupe: Supports immune system and keeps blood pure and the body glowing.

- Cherries: Builds blood, mild laxative.

- Cranberries: Kidney cleanser. Good for the urinary tract.

- Grapes: Lymphatic cleaner, blood purifier, bowel mover, and high in vitamin C, magnesium, and potassium.

- Grapefruit: Same deal as lemon.
- Kiwi: More Vitamin C than an orange. Boosts immunity.
- Lemon: Really gets things moving! The best and quickest detoxifier around purifies the system, high in vitamin C, calcium, magnesium, and potassium.
- Lime: See lemon.
- Mango: Another digestion aid.
- Orange: Blood cleanser, stirs up acids, mucus, and more for elimination; lowers cholesterol, stabilizes blood sugar.
- Papaya: Digestive enzyme aid.
- Pear: Revs up digestion.
- Peach: Stimulates digestive juices, builds blood, moves bowels.
- Pineapple: Protein digestive aid—stimulates kidneys, causing you to run to the bathroom more often for pee pee breaks, which is a very good thing provided the *la toilette* is nearby.
- Pomegranate: Kidney and blood tonic, cardiovascular support.
- Watermelon: An excellent flusher!

If you decide to wield a knife, put yourself in a Zen-like trance (maintaining a focused "sharp object" awareness) while chopping, slicing, dicing, or otherwise preparing your fruit. View this prep time as a mini retreat/escape/stress-busting tool. Really engage all your senses. Focus on the gift of the juicy pieces you'll soon savor. This is the perfect opportunity to be in the moment. Ahhhhhh—as you peel, pare, and carve the fruit, think about what each piece has gone through to get to your home, into your mouth. A seed was planted and nature—the sun, the rain, the air, and more—did their thing and before you know it, divine treats came to be. And then someone picked, packed, shipped, distributed, bought, and displayed the fruit for your pleasure. Now it's your turn. You selected, paid for, carried home, washed, prepared, and consumed. And the process doesn't stop there. Your magnificent body works its magic. Astounding! (On that note, fruit digests quickly and cleans you out swiftly. Stay near a bathroom.) Of course, you could also vent by slicing and dicing. It's very therapeutic to slice cucumbers and shred carrots.

And don't forget to be a smooth operator. Yum! Smoothies! Fruit can also be frozen to create popsicles and sorbets. Dump fruit chunks into a blender and whir away, adding shots of water (nothing else!) to bring to the desired consistency (none for sorbet, some for smoothies). Frozen bananas=awesome dessert. Are you feeling all fruit loopy yet? Sweet!

DAYS 9 + 10 (MONDAY + TUESDAY): VEG OUT + ABOUT!

I never worry about diets. The only carrots that interest me are the number you get in a diamond.
~Mae West

Well, Mae, vegetables can cause us to sparkle brighter than any ol' diamond, but I do appreciate your point. Diamonds are a girl's best friend after all, but second to a sparkly body+mind+heart+soul.

Anyhow, it's time to veg out for two days. Veggies, like fruit, have amazing healing powers. They are full of vitamins, minerals, phytonutrients, antioxidants, fiber, and water. Here's a smidgeon of what good some of them do for you:[17]

- ◆ Artichoke:* Aids digestion, stabilizes blood sugar.
- ◆ Artichoke heart:* High fiber, able to increase bile production.
- ◆ Asparagus:* Loads of potassium and fiber that cleanses the digestive system; a diuretic.

---
17 * = fantastic detox veggies—all have a diuretic effect over and above the others.

- Beets:* Outstanding liver cleanser.
- Broccoli: Strengthens bones.
- Cabbage: Prevents constipation.
- Carrots: Eyesight improver and bowel mover in one!
- Cauliflower: Strengthens bones.
- Celery:* Excellent cleansing properties that aid digestion; a diuretic.
- Dandelion greens:* Stimulates digestion, liver function, and urination.
- Mushrooms: Controls blood pressure, lowers cholesterol.
- Onions: Lowers cholesterol, fights fungus, kills bacteria.
- Sweet potatoes: Excellent vitamin A action; lifts mood.

Enjoy a wide array of veggies raw, steamed, boiled, baked, any which way but battered, buttered, or otherwise oiled and fried. You can sprinkle on herbs and a pinch of sea salt to jazz things up. It's much easier to eat your peas and carrots these days thanks to the bounty of prewashed, precut, presliced and diced packages found in your produce and freezer departments. As always, no other ingredients in the bag—no special sauces or seasonings—nothing but veggies.

For future reference when you're back on the party circuit, the *Journal of Food Science*[18] reported that amino acids in asparagus may protect liver cells against toxins in alcohol, alleviating cellular damage and minimizing hangovers. Yay! And while we're on the subject, have you ever wondered why your pee smells weird after consuming asparagus? I couldn't resist sharing this answer I found after a quick Google. It's from Cecil Adam's blog, "A Straight Dope Classic From Cecil's Storehouse Of Human Knowledge." Here's how he speared it:

---

[18] Y. Kim, Effects of *Asparagus officinalis* Extracts on Liver Cell Toxicity and Ethanol Metabolism. *Journal of Food Science*, Volume 74, Issue 7, p. H204-H208, September 2009

> *Benjamin Franklin, in a wide-ranging discussion of bodily discharges, once noted, "a few stems of asparagus eaten shall give our urine a disagreeable odor; and a pill of turpentine no bigger than a pea shall bestow upon it the pleasing smell of violets." It is said that in a venerable British men's club there is a sign reading "DURING THE ASPARAGUS SEASON MEMBERS ARE REQUESTED NOT TO RELIEVE THEMSELVES IN THE HATSTAND." Serious scientific research in this field dates back to 1891, when M. Nencki tentatively identified a compound known as methanethiol as the culprit. The odor appears within an hour after eating just a few spears of the offending vegetable. According to Allison and McWhirter (1956), the ability to produce the odor is controlled by a single autosomal (i.e., non-sex-related) dominant gene. In a sample of 115 persons, 46 were rendered fragrant by asparagus and 63 were not. (This leaves 6 mysteriously unaccounted for. Urology is an inexact science, I guess.) In 1975 one Robert H. White, then with the chemistry department at the University of California at San Diego, found that the aroma was in fact caused by several thioesters...compounds that result from the reaction of an acid with a sulfur-containing alcohol. (They tend to be smelly.)*

So now you know.

DAYS 11 + 12 (WEDNESDAY + THURSDAY): STILL VEGGING + FRUITY!

And you also know the drill from the prior four days. Consider mixing things up a bit by trying vegetables and fruit you've never seen before or, better yet, never even heard of. This shows the universe that you're ready for new things to come into your life.

DAYS 13 + 14 (FRIDAY + SATURDAY): SOUPER YOU!

The soup you slurp (pinkies up!) today is similar to the "best, next best, and next next best" juice sources. The best is to create vegetable soup from scratch (see recipes below), the next best is to buy your meal from Whole Foods or some other place that offers freshly made, healthy veggie broth-based soup, and the next next best is to do as I do and stock up on cartons and cans of soup off the shelf. My favorite brands are Health Valley Organic, Pacific Organic, and Amy's Organic Soups. Just be mindful of the ingredients, including sodium content. It's all about being easy, chickies. I mean, doing easy. You know what I mean!

No matter what soup source you tap into, make sure the base is a pure vegetable broth and that only veggies, herbs, and spices find their way into the pot. No cream, no beans, no pasta, nothing else. Definitely no bisque, not even tomato. Debut day is right around the corner, so hold onto your super-duper soup spoon (ladle!) for bisque (lobster!) bliss, which is a mere couple of days away.

Here are some easy detox souper-you potions. As you can see, any veggie tossed into a pot of veggie-based broth or plain water does the trick. The produce and freezer sections have prewashed, diced, and sliced veggies that superize your soup. Spice things up with some pepper and sea salt (and only sea salt, not table). Season with herbs as desired. Sprinkle red pepper flakes for some punch. *Bon appétit!*

Rox's Quickie: Add as much spinach, red cabbage, broccoli, and mushrooms as you desire to 10 cups of veggie broth. Sprinkle garlic, sea salt, pepper, and herbs to taste. Bring to a boil, reduce heat, simmer until desired tenderness, and enjoy.

Concert Chick's Fast Fix: Fill a pot with 10 cups of veggie broth and add the juice from 1 lemon, 1 cup seasoned tomatoes, ½ cup pure Grade B maple syrup, 1 tsp. cayenne pepper, ½ cup diced carrots, ½ cup diced celery, and 1 diced onion. Bring all to a boil, reduce heat, simmer until desired tenderness, and enjoy.

Donetta's Delish Pot: Add fresh cabbage, fresh mushrooms, and a 28-ounce can of stewed, salt-free tomatoes to a pot filled with 10 cups of vegetable broth. Season. Bring all to a boil, reduce heat, simmer until desired tenderness, and enjoy.

THE "REHAB RED CARPET CONCERT CHICK BAR" WHERE EVERY HOUR IS HAPPY!

It's time to pop those tail feathers up and shake 'em like a martini in the making, chickies! Actually, shaken *and* stirred. Only without the olives and the vodka.

The only authorized beverages while you're detoxing are prescribed in the following bar menu: water (lots!), tea (iced or hot), and one 4-ounce glass of wine on each grape day (really!). This means no coffee, juice, milk, energy drink, soda (even diet), or other alcohol is permitted.

Serve all drinks in a wine goblet, champagne flute, highball glass, or any other "barware" vessel. Add a flexi-straw and top with a little paper chicktail umbrella for good luck. It's about style *and* substance, glitter girl.

LE CHICKTAIL™ MENU

L'EAU

> *"I never drink water because of the disgusting things fish do in it."*
> ~W.C. FIELDS

Ah, that W.C.! Is he a funny guy or what? Go ahead and have a laugh and then erase his words from your memory. *You must drink water!* If you develop only one habit during rehab, let it be drinking water, and lots of it. The average human body is 60 percent water. In fact, 85 percent of your blood, 75 percent of your brain, and 70 percent of your muscles are water. Overall, there are about ten to twelve gallons of water in our bodies at any given moment, and we must keep rehydrating and flushing throughout the day. Just as you step into the shower to wash the outside of your body to remove any crud, you need to take an internal shower to rid your body of internal dirt (toxins). Drink up!

The benefits of *l'eau* are plenty. Water is vital to life. Digestion, absorption, circulation, excretion, transportation of nutrients, tissue building, and maintenance of body temperature are all impossible without water. Water fills you up, so if you think you're hungry, try a glass of water with lemon and see if that does the trick. Water may reduce food cravings. You'll be less likely to snack if you drink water whenever you think you're hungry between meals. And water actually reduces water retention. It constantly flushes out the old with the new.

The standard rule of thumb is to drink eight to ten 8-ounce glasses of water a day, but as Concert Chicks, we are anything but standard, so the rule of wing is to drink enough to keep your urine light-colored or clear. Take a peek at your pee the next time you're in *la toilette.* If it's bright or deep colored and there's not much of it, you may be dehydrated. If you're peeing often and the color is light or clear, you're most likely sufficiently saturated.

Never, ever, ever, never turn down water. Ever! When you're at the salon, restaurant, waiting anywhere, you're usually asked if you'd like some water. Always respond, *"Oui, s'il vous plaît"* and then, *"Merci."* Keep flushing!

There are many varieties of *l'eau*. Stay away from flavored waters that more often than not contain sugar and other ingredients that you may not even be able to pronounce. Always read labels! Any spring water is fine. If you want fancy, the classics are Evian and Smartwater (no bubbles) and Pellegrino and Perrier (with bubbles). A Concert Chick fave in the flavored water category is VitaminWater Zero, especially "revitalize" (green tea, Vitamin C + egcg), "rhythm" (starfruit-citrus, potassium + magnesium), and "go-go" (mixed berry, Vitamin E + ribose).

LE THÉ

Tea rocks whether poured on the rocks in a Tervis tumbler or served hot in a Limoges teacup. Tea comes in a vast variety of flavors packed in assorted ways—loose, bagged, flowering, herbal, green, black, white, and more. Any tea will do as long as it's unsweetened. Herbal teas are milder and gentler on your system. Feel free to add a squeeze of citrus for natural flavoring. Do not add sweeteners, even those naturally occurring, such as stevia, honey, or agave. But do enjoy these adds post-rehab.

In addition to the must have "poop" tea mentioned in the prescription descriptions in the Swag Lounge, give dandelion root tea a try. It's a known liver stimulant that is also good for revving up sluggish digestion and it has a natural laxative effect. Yogi and Tazo teas are my tried and trues, but I recently discovered the Dr. Tea brand and I'm obsessed. Imagine Candy Bar Black, Caramel Rooibos, and Mint Julep Green. Yummy sippies!

LE VIN

This is only a day 5 and 6 splash. Pour four ounces into a fabulous wineglass, swirl, sniff, and take forever sips to savor this treat. Rock 'n Roll Wine's Reggae Rhapsody, Barefoot Wine's Sauvignon Blanc, Santa Margarita Pinot Grigio, any Sancerre, and La Crema Pinot Noir are Concert Chick faves.

SIPPING + SUPPING TIPS

Here are some ways to enjoy your meals mindfully and peacefully while in rehab and beyond.

- ♦ Go slow.
- ♦ Put your utensils down between bites.
- ♦ Chew, chew, chew your food and chew some more.
- ♦ Swallow one morsel before going for another.

- No other activities while you eat.
- Eat mindfully—engage all your senses.
- Eat consciously.
- Eat while sitting (though not while in your car), not standing. And definitely not on the run.
- Pack your workday lunch in a picnic basket—how much fun to eat at your desk this way! Or better yet, go outdoors.
- Say grace before each meal.
- Drink a glass of water before and after meals, not during (it interferes with digestion).
- Skip the ice in your water (your body absorbs whatever is introduced at body temp).
- Don't eat out of containers or bags. Put your food in a bowl or on a plate.
- Use smaller bowls and plates to make servings look larger than they are.
- Eat with your hands for a sensual experience.
- Set your table with the good dishes that only come out for special company. You are special!
- Accessorize your meals! Think placemat, cloth napkins, candelabra, soothing music.
- Add cute, colorful chicktail umbrellas to all beverages.

BITES FOR YOUR MIND+HEART+SOUL

Nourishment beyond physical food is the icing on the cupcake, and in our world, it's topped with not only neon sprinkles, but electrifying sparkles as well—some swell energetic nutrients that cause you to glow and grow (up, not out). Life is indeed sweet! Your goal should be to *grow* through life, not simply to *go* through it. And I don't mean growth of girth by scarfing down greasy burgers and fries and cleansing your pallet with a double mocha shake. I'm talking about mind, heart, and soul expansion. A mind, heart, and soul wide open; a mouth, not so wide open. What does this mean to you? What's "eating" you? What can you do about it? What *will* you do about it? Chew on these queries for a bit and then explore further in your journal.

While you have pen in hand, make note of what you feed your thoughts, what your thoughts feed you, and how you can feed your "monkey mind" bananas. Swing over to Chapter 6, your soul food pantry, for some inspiration. Sometimes your soul needs a Twinkie, but during detox, you'll be shifting toward the twinkle. Help yourself to those kinds of treats often. Create a "menu" in your journal of nonfood mind, heart, and soul nourishers, with nary a drive-thru sack in sight or bite.

Now that you know how to fuel it, fuel it, it's time to move it, move it. Chapter 5 will teach you how to be a player.

Chapter 5

You Gotta Move It, Move It To Lose It, Lose It!

Exercise, not philosophically and with religious gravity undertaken, but with the wild romping activities of a spirited girl who runs up and down as if her veins were full of wine.
~Lola Montez

In this chapter, you'll learn how to get busy with your physical self while detoxing. Our bodies are designed to travel. If this wasn't the case, we wouldn't have been blessed with so many moveable parts. Most programs have a "workout" aspect. I think the energy of the word "workout" is heavy. Come on…*work*? Out with that! In Rox Detox land, "workout" is "play." Happy dances, sassy struts, wings flapping, booties shaking just because we can. I hear the recess bell ringing. Your "best self show" is now in production.

While your body is the primary focus here, there will be reminders of mind, heart, and soul movement too. Sweet music happens only when the full band shows up ready to perform. In other words, let's get physical, but know that you gotta go mental (and spiritual and heartful), too. Woohoo!

The goal of rehab play isn't to train you for that marathon or to six-pack your abs. You may very well get so dang excited about how great you feel that you'll decide to do these things later. But for now, your full attention is required on simply incorporating movement in and throughout your day.

LET'S PLAY!

Being the curious chicks that we are, this chapter is set up as a series of questions. Who, what, where, when, how, and why? Some sections will necessarily address more than one query because it makes sense to do so. And I promise, there are no trick questions. Let's kick things off with the easiest one (and one it is, as in word).

WHO?

YOU!

WHAT?

Play encompasses the three essential components of any solid fitness program: cardio, strength, and flexibility. For the next two weeks, you'll be strutting, pumping, twisting, swinging, twirling, whirling, and glistening. You'll be wringing your body out like a sponge, releasing the toxins and excess that weighs you down. Let's take a peek at each, shall we?

1. CARDIOOOOOOOOOOOOHHHHH, YEAH!
HEAVY BREATHING + HEART BEATING (PHONE OPTIONAL)

As a Concert Chick, you need endurance for all that red carpet sashaying you do. And the way to go about this is through anything that gets your heart pumping and your breath panting. Rehab fave cardio plays are strutting, dancing, and drumming. If you enjoy other ways to get your heartbeat up, by all means, keep enjoying 'em.

STRUT YOUR STUFF

Walking is the easiest, safest, cheapest, most doable form of play on the planet. It can be done anywhere, anytime, with anyone (or no one), and without any special equipment other than a good pair of walking shoes (it's always about the shoes, isn't it?). Besides, it can be used for transportation, so when your limo breaks down, you know that you can get from here to there, which is a very good thing.

> *Lots of people want to ride with you in the limo, but what you want is someone who will take the bus with you when the limo breaks down.*
> ~ OPRAH WINFREY[19]

Pay attention to the way you carry yourself. Standing tall and confident is where it's at. Keep your chest lifted, abs tight, butt tucked under hips, shoulders down and drawn back and relaxed. Your chin should be parallel to the ground, eyes looking straight ahead, with your elbows bent at a ninety-degree angle, staying close to the sides of your body. Your wings should be relaxed and swing from your shoulders in opposition to your legs, but not across the front of your body. Lean slightly forward from your ankles, not your hips. Peel up from heel to ball of foot, and then push off.

You may experience finger swelling during your walks, making it extremely difficult, painful even, to slide on your gorgeous 15-carat chicktail sparkler on your now sausage finger. This results from extra fluids collecting in your hands, and, thank the stars, it's only temporary. Elevate your hands for immediate relief. Waving to peeps on your path also helps and is a nice thing to do.

---

19 This quote has nothing to do with moving it, but since all aspects of ourselves are interconnected, I thought I'd throw it in here at the mention of "limo." More on what it is about can be found in Chapter 8.

Being able to walk is a gift. Show gratitude for your legs and feet by using them. Walk at a comfortable pace. Move quickly enough to elevate your heart rate and to work up a glisten. As Harry Truman once said, "Walk as though you have someplace to go." As a Concert Chick, you surely do!

SHAKE YOUR BOOTY FOR INNER + OUTER BEAUTY

> *"Every day I count wasted in which there has been no dancing."*
> ~Friederich Nietzsche

As the Cheetah Girls sing, "Come on girls, shake your tail feathers!" There's no better way to express yourself fearlessly than through freestyle dance. No one moves exactly like you because there is no one in this universe like you. So grab a feathery boa, slip on a sparkly tiara and a pair of glittery dancing shoes, and move it, move it! No matter what's going on with your tail feathers, you're shaking things up superbly!

The Rox Detox is all about letting go of whatever weighs you down to make room for the abundance the universe wants to shower upon you, so it's only fitting that we promote a-bun-dance! If you think you have too much bun in your pants—dance, dance, dance—freestyle in your home, on the dance floor, in the elevator on your way to your office.

You'll burn lots of calories, break a sweat, and use every muscle in your awesome, miraculous body. The Mayo Clinic—yes, *that* clinic so listen up—discovered that one hour of dancing can burn more calories than swimming or riding a bike for the same amount of time.

Here's a snapshot of how many calories you're burning per hour for various types of dance:[20]

---

[20] Based on a 150-pound person, Source: Adapted from "Compendium of Physical Activities," Medicine and Science in Sports and Exercise, January 1993, with assistance by Barbara E. Ainsworth, PhD, and Melinda Irwin, Department of Exercise Science, University of South Carolina, Columbia.

400	375	300	200
ballet	country western	belly	cha-cha
jazz	disco	flamenco	mambo
jitterbug	Irish step	Greek	samba
modern	polka	Middle Eastern	tango
tap	square	hula	waltz
		swing	

According to the National Heart, Lung, and Blood Institute, dancing lowers the risk of heart disease, decreases blood pressure, and increases endurance. Pump up the volume and move it, move it.

Dancing is also good for your brain. According to Mehmet Oz, MD, who carries major cred in my book, "Moving the body in a coordinated fashion and following along with complex movements in sync with music requires lots of brainpower. Dancing also works your heart, so you're pumping more blood upstairs." Be smart, sugar tart, and move it, move it.

Dance is also one of the best stress busters around. Shaking your booty even improves your coordination and your memory so that the next time a pal tells you about that unbelievable Manolo Blahnik sale, you'll remember where to be and when, and not trip all over yourself three minutes to closing as you make a mad dash for the rack that *was* packed with fabulous shoes in your size.

And there's more! A study[21] found that "the only physical activity to offer protection against dementia was frequent dancing." So there! And if you still aren't convinced, Dr. Oz, when asked what one piece of health advice he'd give, shared this juicy opinion: "Take up dancing! It incorporates everything you need for a healthy life: It exercises your body (especially your heart), challenges your brain (choreographing your limbs requires concentration), and you can do it with someone (bonding with loved ones brings meaning and joy to your lives), and it's the best way to ensure longevity." Wowee-zowee Zumba! So you see, shaking your booty does

---

21 Joe Verghese, MD, et al, "Leisure Activities and the Risk of Dementia in the Elderly." *The New England Journal of Medicine,* June, 2003; 348: 2508–2516.

enhance your inner and outer beauty.

Do you think you have two left feet? Well, that needs to be changed pronto because as far as I know, Kate Spade boxes usually contain pairs consisting of one left and one right. If yours do not, I apologize for any perceived insensitivity. No matter what your shoeboxes hold, you can always take lessons. Many community centers offer classes, and your local library most likely has a collection of DVDs you can check out.

Now that DVDs have been mentioned, it's time to reveal Rox's top (and bottom) secret weapon of ass destruction that was alluded to before. The **OMG** discovery is—ta-da!—the Brazil Butt Lift (BBL). No, it's not some scary surgical procedure and no, we don't own the company (wish!). It's a dance program designed to shape up your butt, reduce your hips, and lift your glutes. The program combines Brazilian dance, cardio, and lower-body sculpting moves to burn fat and build muscle. Leandro Carvalho, trainer to world-famous supermodels like Alessandro Ambrosio (Victoria's Secret!), merged moves from ballet, samba, and the Afro-Brazilian fighting style of capoeira to create this program. All three major butt muscles are played from multiple angles to reduce your hips and saddlebag area, slim your thighs, and lift your butt without bulk. BBL is a 30-day program, but includes a 6-day supermodel plan that jives nicely with your rehab sked. Hip-hop over to the Swag Lounge for the **BBL DVD** info.

If you're a chick who sits behind a desk for long periods of time, get up and do a little dance every hour or so. Whether you have to use headphones or are lucky to work where there are some noise zones, get your cubicle rockin'. It's contagious. And what a great display of leadership—a butt and a morale booster in one!

And then there's pole dancing, another beloved Concert Chick move it, move it move. You know you want to give it a spin, just once. Swing on over to the Swag Lounge for more info. What will your stage name be?

From this day forward you are encouraged to prance (naked even) and dance, you glittery goddess you.

JUST BEAT IT!

No, no, not as in "get lost!", but as in Drums Alive! After I was introduced to this high-energy, fabulously fun, "oh, yeah, I'm a rock star" play, I was instantly hooked. Prop a stability ball on any base that will keep it stable, grab some drumsticks, crank up the tunes, and rat-a-tat-tat to de-stress and get rid of fat. Nothing like a good drumming to calibrate your body+mind+heart+soul. It's all about the drum roll, please, to eliminate that belly roll, *s'il vous plaît*. March to your own drummer, oh dear one! As always, the skinny is in the Swag Lounge.

2. CHICK POWER!
YOU CAN'T GO WRONG BEING STRONG

Most chicks resist things that rob them of the joys of being a girl such as looking like a boy (unless you're Shiloh, but that's a subject way beyond the scope of this book, though she is beautiful and I think everyone should let her be). We mustn't fear strength training. Dropkick those visions of bulked-up, something-up-the-butt walking meatheads out of your head. Yes, weightlifting builds muscle mass but you will not be massive unless you're dabbling in steroids or have a natural propensity to develop ham shank quads. The goal is to lose fat and gain muscle. Muscle uses more calories and speeds up your metabolism, which means you can eat more. Need I say more?

Don't be afraid to throw your weight around (but not in that psycho lunatic or egomaniacal chick way that some of us see often and despise much). Nope, it's all about firming, strengthening, lengthening, and toning—nothing frightening unless that's your thing. There are other reasons for throwing your weight around. You'll get strong—yes, plenty mighty to carry at least a dozen shoe boxes filled with awesome Stella McCartney clogs. *That* strong. And as a special bonus, chick power helps prevent osteoporosis.

A pound of muscle and a pound of fat weigh the same (how profound!); however, a pound of muscle is more compact (translation: two people can weigh the same, however, one wears a size 4 and the other a size 12). That is precisely why you should throw out your scale and ignore size tags. Those numbers don't mean a flippin' thing. All that matters is how you feel and how your clothes fit. I know we've been over this before, but I'll keep going there as opportunities to do so present themselves, so bear with me and you'll be happy when bare and in that pencil skirt you can finally wear.

The "chick power" play covers your upper and lower body. You'll be enjoying this play twice a week (one upper, one lower). Your daily prescriptions tell you what's when, but feel free to change things around as long as you skip a day between power play.

Here are the general guidelines no matter what you're pumping. Use light hand weights that are heavy enough to give you a challenge. You want your muscles to feel some fatigue. Three to five pounds should get you there. Do at least one set of eleven reps for each move or four sets of select moves that address what you need the most. Consciously devote each set to your body+mind+heart+soul, so by the time you've finished moving, each aspect of yourself will have some undivided attention, affection, and intention.

Here's how to do this. On the inhale, bring to mind a word that represents something peaceful, positive, and desired by you. On the exhale, think of something you want to let go of. Don't worry about correlating specific actions to the area you're focusing on. Mainly fill your play with wishes and releases. For example, say you're doing a wing curl. The first set is devoted to your body. As you inhale and lift the weight say, "one, love," then lower letting go of "fear." Up "two, health," down "limitation," up "three, light," down "heaviness." Then do your second set focusing on your mind using words such as "open," "closed," "calm," "chatter," "still," "scattered," "brilliant," "worry." The focus of your third set is your heart: "love," "fear," "open," "walls," "acceptance," "judgment." The final set belongs to your soul: "untethered," "blocked," "soar," "trapped," "free," "creative," "suppressed." Consciously see and feel yourself receiving what you desire and releasing that which serves you no more. Before you know it, your sets are up and your intentions set.

Here are specific moves for your upper and lower parts.

MOVES FOR YOUR WINGS + OTHER UPPER BODY THINGS

Your upper body play covers your wings, boobs, waist, belly, back, and shoulders. We'll go top to bottom, beginning with moves to help stop the "applause flap." You know what I'm talking about. Your fave band ends its set with your fave song and the crowd goes wild. A hearty round of applause follows, and there are some upper arms clapping and waving to the hot drummer all on their own. Yikes! Extra moving parts and bits can cause strapless gown, tantalizing tank, and hot sundress shyness. We are so done with *that*.

Flap To Zap Those Wings: From a standing position with wings at sides, a weight in each hand, feet shoulder width apart, knees ever so slightly bent, lift wings out to shoulder level, keeping elbows slightly bent and palms down. Lower and repeat.

Press + Squeeze To Please Your Lats + Boobies: Hold weights above shoulders with palms facing forward and elbows out to sides. Straighten wings, pressing them overhead and slightly in front of your body. Return to starting position, turn palms to face each other, and press wings together, tightening your chest muscles. Push back to start and repeat.

Curl Up With A Good Bicep: Start with your wings at your sides, a weight in each hand, palms facing up. Keeping elbows pulled into your sides, bend your elbows, and pull the weights up to your shoulders. Lower and repeat.

Kickbacks Are Great (The Legal Kind To Enrich Your Triceps): With your elbows back like a duck and shoulders relaxed, straighten your wings, pushing the weights backward. Don't drop your elbows as you return to start. Repeat.

Touchback + Push: With your elbows bent and your wings raised out to each side, try to touch your elbows in back, squeezing your shoulder blades, then push your wings forward. Pull your wings back and repeat.

Pec Respect: Remember the old ditty "I must, I must, I must improve my bust" and the accompanying movement? Well, here we are, at it again. Put your wings/hands in prayer position across your chest, higher than if you were actually praying, thumbs at chin level. Press your palms together to make your boobs "pop." That's it. A little isometric chest play (pop pop pop perk!) and since your hands are in the position, go ahead and pray for something uplifting, like your boobs in this case.

Boob Press Express: Lie on your back, knees bent, feet flat on the floor shoulder-width apart. Hold weights in each hand up near your shoulders. Push wings up, let weights kiss, and then lower. That's one set. Do ten more.

Bicycle Your Belly Away: Lie on the floor and lace your fingers behind your head. Bring your knees in toward your chest and lift your shoulder blades off the floor without pulling on your neck. Straighten your left leg out while simultaneously turning your upper body to the right, taking your left elbow toward your right knee. Switch sides, bringing your right elbow toward your left knee. Continue pedaling away.

Waste Waist Not: Stand tall, feet shoulder-width apart, knees slightly bent, with your wings down at your sides, a weight in each hand, palms facing in. Let your right hand slowly drop toward the floor, keeping your body in position. Return and repeat on your left side.

Now it's time to get down with your bad self! Your butt, quads, hamstrings, and calves need some lovin', too.

GET DOWN, GET DOWN JUNKY BOOTY + BIRD LEGS BAN

This section is for you if you have more junk in your trunk or on your thighs than you want. Popping in your Brazil Butt Lift DVD may not always be convenient, so here are some lower body move it, move its for perky tail feathers and shapely non-bird legs so you can wiggle effortlessly into your party pants and strut your stuff.

Super Chick To The Rescue: Lie on your stomach with your wings extended in front of you on the floor. Lift your legs and wings at the same time about two inches off the floor, squeeze your butt and hold for a count of two and then slowly release to the floor. Imagine soaring over the Big Apple with tiara on, bangles jingling in the breeze, boa flowing behind you, with your super shoes picking up feathered tailwinds. Go, girl, go! Take this booty rescue flight ten times.

Squat For Swag: Place eleven bits of swag such as chicktail rings and other sparkly things, Nickelback concert or Air France tickets, a bottle of Chanel nail polish, a tube of Hardy Candy lip gloss, Lady Lanell flip-flops, anything that gets you going, across the floor, one in front of the other, about six feet apart. Meandering is OK. Squat to pick up swag one. Keep your chin up and back straight. Stand up and step forward, then squat down again, pick up swag two, and repeat the drill until you've collected all the swag. Depending on what your swag spread looks like, you might not be able to carry all with you through the receiving line, so feel free to toss the treats aside or tuck them in your sports bra or boyshort waistband as you go, or carry a tote or basket to collect your goodies. You'll know when you've reached the toppling point. Remember to keep good form.

Ball To The Wall: Place a fitness ball between your lower back and a wall. With feet hip-width apart and toes pointed forward and under your knees, with hands on hips, slowly roll the ball down the wall, lowering your body as if you're going to sit on a princess throne. Roll back up to starting position and repeat.

Plié-Up-On-Your-Toes Squat: It's now time for some Concert Chick ballet. Don your tutu and tiara and summon grace. Stand with your feet a little wider than hip width apart, toes turned out slightly, and hands behind your head. Stick out your butt a bit, and then slowly bend your knees until your thighs are parallel to the floor, without allowing your knees to drift beyond your toes. Lift your heels and hold for a few secs. Return to starting position, squeezing your buttocks on your way up. Contract your abs to prevent capsizing. Repeat.

Duck Walk Like A Chick: Stand with your feet shoulder-width apart, toes pointed out to the side. Squat until your thighs are parallel to the floor. Keep your tummy tucked, butt slightly back, and hands behind your head. While in this position, walk forward by pushing off each heel. Move your right foot first, then your left. This is one rep. Take ten more steps. Quack, quack!

Pelvic Play Lay: Lie on your back, feet about an inch apart, arms at sides, and abs tight. Squeeze your buttocks until your pelvis lifts slightly (about an inch) off the floor. Hold for two counts and release. Repeat ten times.

Bent-Knee Butt Tuck Back: Lie facedown with your elbows bent out to the sides with your forehead resting on your hands. Bend your left leg to a 90-degree angle (the sole of your foot should be facing the ceiling) and lift your leg so that your thigh is about two inches off the floor. Slowly release to starting position and repeat ten times. Switch sides.

Get Sideways With A Side Raise: Standing wing's-length distance from a chair, lightly rest your left hand on the back of the chair and put your right hand on your hip. Placing the majority of your weight on your left leg (keep slightly bent), squeeze your butt and lift your right leg out to the side about eight inches from the floor. Repeat ten times, and then switch legs.

Up The Rear With Your Leg Raised: Stand in the same position as the side leg raise, but with both hands lightly resting on the back of the chair, knees slightly bent. Place your body weight on your right leg, extend your left leg out directly behind you while straightening, but not locking, the knee. Keeping your buttocks squeezed, lift your left leg about six inches. Slowly release and return to starting position. Repeat ten times and switch legs.

Relevé Hooray For Your Booty: More tutu + tiara time! Channel your inner ballerina and do this move to tone your lower body pronto. Warning: this one can be tough. Stand on your right leg, toes turned out. Rest your left foot on your right calf (if you can rest it on your left, put this book down and join *Cirque du Soleil*—you are so missing your calling). Raise your arms overhead ballerina style, elbows slightly bent. Contract your abs and lift your right heel off the floor, coming onto the ball of your foot. Lower the heel. Do eleven reps slowly, eleven reps quickly, and then switch sides and do it all over again.

Shoe Lift: No, this has nothing to do with Tom Cruise (sorry TC, Rox forced me to go there). This very simple move can be done anywhere. Imagine that you're wearing Sam Edelman ballerinas, feet flat on the ground. You're now going to switch to YSL platform pumps with 5" stiletto heels. Up on your toes you go! OK, that's enough. Time to get back into your flats. "Switch" shoes ten more times.

3. BE FLEXIBLE!
OOH LA LA + AHHHHHHHHHHH...THAT FEELS SOOOOOOOOOOOOOO GOOD!

Flex appeal rocks! There are many perks to stretching. Good muscle elasticity promotes agility, reduces the risk of injury, and creates the potential for greater speed. You're elongating both muscle and connective tissue. Your posture improves and you move more gracefully, both of which are key to red carpet success. Stretching also helps you maintain flexibility in your joints and muscles. You'll experience a greater freedom of movement and increased physical and mental relaxation as your muscles release any tension or soreness they may hold.

Before you turn into bendy chick, there are safe stretching rules that you must abide by. As much as Concert Chicks like to stretch the rules a tad, there's no budging on these:

Thou shalt...

...never stretch a muscle that hasn't been warmed up.
...stretch until thou feel tension, not strain or pain.
...not bounce. Stay static.
...hold each stretch for twenty seconds.
...not hold thy breath. Breathe slowly, deeply, and rhythmically.

OK, let's stretch it starting at the top, maestro!

BENDY CHICK BASICS

Stretch It To The Max: Lie on the floor flat on your back with your wings stretched overhead. Reach your wings to the wall or some point behind you while at the same time stretching your gorgeous gams to the opposite wall/point of interest, so if viewed from above, you've grown at least four inches on both ends.

Swan Neck: Gracefully tilt your head forward as you press your chin toward your chest. Breathe a bit and lift your head back up. Slowly lift your chin, tilting your head back. Gently return to center. Lower your right ear toward your right shoulder. Return to center. Repeat on the other side.

Oooh + Ahhhings For Your Wings: Stand or sit and place your right hand on your left elbow with your left wing parallel to the floor. Let your right hand guide your left wing to the right. Repeat with your other wing. Next, interlace your fingers, palms out. Extend wings in front at shoulder height and gently push forward. Hold and repeat.

Calf Call To Walk Tall: Stilettoed or not. This move stretches your calves and Achilles tendons. Place both hands against a wall, a tree, or other supportive surface. Put one foot behind you, keeping your rear leg straight and your heel on the ground. Lean in toward the surface. Hold for twenty seconds, and then repeat with your other leg.

Super Quad Squad: Put one hand on a tree, wall, or other supportive surface. With your other hand, reach behind your back and grasp the ankle of your opposite leg. Pull it up toward your butt until you feel tension along the front of your thigh. Keep your quad facing straight ahead, moving only your lower leg. Hold for twenty seconds, and then switch to the other side.

Make Your Hamstring Sing: Stand on one leg, propping your other leg parallel to the ground on a bench, rail, chair, or tabletop. Slide both hands toward the propped up ankle as far as they'll go (don't strain). Hold for twenty seconds, and then switch sides.

Chin Chin For Your Shin Shin: Stand about nine inches from a tree, wall, or other supportive surface with your back to it. Keeping your feet on the ground, allow your upper back to gently meet the support surface. Hold for twenty seconds. Raise toes on your right foot, leaving your heel on the ground. Hold for five seconds and release. Repeat three times and switch feet. Toe tapping makes your shins happy, too!

YOGA
HOW TO GET AHEAD BY LYING ON YOUR BACK

Ahhhhh—this biz of life—just like the entertainment biz. A girl's gotta do what a girl's gotta do. Concert Chick style, of course. Yoga is my all-time number-one go-to for body+mind+heart+soul bliss play. If you're already hooked, you know of what I speak. If not, you're in for a treat!

The beauty of yoga is that every posture can be modified to fit your level in terms of experience or just how you feel that day. What happens on your mat stays on your mat!

There are many superb yoga instruction resources out there so there's no point in recreating anything here. My personal faves can be found in the Swag Lounge. But I will share *the* best pose that you can use as part of your cooldown or anytime you're down or just wanna get down.

This simple pose can do more for your body+mind+heart+soul than anything else. It's a powerful calmer and energizer in one. Some claim it relieves mild depression. I'm not sure what the official ruling is on that, but I can tell you firsthand that I've had awful days and feel immediate relief once I assume the position. It relaxes your body, reduces headaches, beats fatigue, and lowers blood pressure. It also allows the time for your body+mind+heart+soul to embrace all the benefits of the other moves you may have done before melting into the floor.

All you have to do is lie on your back and spread 'em. That's it. Rest your arms about a foot away from your body, palms up, with your legs a little splayed—shoulder width apart, allowing your feet to fall outward. If there's pressure on your lower back, put a bolster under your knees. You want a tension-free, neutral body. Close your eyes. Breathe deeply. Stay like this for ten minutes. This is called "Shavasana," "Relaxation Pose," or the "Corpse Pose." Whatever you call it, a chick needs to do it.

Before we leave this section, I must mention that yoginis have *the* most awesome outfit selection. Think low-rise, body-hugging, pull-on boot legs, sassy capris, palazzos with or without side slits, hot shorts, cashmere wraps, flip-flops high or low with or without sparkles, and chandelier earrings. Is it any wonder why yoga is divaliciously divine?

WHERE?

Anywhere and everywhere! In or out or both. Many people prefer gyms and that's fantastic for them. Not for me. Playing outdoors is where it's at for this chick. I walk along the beach in the wee hours of the morning. Nature's gym offers plenty of pluses. First of all, it's free (more shoe money!). And there's something about breathing fresh air rather than sucking in stale air conditioning and someone else's sweaty armpits. Sunlight not only provides vitamin D (which is needed to absorb calcium and phosphorous—crucial to good bones—possibly slows down the growth of cancer cells, and fights infection), but in addition, ultraviolet light is required to break down cholesterol, and produces that good-feeling hormone serotonin. To me, sunlight trumps fluorescent bulbs any day. Don't forget sunscreen!

Playing outside also requires you to focus on more than pedaling a stationary bike or pumping up and down on an elliptical machine. Most gym equipment can be operated on automatic pilot. Walking outdoors requires you to pay attention. Think big buses and crazy drivers. And gyms can be noisy. I try to avoid the hustle and bustle I can't escape from during the day. Nature sounds are more soothing to your soul and heart. You get the ultimate body+mind+heart+soul connection when you're in the environment in which you were created, even in the middle of rush hour in the Big Apple with Yellow

Cabs honking up a storm. On that note, the elements also add to the fun. Have you ever played in the rain? There's something about the energy and being part of the bigger world out there. You know what's best for you. Just move it, move it somewhere.

WHEN?

Whenever you'll do it, that's when! There's always time, so let's get that "no time" nonsense out of your head and mouth once and for all. Refer back to my lecture/rant in Chapter 3. Would you go to the office with your jammies on because you didn't have time to get dressed? Would you consider not brushing your teeth? Do you always have time to shower? To eat? Of course you do. Moving your body for health must rank just as important as these other must-dos. The only question is, when is the best time for you? And the answer is: anytime that you'll do it.

First thing in the morning works best for me. My days typically take on lives of their own the moment I cross my office's threshold. I just won't play later in the day. I roll out of bed, throw on any old thing, and head out the door. I don't brush my hair or my teeth. I just get out there. It's usually around 5:00 a.m. when most of the people I know are sound asleep and questioning my soundness when they are awake. The quiet of morning allows you to focus on yourself and the new lifestyle you're starting. The cobwebs are cleared and you've sent the message to the rest of your parts that your mental, spiritual, physical, and emotional wellbeing is *the* priority. But not every chick is an early bird. The mornings wouldn't be as peaceful if we all played before the sun broke through the horizon.

If morning is no-way, no-how or if you're a night owl, you have a day filled with options. Midmorning play helps curb your lunch appetite. Lunchtime also works as long as you make sure you leave some meal moments. Mid-afternoon nips stress and can ding your dinner hunger. Playing after supper works to help you unwind from the day. Your best time to play is a very personal decision. Only you know when you'll be in the mood. The bottom line for your bottom (and top): Morning, noon, or night—anytime is right!

HOW?

Some how-tos were mentioned in the "what?" section. Here you'll find the generals to lead your way no matter what you play. Here's your sked at a glance:

- cardio every day but Sunday, which is a day of rest (if God needed it, you do, too)
- twice-a-week chick power (one upper and one lower or Butt DVD)
- twice-a-week yoga
- stretch
- warm up, cool down before and after
- undercover play all day, every day

GET HOT! BE COOL!

As much as a Concert Chick likes to get right to it, you must take a few moments to prepare your body before play and then to recover after play. You do this by warming up and cooling down your heart and muscles. Taking time to get ready and to recover reduces the chance of hurting yourself. This is a good and necessary thing.

To "get hot!", a simple march in place for five minutes works. Or, if you're heading out for a walk, spend the first five minutes strutting slowly and gradually building up to your play pace.

And when you're finished playing around, it's time to "be cool!" and you do this in the same way as pre-play. When you're at the five-minute mark of your, for example, walk, start slowing down to finish with a steady heart rate. Wrap up with a feel-so-good stretch (see the "flexibility" section above for details).

SECURITY CHECK

Not every Concert Chick is as lucky as Rox to have the world's best bodyguard, John "the Big Dog" Anderson, watching out for her. But he knows an awesome chick when he sees one, since he, among many other things, provides security for major concerts and professional sports teams and their owners and celebrities. You may recall him from Chapter 2, where he was one of the wise guys who shared a sparkly chick tip. The Big Dog has given his blessing to this Rox Detox "safety first" section of the playbook.

Always be aware of your surroundings when you're out and about. Avoid walking alone unless you know the area very well. Always walk facing traffic. If you walk in the dark, wear reflective clothing and/or carry a small flashlight or clip on one of those flashing red light reflectors. At first, I felt like a big blinking dork wearing one of those gadgets, but after almost not seeing a walker one night while I was behind the wheel, I am now a blinker believer! If you're driving to your walk start, park in a lighted area and carry your keys in your hand along with an ID and cell phone. It's not a bad idea to carry mace or pepper spray but know that it's hard to control the spray direction—a slight breeze and it's right back at ya. Not good. Leave the fancy jewelry and watch at home. Vary your walk routine in case some creepy stalker has been watching you and is now familiar with your time and route. And if you walk along a sidewalk where vehicles are parked, be alert for anything out of the ordinary. Trust your instincts. You don't want to be pulled into a car and held for ransom or worse, the other *r* word. Don't be paranoid, just aware. One more note on this topic: be prepared to see things you'd rather not. I was flashed one morning and it wasn't pretty—pretty petite, but yuck nonetheless.

Now that you know how to protect yourself from others, here are some ways to protect yourself period. No matter what you're playing, focus on the flow—lift, lower, bend, squat, up, down, and all around with fluidity. Drop the "no pain, no gain" mantra from your mind. In the absence of pain, you allow the life force to flow through you. Sure, you want to push yourself to the edge and perhaps a tad out of your comfort zone, but if you're sore afterward, you're out of play, which is not the Concert Chick way. You're going for soaring, not sore-ing. Stay in the game!

COP AN ATTITUDE + THEN A BUZZ

Play with attitude. Maintain good form and posture in all you do, tossing in a skip and a jump and a hop or two. Take a leap. Turn around three times for good luck. Strut backward (this really works your back and front thighs, hamstrings, and abs). Flap your wings. Sing a song. Wear a tiara, a tutu, and/or a thong. All this Concert Chick sass will reduce your ass and other mass that weighs you down. I can't tell you this enough!

For example, say you're strutting down the boardwalk. Alternate five minutes of regular walking with some weaving, bobbing, curb jumping, tree climbing, branch ducking (nature's limbo—how low can you go?), slinking around parking meters, and sashaying up and down stairs and under railings. Skip. Hopscotch. There are many opportunities for "I am Concert Chick" moments that sends the world a message that you've "got places to go, people to see, things to do, and *oui*, I am a tad crazy so get out of my way." And smile. Always! You never know when your photo will be on the cover of *Star*!

Attitude is why I walk in the morning when most peeps are asleep. Not that it matters what others think; however, I'm less inhibited in the company of birds, bees, flowers, and trees. And if you're out there in broad daylight—good for you! Practice ignoring what others think about your play. You might look a little strange, but who cares and who doesn't from time to time? You're taking care of yourself, improving your life, having fun, getting some fresh air while the "judgers" are perched on their overstuffed sofas looking out their front windows during commercial breaks or passing you by while driving their cars to Dunkin' Donuts. This is a great time to reread Chapter 2.

Attitude is easy to express no matter how you're moving it. Wear a tutu and tiara to yoga class; fearlessly move into child's pose while others are in crow. Do a little dance between chick power sets. Dancing and drumming are wide-open opportunities for attitude play.

Here's an excellent example of the kind of attitude we're talking about. A French woman named Jeanne Calumet, who lived for 122 years, rode her bike every day into her nineties. While celebrating her 100th birthday, she told a reporter, "I have only one wrinkle and I sit on it!" Madame Calumet knew how to move it, move it for a really long time, and I bet she was sparkling to the end!

DON'T HOLD YOUR BREATH

No matter what your game—strut, dance, drum—breathe. Breathe! Breathe! Don't forget to breathe! Take the old talk test. If you can't talk, you're trying too hard. Carry on a conversation with yourself (it's OK!) or with a play pal. You may very well discover the solutions to world peace as you play, or at least how to respond to that work issue. Singing is also a great way to keep your breathing in check, as well as a surefire play attitude in and of itself.

According to Dr. Oz, "Deep breathing helps relieve stress: it moves oxygen and lymphatic fluid through your cells, improving all bodily functions and helping you to think more clearly." It's free! And you're doing it anyway, I hope, so why not kick it up a notch or so and go deep?

PLEASURE YOURSELF

Music and rhythm find their way into the secret places of the soul.
~Plato

As you know by now, your playtime should feel good. And what sets the tone best of all? Tunes! Let music be your muse. Create a playlist of songs that gets you moving, park it in your iPod, plug in those fancy crystal-encrusted ear buds, and jam. Listen to self-improvement, motivational, or spiritual programs. How cool would it be to not only emerge lighter in body+mind+heart+soul but also brighter because you now speak a foreign language? *Très* cool. Just be careful. If you're bopping to the beat with major volume you may not hear something you should, such as cars, trains, buses, and ambulance sirens.

GOING UNDERCOVER

My day job is all about transparency, disclosure, letting the whole world know all I do, who I see, even when I pee. The who, what, where, when, and why is everyone's business. And it sucks, though it's part of what I signed up for. But there are some things that I simply do not declare or share.

Like how I play all day at work. When I'm talking on the phone, I'm walking around my office, stopping every so often to do a few leg lifts or biceps curls. I run down the hall. I take the stairs. Every moment is an opportunity to move it, move it. You can, too! And because you're a Concert Chick, I'll let you in on a cache of top-secret stuff—very covert ways to sneak play in your day all day long. So give me the secret wing shake (two snaps, a hop, and a twist midair), say the code word (*player*), and make a no-fingers-crossed pledge to commit to *it*. Welcome! You're now an undercover "Operation Stealth Health" agent on a mission. Go ahead and reward yourself with a fabulous trench coat for becoming a covert player. But remember, the only thing to be flashed is a smile.

Pssssssst...here are your assignments should you choose to accept them (Come on! Do it! You know you want to join the fun and play all day):

While Out + About: Get off the bus or metro a few blocks before your stop and walk the rest of the way, at a good clip. Take the stairs instead of the elevator. Don't drive around the lot in circles looking for a spot near the entrance. Save your gas and lose your ass. Park your car far away and enjoy the extra moves (don't forget where you left your vehicle and keep your eyes out for weirdos, including the aforementioned flasher—poor little guy). Skip, hop, dance to your destination (of course, these moves will probably take you out of secret service detail so be prepared to blow your cover).

While In Front Of The Tube: While you know very well by now that it's a fact of life that this chick will never promote boob tube time, this chick realizes that it's happening in millions of households at this very moment, so here's how to save your butt and more if you're a TV sweetie. Play during commercial breaks. Keep hand weights by the remote and do curls or any of the other chick power moves you learned earlier. Drop down on the floor or sprawl on the sofa and crunch your abs. Get off your bum to change those channels and do a lunge or two on your way to the tube and back. Stand with your arms stretched over your head with your fingers interlocked. Slightly bend your knees and tuck your butt. Slowly bend to the left and hold this position for the length of the commercial; bend to the right side and hold until the next ad ends. Sit in your La-Z-Boy (upright position or else—shudder—I don't want to think about it) with your legs in front of you. Lift one leg up a few inches and hold for five seconds. Repeat with the other leg. Pull in your stomach muscles as hard as you can. Jog in place, pretending that you're running after or from the bad guys as you watch *Law & Order* or on the playground with Cartman (*South Park*).

While Shopping: Power walk one lap around the mall before you power shop. And then, evenly distribute shopping bags in each hand and do wing curls before you enter yet another store. If you find yourself standing in line in Nordstrom's shoe department or any other place, don't whine—squeeze your butt as hard as you can instead. Hold, release, and repeat. Rise up and down on your toes (recall flats-to-stilettos move). Sit on a bench in the mall for a brief respite and then decide to hit Saks. Slowly make your way up and then change your mind and sit back down. You really shouldn't. Oh, yes, you should. Slowly make the ascent again. No, back down! Do this mind-changing squat thing ten times. On the final rise, stand all the way up, march into Saks, and buy some fabulous boots to match your trench coat or some sassy camouflage capris—by now you have surely reached a new level of covert play.

While In Your Office: Sit at your desk with your feet flat on the floor. Squeeze your butt and pull in your abs. Hold for a few seconds and relax. Do throughout the day for some awesome abs and bootilicious bun tightening. This also works wonders during meetings and may even keep you from yawning, which is handy, especially when the boss is making a presentation. Take a walk around your entire floor. Twice. Be brave and go for a third lap (it is a charm, after all). Return phone calls and reply to e-mail in person. Hand-deliver documents to your pal's cubicle or even to the office building seven blocks away unless it storming. (This is also an escape tactic that comes in handy at times). I used to work with a woman who did cartwheels down the hallway. You don't need to go that far, but if you do go there, you might want to exhibit your gymnastic prowess on a day you wear slacks. To tone your thighs, slide forward in a chair until your butt is at the edge. Stretch legs in front of you and lift them until they're parallel to the seat. Repeat five times. Do not perform this on a chair with wheels. This I know firsthand. Ouch. During lunch, climb five flights of stairs or the same flight five times. Sit at your desk and bring the palms of your hands together in front of your chest with your elbows pointing out to the sides. Press hands together as hard as you can. Hold for a few seconds. This works your chest and wings. Use your coffee break to walk around the block instead of grabbing a cigarette or gossiping by the water cooler. It's all calorie-free fun and great for karma building.

While Thumping Your Leg + Twitching: Fidgeting is a proven way to burn calories and to get your blood pumping. I have a hard time sitting still, so it was great news to me to learn that fidgeting does the body good (though when I'm kicking my leg back and forth under the table, sometimes it doesn't do other bodies good).

While Doing Chores + Running Errands: Movement is in the house! Housework is a grand opportunity to sneak in some activity. You'll burn calories and have fun doing what otherwise might be a major grind. Exaggerate your scrubs, scours, scrapes, and sweeps. Dance around the room with your broom. Bebop and hip-hop with your mop. Do lunges and squats as you vacuum, or biceps curls with cleaning product containers. How about some leg lifts while you're doing the dishes (rear and side)? Even putting away groceries can be a mini-movement moment. Lift and squeeze anything you can. Bring shopping bags in one at a time. Really reach when you put those tins of escargot away in the pantry. Do some bicep curls and tricep dips with the cans of *foie gras* before shelving them in the cupboard. Or how about pumping iron literally by doing some knee bends and toe raises while you're at the ol' ironing board. Just be careful with that iron—hot, hot, hot. Gardening is not only a popular tension tamer, it's great play. Digging, weeding, raking, shoveling, and packing bags full of leaves—these are all great ways to play that connect you with nature. And while you're washing and waxing your car—really stretch across the hood and roof. Think Jessica Simpson as Daisy Duke!

While Grooming/Pampering: Play with your butt while you're brushing your teeth. Do squats, kickbacks, and cheek squeezes as you brighten your smile. Constantly contract and release your abs. Sneak in a stretch while in the tub. The soothing water warms your muscles, making them more pliable. Sit upright and lean forward from your waist, reaching for your toes. Hold for twenty gentle seconds. Soak, savor, stretch. And in case you're wondering, yes, zipping up those thigh-high boots qualifies for play in addition to adding to your hotness.

While in a Train, Plane, or Automobile: Remember being told not to play in traffic? Or maybe it was suggested that you do go play in traffic, which was a very mean thing to say and I'm sorry you had to hear that. Anyhow, what was once wrong is now right. Rather than being stuck in traffic, play in traffic. There's not much you can do about it other than stay home, so skip the not-good-for-you road rage and turn those idle moments into sweet cheek ops to play with yourself. Squeeze and release your butt muscles. Stretch your neck to the right and to the left and then front to back—a great relaxer. Contract your abs and release and repeat until the light turns green. Red means stop in traffic land, but it signals *go*! when it comes to stealth health. It's code for "play now!" Just be careful. Put your car in P if you tend to get all Zenny while in play mode. Moving it, moving it for your body+mind+heart+soul doesn't have anything to do with moving into the car in front of you or into the intersection. That would not constitute stealth health in any fashion.

WHY?

For the perks, silly goose! And what exactly are the perks of playing around besides a perky butt? Plenty! How does total body+mind+heart+soul health sound? When your play becomes a habit, you'll find that things that may have bothered you no longer do. The American Heart Association recognizes that stress contributes to heart disease—there's a tremendous value to reducing tension in your life, and you can do this with movement. Play clobbers stress and improves your mood. If you're prone to bouts of depression, don't be surprised if they are fewer and farther between.

Reflect on your life, your career, and your relationships while you move. Think of where you've been, where you are, and where you'd like to go. You can even pray while you're moving. Meditating on the move is just as effective as mountaintop, navel-gazing, lint-plucking swami stuff. Let your play be "in the moment" practice. Count your footsteps. Notice trees, plants, and flowers you haven't seen before. Greet every bird, butterfly, squirrel, and any other creature you see. I carry a voice recorder so I don't lose all the fantastic ideas that come to me as I walk. One day I recorded over fifty notes! You'll be amazed how things fall into place when you get out there. I tend to drip in creativity as much as I do in sweat—oops!—I mean, glisten.

Play in rehab may very well be the most therapeutic of all your treatments. OK, not as much as napping and soaking in a bubbly bath, but close. The more you move, the healthier you will feel and actually be, not to mention how hot you will look in your low-slung Miss Me jeans. Moving enhances your body+mind+heart+soul connection.

For you see, your physical self is not the only beneficiary of your playing around. There's no question that it's good for your body, but it's also very good for your mind, heart, and soul. Long before you wake up one day with leaner legs and a firmer butt, a better-functioning heart, more stamina, and a revved-up metabolism, you'll have a heightened sense of self-worth and accomplishment. You'll immediately feel in control of yourself. Play helps you lose all the sludge and pudge and helps you gain your authentic self again, only with more perkiness.

As I'm typing this paragraph one of my favorite get-up-and-dance songs shuffled on—"I Like to Move It" by Reel to Real. Time to get up and move it, move it to lose it, lose it! Shall we dance? OK, you dancing machine, the song ended. Get a hold of yourself and sit down. Is your heart pumping a bit faster? Your mood uplifted? See how easy it is to move it, move it? The benefits are so good and plenty. Savor this sweet sampling for a second and then read on.

THERE'S NO QUESTION ABOUT IT!

Notice the change in punctuation marks? There isn't a question posed in this section, only an outright order. So listen up! By the way, bossiness is not a desirable Concert Chick characteristic, but there are a few things that can really tick off a chick, and one of them is making excuses. Others are lack of self-responsibility, bad manners, flat champagne, and missing *the* shoe sale of all shoe sales by one day. But I digress.

We've had the "time" chat in Chapter 3 and in the "when?" section, but we're going there again, as there are some excuses exclusive to playtime that we must kick to the curb. As long as you're a reasonably healthy person without medical limitations, every excuse is a feeble one. Here's a list of the common "I don't wannas" including some "you just gottas". Excuses are just not part of a Concert Chick's vocabulary, no matter what the topic, but especially on matters pertaining to your well-being.

"I Have No Time.": Yeah, right. No freakin' time to take care of the body that takes such good care of you 24/7 no matter how you treat it? But you do have time to watch television, goof off, text, social network, twiddle your thumbs, shop, gossip, and just sit on your ass? Ten minutes here and there will not kill you. In fact, not only will play keep your *derrière* from dragging on the floor, it could very well save your life.

"I'm Too Tired.": Wake up! Exercise gives you energy. Not only will you be arousing your healthy state, you'll be able to put to rest all the things you have to do that you claim exhaust you. See how all this fits together so nicely?

"My Body Aches.": Only if you do too much, too soon. And if you do feel a smidge sore, that's what Tiger Balm and Biofreeze are for. You're giving me a headache with your bellyaching. Start slow. Just start.

"My Job Is Too Demanding.": Of course, the planet will stop spinning, the market will crash, and a plethora of other disasters will occur if you aren't checking e-mail or otherwise at your desk. Not! You must take care of yourself or you will burn out and not have a job. And then you'll have plenty of time and energy to move. Only thing is, your move it, move it may entail packing up your

apartment after you lose your job due to whining and now you can't pay your rent. Sure, pounding the payment looking for work is great play, but there's a better way. Think Operation Stealth Health!

"Times Are Tight—I'm Short On Cash.": Such a cheep-o, lame-o, no-go excuse! It's getting sick that will really cost you! Forget tight times. Think tight butt and gut. You're wealthy when you're healthy. Take that to the bank! You might not have much dough in your pockets, but if you don't get moving, you'll be like the Pillsbury Dough Boy (the girl version). The Rox Detox play doesn't require much. Good shoes are a must, so no scrimping there. The last time I checked, those Stuart Weitzman's you had to have are pricier than those New Balance's you need. Oh, yeah, and no shoes are required for yoga. As for play clothes, anything goes. And if you play at home, you can wear your birthday suit. Otherwise, depending on how you want to play, you might need a yoga mat, a pair of drumsticks, and/or some light hand weights. Hello, Tar-jay! You do not need to join a gym. Nature provides one for free. Steps and stairs can be found in many places. I bet your local library has many DVDs and manuals that you can check out for no charge other than the taxes you pay, which you must do no matter what, so you may as well get something in return, *non?* The Internet is loaded with info and freebies to download. Chances are good that you have at least one electronic device that you can upload the many free/near-zero-cost apps out there.

"I Hate To Get All Sweaty.": Gimme a break. No hanging out at the corner tiki bar or beach? No sex (excellent play, by the way) life? It's not sweat anyway. It's glisten! And it's one of the main vehicles that moves your toxins out. A/C and a shower can fix that post-play in a flash and a splash.

"I Have No One To Watch The Kids.": Oh, this one is as easy as A, B, C, 1, 2, 3. Play with your children or take turns with your peeps watching each other's kids so everyone can play.

"It's So Boring.": So, unbore it. Add some variety. Play with a friend. Reward yourself. Do what you love. The Rox Detox play focuses on things you do in your own way—dance, strut, drum, yoga. It's all about the *f* word. Fun! Don't make me use the other *f* word.

"It's Too Difficult Or Tricky.": Did you see the words "high impact", "heavy weights", "grueling workout", "cage fighting", "mud wrestling", "roller derby", "synchronized swimming", or "dodge ball" mentioned anywhere in this book except here? I didn't think so.

"Getting Fit Is A Luxury.": Here's where you're really wrong. It's a necessity if you desire to be healthy and happy, and I hope you do. How about luxuriating in the afterglow of some great play?

"I Have Too Much To Do.": I'm sure you do, sister! You do not hold an exclusive on that status. You're alive and in demand and breathing...at least for now. If you don't find the time to take care of yourself, you won't be able to do a damn thing later. Then what?

"I'm Too Fat.": No, you are not fat. Fat is not you. It's just a layer of lard that's covering up who you really are. But if you insist, you will always be a fatso unless you move it, move it to lose it, lose it. It's time to face the music. Don't be a chicken. Come out of hiding. The real you deserves to be seen. Reread Chapter 2 immediately for an attitude adjustment. Embrace your inner chick and shake those tail feathers, no matter how much plumage you have!

I hope you enjoyed playing around as much as I did. I don't even smoke, but I feel like having a cig. Next stop, your nest, for some well-deserved, post-moving it moving it reflection and rest and inner bling flashing.

Chapter 6

Sparkles In: That Inner Bling Thing

To appreciate your own inner beauty, reach inside your head and turn off the Barbie switch.
~Veronique Vienne

True confession time. I think Barbie is cool. *Way* cool. She has an awesome wardrobe, sassy shoes, sparkly accessories, perfect hair, a dream house, and a convertible, though my Joe is better than her Ken and I think an 18" waist is sorta freaky on a grown-up. It's time to get real, girlie girls, and check out of fantasyland for a bit. It's a great place to visit, but what you need first is the stuff that really is. So, turn off *that* switch and turn on your inner light with the power presented in this chapter.

Every red carpet celebrity needs to get off the stage and away from the camera and bright lights to recharge and rest between gigs. And so do you. It's imperative that you take time out to tune out. Every so often you just gotta scream, "Stop the music!" If you don't nurture your inner world you won't be able to thrive and survive in your outer world. You won't have it all when you emphasize your looks and neglect your mind, heart, and soul—a.k.a. your "inner bling." If your body is your only focus, you're nothing more than beautiful wrapping on an empty box—pretty sad considering the precious gift that you are. Up your inner energy and your outer will follow. Your body will lighten as you enlighten. It's nature's law and present to you. Don't take it for granted.

> *That which is strikingly beautiful is not always good; but that which is good is always beautiful.*
> ~NINON DE L'ENCLOS

SPARKLE THERAPY
A DOZEN EGGS TO PUT IN ONE BASKET

This chapter is your secret rest nest—a quiet, nurturing between gigs place where you can reflect, recharge, refresh, rest, rehab, restore, renew, and more to create energetic space to invigorate and illuminate your inner bling. This nest holds a dozen eggs, collectively known as "sparkle therapy." An egg symbolizes rebirth, which in many ways is what you're doing in rehab—the rebirth of your marvelous self. Consider these seeds your priceless nest eggs, far more valuable in the long run than any external assets if you invest your time and energy in exploring them wisely on a regular basis. Your daily prescriptions remind you to take an egg out of your basket—an egg a day keeps the dimmers away! An easy fun way to also remember is to write each sparkle therapy suggestion on a small strip of paper, add some glitter glue, insert each into a red plastic egg (the kind used at Eastertime), and place in a basket (yes, all your eggs go into one basket in rehab). You can add the rocks + rolls you created during the pre-rehab ritual. Whatever you do, know that it is here, in your nest, that you'll discover how to grace and adore your inner world. You'll then transition this bright light into Chapter 7, where you'll learn how to gratify and adorn—light up!—your outer world.

Only you can reveal your authentic self. You can pay people to do your laundry, clean your house, cook your meals, change the oil in your Mini Cooper, but no one at any price can sit in stillness on your behalf and explore what's it your head, your heart, and your soul. The sparks held in each egg can help with the reveal.

Before you go on your egg hunt, let's talk about the stuff that can cause serious scrambling and many Humpty Dumpty moments if not whisked away. Yup, the big *s* word that dulls our internal diamonds (and you know it isn't "shoes"): *stress*.

THE BANE OF A-DRAMA-ME STRAIN

Stress—the confusion created when one's mind overrides the body's basic desire to choke the living crap out of some jerk who desperately needs it.
~ Contemporary folk wisdom

Stress was designed to keep us alive, not kill us. It goes back to our God-given, primal "fight or flight" instincts, whereby whenever danger was sensed, we'd react in one of two ways to survive: we either took flight—hightailed it outta there ("Holy shit! It's a T. rex! Run for your life!")—or we decided to fight. We grabbed our clubs, loaded our slingshots, and faced it head on ("Step back, Spinosaurus, or else!" followed by a silent "Holy shit, did I just say that?", but say that we did because it was either him or us). Either way, we acted appropriately, albeit rather stupidly at times, but the urge was pure survival of the fittest. But long gone are the days where we must fear that woolly beasts are crouching behind our hibiscus bushes preparing for a full-on attack when we roll out our cans on trash day.

I personally think the *s* word is overused. Oh, it's real, all right. But it's tossed around so casually these days that it has morphed into yet another lame excuse for all sorts of irrational, sometimes criminal, behavior. From drowning sorrows in cheep scotch because someone's boyfriend didn't notice her brow wax to drowning children because someone's boss didn't approve her travel to the convention in Kalamazoo, we've gotta get a grip! Even though there are many legitimate reasons for being scattered and tattered, we have to do whatever we can to keep our lives from being shattered. We must learn to embrace stress to minimize its mess. Since it'll always be a part of your life, you may as well put it to work for you. Give it a fancy title, as in "meet my virtual assistant, Stress." How cool are you to have one? Very.

Modern time stress typically alerts us to something we have to deal with, be it that monster of a problem (no job!), that long overdue memorandum (boss is pacing outside your cubicle!), or that little mole that is now the size of a quarter (WTF is it?—better call the derm stat!). This is stress at its best. And it doesn't have to involve big, scary obvious things. It may take the form of insomnia, causing you to toss and turn all night. One day it dawns on you that you really don't want to serve folks stew and brew for the rest of your life. So don't! Do sleepwalk to the nearest educational center or institution the next day, sign up for classes more in line with what you do want to serve up in your life, and enjoy a good night's sleep. Stress can be a great motivator—the swift kick in the ass we may need from time to time. It's all how you look at it, and not only how you look at it, but primarily how you react to it. Herein lies the real problem. And the solution is entirely within your control.

For you see, the source of most of your stress isn't what you think it is. There's no denying that life is filled with button pushers and really sad and awful things. The truth of the matter is that much of our life strife is of our own doing and not due to annoying people, traffic jams, broken nails, Wolford snags, jobs lost, decreasing medical coverage, and increasing cost of cable TV. Most often, we are the source of our problems.

It's natural to think that if we could only get away from the external crap, we'd be happily stress free forever. But that's not how it works because the crap is here to stay unless we take up living in a bubble, and we're not talking Perrier-Jouet here, girls. No matter where we escape to, no matter what or whom we escape with or from, we'll still be there, and chances are good, so will the condition we thought we left behind. We may as well learn to play with it, instead of letting it play us.

To do otherwise is to concede that everyone and everything outside of you dictates how you feel, show up, and live your life. That is simply a big fat lie. OK, so the lie is simple. Not so simple is facing the truth. But if you put the energy you waste driving yourself crazy toward sane moving on, you'll be happier, healthier, and certainly experience less loony moments. Since it's practically impossible to run from and refrain from stress, we must reframe it. It's time to stress for success.

And just how do we do this? How do we go from frazzle to dazzle? Nuke it, baby!

NUCLEAR REACTIVITY

The single best thing you can do for your health and happiness is to nuke any nuclear reactivity you possess or, rather, that possesses you. It's highly toxic and must be eradicated if you truly desire a salubrious life.

Here's a real-life example of how toxic and ridiculous reactivity can be. Two co-workers are walking down the hall. Their boss passes by without a word, as if they didn't exist. No hello, no smile, nothing. One thinks to herself, "What's wrong? What did I do? I wonder why he's upset with me." And then she proceeds to tell everyone who'll listen how insensitive her ass of a boss is and asks whether anyone knows what's wrong with him or, better yet, whether anyone knows if she's in trouble. Is she going to be fired? Was her report rubbish? This dramarama could—and usually does—last all day and more days. Too many days. Meanwhile, her co-worker who also didn't get a "good morning, how are you?" simply thought the boss seemed preoccupied—probably had something else on his mind and didn't see them as he passed by. The co-worker who responded in this manner worked all day without a second thought about the two-second non-exchange in the hall that morning, while the other is already on the sixteenth replay and it isn't even lunchtime yet.

Same event, completely different results. One simply noticed, one seriously (over)reacted. One person's day was shot to hell (and by the way, she got others fired up, too—drama is viral); the other's day went extremely well. Why? We see the world through our own experiences and perceptions. We all have our own stories, premises, and sensitivities that we filter everything and everyone through.

Overreacting can cause you to stuff your closet, drawers, mouth, and mind to toxic excess. If you keep it up, your immune system could shut down, laying out the welcome mat for all sorts of illness that will definitely put a damper on your life. You could be inviting hypertension, a stroke, or a heart attack to hang out with you. Heck, you could even drop dead.

When it's all said and done, you are the only one who can dim your light. You control the activation switch, or rather, the reactivation switch. This statement of fact isn't contrary to the Rox Detox push to rid yourself of the people, places, and things that dim your light. It's just that there's so much you can't ditch, so you may as well fortify your inner repellant. That's where the eggs come in. They are loaded with proactive measures to strengthen your immune system, thicken your skin, and help you get a spine. No, the goal isn't to get all Barbie badass, but rather to illuminate your light with highly charged positive energy so that the effects of negative people, places, and things will not affect and infect you as much, if at all. Are you ready for some sparkle therapy? Let's get cracking those eggs! But first, a message about the Rox Detox solitary confinement wing that houses your rehab nest.

SOULITUDE™

Loneliness is inner emptiness. Solitude is inner fulfillment.
~Richard Foster

To receive the gifts placed in your nest, you must get comfortable with hanging out with yourself. There's a big difference between being alone and being lonely. In rehab, these spells of "soulitary" confinement are called "soulitude," which is simply nourishing time you spend with your soul to reflect, nap, transform, shrink, expand, glow, incubate, polish—to enhance, not exhaust, your essence. Your gig in rehab is for the most part a solo act with your marquee now reading "Appearing Live to Thrive...Souloist (insert your name)."

For many people, it's very uncomfortable, scary even, to go solo, because your companions become your thoughts and feelings, many of which you've never met before. But you must create the space for your body+mind+heart+soul to hang out with each other for a while, communicating and connecting through private exchanges and stillness. View your nest as a little cocoon that you enter in rehab. Your very own metamorphosis maker. And if you aren't buying that, just think this: More cocoon=less loon. That should do it. Hop into your nest and break an egg!

EGG #1: PRAY

No, we're not getting all religious on you but we are summoning your spiritual side. In rehab, spirituality is your connection with something/someone at a higher level that guides, supports, protects you—gives you those little nudges from above—your source and creator, be it God, Kali, Buddha, Shiva, Allah, Kuan Yin, any one of the many goddesses, or even the Lord of the Rings. For me, it's God,[22] thousands of angels, nature, and the universe as a whole. As for worship, that would be Beverly Feldman but I'm jumping ahead to the next chapter. Who takes care of you? Who makes your favorite shoe?[23]

---

[22] To keep it simple, this is the term I'll use—if this isn't working for you, substitute your own deity in its place as you read along.

[23] I'm not making light of this serious practice, though God did give us a sense of humor and we really do need to lighten up. God also gifted some folks with amazing shoe designing talents.

Prayer is simply communicating with that someone out there. Prayer is powerful. When we pray we are asking—for an answer to a problem we are having, for an end to our pain and suffering, for an illness to be healed, for an idea that will spark a new chance at life, for others' well-being.

There really isn't a right way to pray. You don't have to be in a church, temple, mosque, or other place of worship. On your knees, behind your desk, while waiting for the light to turn green, in line at Walmart, it's all good and you will be heard. Your prayer can be as simple as "Dear Shiva, please direct me to the perfect pair of slippers for the ball" or "Dear God, what can I do to be a better person today?" I highly recommend the latter as soon as you start your day, every day. As for the other, at least two weeks before the event, as needed.

Your supreme authority is everywhere you are and always has time for you. Nothing is too big (please cure my father's cancer), too small (I'd really like a parking spot near the entrance to the mall), too trivial (please let that gorgeous gown find its way to the half-off rack), too impossible (world peace). Pray all day. And always say "thank you".

To further your prayer practice, stock your nest with a rosary, mala beads, a prayer shawl, a book of prayers, a Bible, some holy water, and/or a candle. You don't need props to pray, but the items mentioned here mark the shift into prayer mode and can be very supportive and symbolic of the sacred moments you create for yourself to commune with your source.

A word of caution. You will get what you ask for, or at least what you need, which most often is better than what you thought you wanted in the first place. So if you pray for a new job, make sure you mean it, because a pink slip accompanied by an order to leave your key to the executive bathroom at the security desk on your way out could come next week. A good practice is to say "this or something better" or "this for the good of all involved" at the end of your prayer. Of course, to receive, you must have faith and believe it's possible. And you have to pay attention or the blessing, answer, whatever it is that you are seeking will be right in front of your eyes yet you'll never see it. This is where stillness and mindfulness enter. Proceed to eggs #2 and #3, please.

EGG #2: MEDITATE

Meditation is prayer's partner. As you know, in prayer you ask, and in the stillness of meditation you receive. This powerful duet brings forth rockin' inner bling radiance and resilience.

And have no worries. You won't be asked to twist on a turban, slap on a diaper, and perch yourself atop a mountain and chant "ohmamabananapapacaca" unless this strikes a chord with you. We are going for mindful, not a mouthful. Rox Detox meditation is about mindful stillness and peaceful quiet.

Being a "can't sit still" person since the day I was born, when I first started dabbling in mediation over twenty years ago, the most difficult part of sitting still was sitting still. My mind would race, and oftentimes it still does. I felt antsy, bored, and guilty. Surely there was something I should be checking off my to-do list. How could I just sit there? Our culture, unfortunately, places great value on doing rather than being, and I was a champion at that, though I was determined to sit still because I instinctively knew it was a better way.

And then something bizarre, unexpected, and wonderful happened. I discovered that the more I sat and centered myself (being), the more I experienced peaceful productivity (doing). And it wasn't the typical doing (any dodo can do), but rather doing better, with more clarity and consciousness. There's a big difference between being busy and being productive. Being productive is constructive. Doing busy can be counterproductive and destructive. I suppose that's why filling time with activity but not necessarily seeing results for all the effort is called busywork. You may have seen the office plaque that reads: *Of course I don't look busy...I did it right the first time.* Surely something to think about.

It took many hours of silence for me to hear loud and clear that I need this time of just being before I could get to the doing. My daily dose of stillness is now nonnegotiable *and* enjoyable.

All you have to do is sit down, shut up, and listen. And when you do, you invite your silent partners (for me, God, my angels, nature, and the entire universe) into your body+mind+heart+soul to receive messages and insights. No, this is not alien intervention—no anal probes here[24]—but definitely divine intervention, soul strobes! Constant chatter and noise blocks the universe's gifts. It is in the quiet where you will hear the answers. It's truly an amazing process if you give it a chance.

Still not convinced that meditation rocks? There are proven perks, many of which are backed up by science. Meditation can improve everything in your life—your career, your relationships, and your physical and mental well-being. Your body relaxes, your blood pressure drops, and your breathing slows. And the perks keep percolating post-stillness. You'll have more energy because you've given your body the time to recharge itself. You'll be focused and serene. You'll be very aware and in tune with what's going on around you. Are you ready to give it a test drive (in park)? To close your eyes, breathe, and receive?

This Rox Detox meditation prescription is both a simple (just sit there!) yet difficult (just sit there!) practice, but hang in there. If I can do it, you can do it.

1. Find a quiet spot where you can be alone without distraction. This is your time. Pets, parents, and peeps can wait, unless they meditate with you like my "kids" do.
2. Light a candle or stick of incense to mark the start of your quiet time.
3. Sit on a comfortable cushion on the floor or in a chair. Maintain what I call a receiving posture. Keep your spine straight though not rigid. If you are on the floor, sit with your legs in half or full

---

24 That would be *South Park*, Season 1, Episode 0101, "Cartman Gets an Anal Probe".

lotus position. If you're in a chair, sit cross-legged if there's room, or tall with both feet grounded on the floor, *sans* stilettos (it's nice to establish an earthy connection in bare feet—you can slip on your Steve Maddens afterward). Rest your hands on your knees, palms up or down or simply relaxed in your lap.

4. Set a timer for three minutes to start, gradually building to twenty as you get more comfortable. There are some great phone and pad apps just for this purpose that include different time increments and a variety of "time's up!" alerts, such as chimes, gongs, a little bell jingle.

5. Close your eyes gently and take a deep breath in through your nose, inhaling goodness.

6. Exhale slowly and peacefully through your nose, letting go of badness.

7. Repeat inhales and exhales, focusing on your breath. In and out. Receive, release. Simply be aware and breathe, letting any thoughts pass by (there will be some).

8. After your session is over, glow in the calm for a few moments and transition into the "real" world that in time will be more unreal with each minute you are still. *Namaste.*

Welcome "om sweet om." How'd it go? If you're like most people, it was the longest flippin' three minutes of your life. How do you feel? Record your experience in your journal. Any judgment or fear of not doing it right? Any distractions? Did you think it was the dumbest, most ridiculous thing you ever did, a complete waste of time? Please know that there's no right or wrong way to meditate. No worries if your head was swimming with thoughts while you sat. You will have them. You are still meditating. Simply notice the wondering of what you're going to have for dinner, what a schmo your co-worker can be, and how you hope it doesn't rain on the BBQ you're hosting next month. Observe and let the thoughts float by, like balloons on strings or clouds in the sky. Just there. It's the grasping of the string or the desire to rearrange the sky that blocks the perks of stillness. As Davidji, the dean of Chopra Center

University, tells us, having thoughts means you're alive. This is a good thing!

The Rox Detox meditation is a basic practice, though it's very effective. I'd encourage you to try other methods, such as guided meditation, where you are walked through your stillness via voice prompts. This is a great beginner practice because you focus on what you hear rather than sitting still wondering if you're doing it right (but remember, there is no right or wrong way). I'd encourage you to explore different techniques. The Swag Lounge is stocked with resources on this subject.

There are also many ways to keep your basic practice interesting. Feel free to incorporate the items mentioned in your prayer egg. For example, you can simply rest a rosary or strand of mala beads in your hand or assign each breath to a bead, moving along and around the circle on the inhale and exhale. Mantras are also worth exploring. A mantra is a word, phrase, or sound that is repeated on the inhale and the exhale. A popular one is "so hum," which means "I am that." This is the sound of the breath, a way to connect with your source. It works like this: As you inhale, repeat silently to yourself "so," and as you exhale, repeat "hum." "Rehab" and "detox" are other appropriate choices—"re" on the inhale, "hab" on the exhale; "de" inhale, "tox" exhale. "I rock" and "new shoes" work, too. You don't have to repeat your mantra the entire time, just whenever your thoughts take over. A mantra is simply a nice way to say "Stop it, dammit!" to the incessant chatter in your head.

A prayer shawl creates a silent huddle of one. I use the batik sarong I bought in Bali to wear during temple visits and blessing ceremonies. I'm instantly transported back to the Tanah Lot Temple as soon as I touch the cloth. When my dogs see the sarong in my hands, their tails wag because they know it's sit-stay time that they really enjoy, too. We sit in a comfy chair, close our eyes, stay, and breathe. Actually, Oliver snores, but we girls know that's a guy thing and we welcome the opportunity to practice maintaining inner quiet in the midst of outer noise. Treats afterward!

Just like play, the ideal time to meditate is any time you'll do it or when you need to be centered and grounded. There are no rules; however, it's very effective to start and finish your day in meditation, preferably for twenty minutes, but even one minute will start shifting things around. The only rule I can think of—since meditation can be done anywhere—is if you're taking a few reflective moments while driving, skip the "close your eyes" instruction. The same holds true if you're at a meeting that doesn't have an end in sight and you decide to escape to a peaceful place. Be careful—the deadly combination of a boring meeting and a quickie with your soul could bring you to lala land. Not good for your professional reputation, especially if you snore like Oliver.

EGG #3: BE PRESENT

> *The mind is its own place, and in itself, can make a heaven of hell, a hell of heaven.*
> ~John Milton

Meditation is certainly a session in mindfulness, stillness, and being in the moment, but it's a deliberate intention. You decide that you will sit in silence for a spell. This egg holds the "meme brain" of movement, not stillness.

You're alive right now or else you wouldn't be reading this sentence. But by the time you reach the next paragraph, you could be hit by a bus, suffer a heart attack, fall off your rocker and fatally bump your head, or be attacked by one of those woolly beasts we joked about earlier. Anything is possible and any one could kill you. Grim, but real. The reaper is always lurking.

I'm not going all doom and gloom on you. Recall that I wear rose-colored glasses. But life has a funny, strange, startling way of getting our attention, and we must learn to heed its messages. And we do this by staying in the present moment, mindfully.

Buddhists refer to constant internal head chatter as "monkey mind." Think of monkeys swinging from tree to tree shrieking "ooh

ooh ooh ah ah ah" with the occasional underarm scratch. This commotion can drive you freakin' bananas. I experienced an up-close-and-personal live demo of how rowdy those monkeys—thoughts gone wild!—can be. One peaceful morning in Bali, as a group of us started to meditate in the middle of a rice paddy, our leader's dharma talk focused on monkey mind. As if on cue, about twenty monkeys surrounded us, chattering up a storm. Though adorable (OMG! They are so cute, look at how they hug each other.), they can be unbearable (WTF? How can *that* noise come out of such an adorable creature?). They really drove the message home, loud and clear.

Unless you experience a live monkey encounter, it may be hard to fully appreciate the craziness of it all, so here's another way to look at it. Imagine that your head is a popcorn machine and the kernels are thoughts. The kernels rest on the bottom and stay put as long as you're still and calm. But when things heat up, watch out! A pop here, a pop there. It gets hotter. Pop pop pop. More heat, more pops until you're in full-blown popping-your-top mode. Does that work better for you? And you know, the popping is a necessary, unavoidable part of life. Without the noise, the treats of life may not appear. Patiently surrender and it shall pass. I'll take mine with extra butter and a shake of Parmesan, please.

> *The world in which you live is not primarily determined by outward conditions and circumstances but by thoughts that habitually occupy your mind.*
> ~Norman Vincent Peale

Another personal lesson on being in the moment came as I drove along the beach on my way to work one day. I usually start cell phone yakking immediately after I shift my car into D and that day was no different until I reached the end of the road. When I arrived at the turn that moves traffic onto a major roadway, I realized that I hadn't seen the sea once. Pathetic. All we have is this very moment. Make sure you see the sea or whatever beauty surrounds you in the now.

> *You can't change yesterday, but you can ruin today worrying about tomorrow.*
> ~Seen on a wall in the ladies' room at McCormick & Schmick's in downtown Cincinnati

Just as there isn't anything you can do about the past other than practice the lessons today that you learned then, there isn't any point in dwelling on the future, because everything can change in a flash. Tomorrow may never come. Now is all we have. Don't miss a beat. If you stay in the present moment, really paying attention to what you're doing, who you're with, and where you're going, you'll be able to handle, receive, embrace, and enjoy all that comes your way. If you don't, not only do you miss the amazing scenery along the way, the miracles drive by, too, and end up parked in someone else's driveway—someone who is wide awake and alert *now*.

EGG #4: SPEAK UP + BE HEARD

Don't be afraid to speak your truth and ask for what you want. I know the asking part smacks of prayer, but this egg is different. Prayer will always stand on its own. The focus here is on the authentic expression of your unique voice. An ability to express yourself is a powerful gift because, like prayer, what you talk about, comes about! In Chapter 8, we'll discuss the conversations you have with and about others. Here, it's all about the conversations you have with and about yourself, be it in your head, what you "say" in your journal, or voice out loud. Let's start with the practice that you've been busy with in rehab.

Journaling: Your journal is your BFF. You can tell her everything and anything and she will tell you what she thinks. How many times do you start writing, not really sure what to say, and then all of a sudden it's as if someone else is doing the writing with your hand and you end up filling a dozen pages? Expressing your thoughts and feelings through the written word is an excellent detox tool that requires only something to write with and something to write on. There are many beautiful journals out there that can house your heart's and soul's messages. Surely one will call out to you, "Take me home and make me yours. Tell me all your most intimate secrets. I promise to tell no one! I'm here for you."

It's amazing how answers from your soul can and will come to you through journaling. If someone or something upsets you, rather than confronting that person when you're angry, go head-to-head with him or her in your journal. Write down everything you'd love to say to that person or how you'd change the situation if you could. Your journal is the perfect place to give a piece of your mind for peace of mind. It's a simple but effective method of purging your system without speaking words you may regret and want to take back later, but can't. You may find what was driving you crazy when you started is actually amusing by the time you reach the fifth page. From your hand through your heart and head to the paper through the pen, you can release tons of toxic energy from your system.

The Artist's Way by Julia Cameron (a must read!), introduces a wonderful journaling ritual called "morning pages." You simply open your journal after waking and write and write and write until you spill yourself all over three pages. This is an excellent ritual to play with during rehab. Write about anything, everything, nothing, just write. If you're stuck on the first word, start with a doodle, the name of the movie you saw last night, what you're going to have for breakfast. It's truly miraculous what starts to pour out. You'll find yourself wondering, "where the hell did *that* come from?" when yet another profound statement flows from your pen.

Let's tailor this concept a bit to mesh with the detox, let-go flow of rehab. As you release people, places, and things, share how you feel in your journal on what we'll call "mourning pages." No matter how toxic a person is, you'll still feel a loss—of that person and the role he or she played in your life, of your old self. It's important to feel any grief and deep sorrow as you move people out of your life. It's necessary to mourn your losses. The process of letting go and saying good-bye can be painful. Expressing those feelings in your journal is helpful. And that includes the sadness you feel when you donate that ridiculously priced handbag to Faith Farm. Write about that, too.

And please add a gratitude journal to the mix. Regularly record everything you are thankful for. To get you started, I've included space on your daily prescription to pen three things you are grateful for each day. By the way, I am grateful to you for not only buying this book, but for reading it as well. *Merci beaucoup*.

Visual journaling is another way to access your inner bling through images and random words that mean something to you. See egg #5 for the scoop.

Affirmations: An affirmation is a statement of what you desire expressed as if you already have it. So, you want to replace soda with water, do you? Instead of saying "I don't want to drink soda," proclaim, "I enjoy drinking eight refreshing glasses of water each day." See and feel the difference? The first statement is still coming from a negative, wanting place, the second, you're already enjoying the water! Before you know it, your actions will catch up with your thoughts. (This is why it's important to watch your thoughts—they do become your reality.)

One of the most powerful universal affirmations—*every day in every way, I am getting better and better*—was created by Emile Coue, a French psychotherapist who practiced in the early twentieth century. Feel free to use this one, create your own, or refer back to the Concert Chick quiz questions in the "meet + greet" and make these your life-affirming statements.

Write your affirmations on index cards, Post-it notes, chicktail napkins, or any scrap of paper nearby, and place them in conspicuous spots in your home, car, and office. If you're at a loss as to what to write in your journal, start with an affirmation. Write it down at least twenty times a day while in rehab and for as long afterward as it takes to get it. And you will.

EGG #5: CREATE

> *Life isn't about finding yourself.*
> *Life is about creating yourself.*
> ~George Bernard Shaw

This egg invites your inner *artiste* to come out to play. Our mediums differ, but we're all creative souls, desiring—needing—to express ourselves. The world is not black and white. Lines are not neatly drawn. We fight our inherent nature when we always try to stay inside the lines. It's time to cross the line. Get outside yourself. Life is colorful, playful, squiggly, and vibrantly *alive*. Be the human sparkler that I know you are!

To ignite the sparkler within, ya gotta get down and dirty. Play with clay. Paint with acrylics or watercolors. Scribble with chalk pastels. Transform textiles. Decoupage a cigar box to put your crayons in that you'll use later when you're in the mood for some coloring book action. Knit a poncho. String beads. Write a children's book or some chick lit. What creative streaks will you release in rehab?

A fun, easy, breezy way to make art and remake yourself is through a collage. Flash back to kindergarten and you may recall cutting and pasting images of your favorite things from magazines. Today it's called visual or art journaling and dream or vision boards. No matter what you call it, the idea is the same—just do it. Buy a sketchbook to house your visual expressions. Cut and paste images and words that speak to you, reflect who you are, who you want to be, your dreams and intentions. Jazz the display up with glitter, feathers, sequins, and other 3-D extras. The scrapbook aisle at Michael's has taken on a new meaning for me. I've composed pages filled with nothing but eyes (what do I see?) and lips (what do I say?). I also capture visual memories of trips and events that left an impression on me. Enjoy the process.

Along these lines, here's a rehab art project for you. Glue a photo of yourself in the middle of a heavy sheet of large paper or a poster board. Draw a circle around your image. You represent the sun. Next, draw seventeen "rays" emanating from you. These rays of sunshine represent your prep, rehab, and debut days. On each ray, before each day closes, write something that expresses, reflects, and captures how you're doing, what you're feeling, who you're becoming, something you've learned. Surround the "sky" area with your intentions for rehab and images that support your words. Your masterpiece will reveal itself as you reveal yourself.

EGG #6: SEEK WISDOM FROM OTHERS

Even though deep down inside you know what's best for you, sometimes that "best" is right in front of your face but you don't see it. This is where prompts and nudges from others, known and unknown, can assist. Besides, no one person knows everything (more on this in Chapter 8). We are all here to teach and learn from each other. Your like-minded soul friends are great support systems. Don't hesitate to reach out and ask for advice. Seek out mentors, role models, and others on the same path to provide you with reinforcement, guidance, and experience.

I invited some people in my life that I greatly admire and respect to share with you how they deal with people who dim their light. The response was fantastic and most are found in Chapter 8; however, two pertain to this egg. Suzanne is my super sister-in-law and friend. Jane and I met in Bali, instantly connected, and have stayed joined in spirit ever since.

When things get a little crazy I'll say "Serenity now!" to myself and laugh a couple of times...it's from a Seinfeld *episode. Another technique I use came from a training class. We were told that to have a better day you should wake up each morning and yell, "hotdog!" I think it works, because it makes you feel a little silly, which then makes you giggle and puts a*

smile on your face. It's much easier to have a good day when you start with a smile on your face. I also have no need to have the last word...you cannot rationalize with the irrational.
~ SUZANNE NIEMAN, SERVICE COORDINATOR FOR A NOT-FOR-PROFIT AGENCY, ADVOCATE FOR PEOPLE WITH DISABILITIES, CINCINNATIAN, EXERCISE ENTHUSIAST

Most of the time, it's mind-inflicted, so a quick way to "change" your mind is to switch on your favourite music and tune in. I usually start to meditate and connect to my inner self because it knows that I am safe and protected. Other little tricks...hmmm, I sometimes visualise myself at the bottom of the sea and then forcefully swim up to the surface to see light... it's more powerful than it reads, but if you ever will have a low moment (and I hope not), it helps. From the channelings, we were told once that a quick way to connect to a source is to start deep breathing, especially good in emergencies. There's also a little quote that I often refer to, that I got from a card deck. It says, "Being Unique—I am a very unique Creative Being. Criticism tears me down and draws out the worst in me. I look at my real self and express the love and beauty within me."
~JANE CHOW, FASHIONISTA, DREAMER, NEW-AGER, LIGHT-WORKER

Wisdom can also come from inspirational, spiritual, and motivational books, oracle cards, CDs, and DVDs. The Internet provides unlimited access to teachers. Online courses and tele-classes are an inexpensive and convenient way to expose yourself to personal growth, creative expression, and more—anything you're interested in. Don't hesitate to sign up for lectures, retreats, and workshops. Rox shares her personal favorites in the Swag Lounge.

EGG #7: LIGHT ONE UP + INHALE

This egg provides the juice and other euphoria inducers. You're encouraged to get lit, get stoned, hit the bottle, and play with matches. We're talking candles, incense, crystals, rocks, tiny twinkly lights, and essential oils. What were you thinking? Good thing you're in rehab!

Candles + Incense: Lighting a candle (scented soy-based varieties rock!) or some incense (hail to the Nag Champa!) are excellent soul-soothing, calming reminders of your inner bling. The flicker, glow, spark, and scent shift the energy in any room.

Candles are used in many rituals. Churches (all those votives!), weddings (unity candle!), birthday cakes (oh my!). Candles are mesmerizing and can transform any space into a reflective environment. They bring tranquility, softness, and a warm glow to our lives (and to our complexions, virtually erasing little lines—oh yeah!). Contrary to county policy (please do not tell the Inspector General), I'm known to light up in my office. The scent and soothe of the candle's flame keep me centered. Besides, there's nothing like a little file fire to bring some more excitement to the day. Just kidding, Chief!

The burning of incense is also a ritual staple. It's a peaceful and welcome addition to yoga, meditation, and sacred ceremonies. It comes in various forms, including standard sticks and cones, and in many scents. Incense promotes calm, helps one focus, and purifies the mind.

Get Strung Out to Fly: They're not just for the holidays anymore, kiddies! Mini twinkle lights are a way to get lit without fire. I encourage you to get hung up on them. Make every day a celebration by hanging strands in trees, on top of bookcases, around window frames, everywhere. Twinkly lights are festive. They're like little stars—your own personal sky—transforming any place into a magical, festive fairytale. Twinkle, twinkle little star...*oh yes you are*! And a rock star at that.

Hit the Hard Stuff: Now that you're sufficiently lit up, it's time to experiment with the hard stuff. Crystals and rocks are powerful meditation focus tools that carry special natural charges. So, let's get stoned! Sit in silence and stillness with your eyes slightly open, fixated on a crystal or rock you found in a special place like Mount Tomanivi in Fiji or the Godavari River in India. Or keep your eyes closed and hold the stone or crystal in your hand, sensing and receiving its healing energy. If you're not getting off on this, reach for the bottle! Aromatherapy is potent. A variety of essential oils are available for you to tap into. The Swag Lounge deals the 411.

Burn, Baby, Burn: Revisit the lists you created in Step 1. Combine all you desire (peace, love, and happiness stuff) on a sheet of paper[25] and all you want to retire (toxic people, places, and things) on another. You're going to set them on fire! There are two parts to this ritual—one for "letting go" and another for "letting grow." You'll need matches and something fireproof, such as a fireplace, a flowerpot, an ashtray, a crack pipe (just checking to see if you were paying attention!)—anything that can safely hold your burning paper. "Burning Down the House" is only a great Talking Heads tune, and not to be taken literally. Be careful.

Let's "let go" first. Strike a match and set the toxic list on fire, and put it to rest in a safe container. While joyously watching it all go up in flames, ask the universe to support you in your efforts to release all the toxins from your body+mind+heart+soul. After a slight pause to absorb what just happened, say thanks and move on to the next list—the one filled with your wishes, dreams, and intentions for rehab and your life.

Repeat the same match strike and burn, only this time, ask the universe to co-create with you in making all that you send up in smoke come true. You're planting "I'm smokin' hot!" seeds to "let grow." Visualize everything manifesting. Believe it is possible. And then express your gratitude for what is to be. Your angels are on standby!

---

25 I suppose you could really get into this egg's theme and use rolling papers—one for each let go and let grow desire. Your call.

> *As much as I try to be an easygoing, stretch your wings and fly type...I just can't stop trying to burst people into flames with my mind.*
> ~ERIN SMITH, FUN + SASSY, CHEEKY CHICKIE,
> MIXED MEDIA ARTIST EXTRAORDINAIRE

Now that you're all blissy trippy, get your groove on even more with the original source of Zen-zing!

EGG #8: POP NATURAL SEDATIVES

Nature's sparkly stuff is very empowering and can illuminate your inner bling like nothing else. When I'm outdoors, I always feel more connected, balanced, and calmer. As they say, life's a beach. Spend time near or in water. Go for a swim in the salty sea or in a refreshing lake. Climb a mountain or just sit in awe of one. Don't make mountains out of molehills, but believe that just one little mustard seed can move a mountain. Grab a blanket, lie down on the ground under the moonshine, and unfold in the awesomeness of a vast, twinkling sky. Be a cloud watcher and a sunshine gatherer. Hug a tree, run free in a park, hike, bike, canoe, kayak, surf. Breathe in fresh air. Garden. Be kind and compassionate to critters big and small. And please take care of Mother Earth. Whether you believe in global warming or not, I think we can all agree that littering sucks, recycling is good, and participating in a monthly beach cleanup scores major karma brownie points.

EGG #9: GIVE YOURSELF A BREAK

As we touched upon in the meditation and be-present eggs, we must take time to simply "be" and not "do." No multitasking. No tasking of any kind at all. This egg will have you dreaming about napping, deep sleeping, lounging, swinging in a hammock, lying in a chaise, taking a time out already. Essentially and blissfully doing nothing but going slow and chilling out. Are you up for it, sleeping beauty?

I used to sleep four hours a night for many years ever since I was a kid juggling all those responsibilities I mentioned earlier. It's all I knew, so it was my norm. And then I slept for an entire weekend. It was as if my body finally gave up. And the world did not crash when I crashed. And it won't collapse when you do either.

You really do need sleep. There are numerous studies, reports, and articles out there about the effects of sleep deprivation. A quick Google will bring you many. My favorite is from WebMD: "10 Things to Hate About Sleep Loss," by Camille Peri. Ms. Peri's list: causes accidents, dumbs you down, puts you at risk for heart problems and other disease, kills your sex drive, depresses, ages your skin, makes you gain weight, makes you forgetful, increases your risk of death, and impairs your judgment. I'm not seeing one thing on that list that isn't a nightmare. Sounds like permission to sleep an extra hour tonight. Make your dream of at least seven hours come true.

It's when you let go and slow down that you glow and grow. Step back, take a long, deep breath, yawn, and enjoy the ride. The journey is where bliss is found. It's time to unlace your running shoes and strap on your stilettos, buckle up those hot thigh-high boots, or lace up the ballerina-slipper inspired platforms and get your groove on one slow but sure step at a time. After you wake up, of course.

EGG #10: HALLUCINATE TO ILLUMINATE

> *We don't see things as they are, we see them as we are.*
> ~Anais Nin

This perfect egg teaches you a couple of techniques that will bring elucidation to any hallucination. In other words, clarity to the stuff we make up in our minds based on false premises and popular perceptions. It's time to take the blinders off and see what you've never seen before in yourself and others. You'll first take a peek in a mirror and then make stuff up in your head. What you see is what you'll get.

Look In The Mirror: Mirror, mirror on the wall, who's the most unique chick of them all? That would be you! An outstanding "get a grip" practice is self-reflection through others. What you see in people you encounter can be found in you, too. The things that really bug you about someone lurk inside you. And the same wonderful attributes you admire in others are a part of your constitution and are worth bringing out in the open for all to see. The next time you find someone annoying, stop and think how you might be showing up in the same annoying manner. Always look at yourself first. The universe may have put that dork on your path to teach you a thing or two. The person you are in awe of is teaching you to cultivate that very same talent that resides within you. Keep looking (but don't stare—that would be rude) and listening (though pay attention to your gut for the final answer).

Making Up Stories: Another winning technique puts your imagination to good use by having you visualize what you desire in vivid color. It's like a dress rehearsal in your head. Athletes and other performers do this regularly. They see themselves executing their moves perfectly. A basketball player visualizes himself making every free throw, leading his team to the championship, injury free. A musician sees herself wrapping up a brilliant set during a sold-out show, hearing thunderous applause from her ecstatic fans.

Here's a red carpet debut day visualization to show you how this process works:

Sit down in a quiet space and get comfortable. When you're settled in, close your eyes. Spend a few moments in silence, focusing on your breath. When centered, imagine waking up on debut day. The sun is shining, birds are chirping. You slowly stretch and glide out of bed. You feel really good about yourself because you successfully finished rehab. See yourself smiling and light, with a twinkle in your eye and a bounce in your step. Imagine walking to your closet, pulling out, *and* sliding on your favorite outfit, the slinky turquoise mini you haven't been able to wear in a long time. See it gently hugging your svelte body, with nary one lump in sight. Decorate yourself with sparkly bangles and chandelier earrings. See the light from the sun catch the crystals. Envisage buckling the straps to the awesome pair of gunmetal stiletto sandals. You feel and look like a princess. You enter your chariot and are whisked off to your chosen celebration venue. And then you see it—the red carpet that has been rolled out just for you. Your car stops at the curb. There are people lined up on either side of the walkway trying to get a glimpse of the celebrity—you. You step onto the red carpet, smiling as camera light bulbs flash. Envision yourself gracefully walking the red carpet, poised, confident, glowing, sparkling. Before you enter the café, you turn around to thank your fans for being there on your big day. A round of applause follows. You wave one more time before crossing the threshold into your party, your new life.

Amazing, huh? You can easily and with great fun visualize anything your heart desires, be it a perfect interview that lands you a position with the company of your dreams, walking across the stage to accept your college diploma, or strolling though a village in the South of France. The more detail and senses you incorporate, the more profound your experience will be. You're essentially recording a live imprint of your wishes.

EGG #11: MAKE SOME NOISE!

Music sends my heart soaring above those things that could otherwise eat at me.

~Kathleen Fox, Washington, D.C., believer in magic +the positive power + inspiration of girlfriends, someday writer, lover of nature's beautiful gifts + mother of two adorable, furry, four-legged boys.

First you were seeing things and now you're hearing things. Good for you! The noise you listen to in this egg is music and sounds you make or locate.

Music is therapeutic. It can relax, energize, transport, transform, soothe, and move you. Making your own music is quite a tension tamer, too. Drumming, chanting, or singing at the top of your lungs anyone? No matter what, this egg makes your inner bling sing!

Create a variety of playlists to tune in to, depending on what you're in the mood for. I have lists for "good memories," "bestseller writing," "relaxation," "yoga," "meditation," "sounds of France," and "best pole dancing tunes." Aha! You *are* paying attention.

Select a theme song to carry you through rehab and another to accompany you on the red carpet. Make sure you sing your own song often—in the shower or your car, on a bus, while you play—no matter where, belt it out at least once a day. My favorites are Lady Gaga's "Born This Way" and the Black Eyed Peas' "Own It." Rocking your body with some dance moves fine-tunes your inner bling.

Sometimes going quiet and still with a song is what you need. One evening as I was writing with tunes in the background, I started to cry out of the blue when "Ordinary World" by Duran Duran shuffled on. "What's this all about?" I thought. As I repeated the song, strong feelings surfaced about my brother Dennis who committed suicide many years ago. I thought I had peace around his passing, but apparently I had more work to do. I played the song over and over and over again and wow. What a release! Now I can listen to "Ordinary World" and simply enjoy it. It's really an extraordinary world! I call this my "lyric therapy." Try it and see what pops up. Truly powerful stuff all the way around with this sound technique.

Noisemakers As Consciousness Raisers: Wind chimes, bells of any kind, crystal singing bowls, and Buddhist gongs are used in various ceremonies and rites. Each sends a "come back to the present moment" message when rung, jingled, tapped, or otherwise resounded. My office is across the street from a church. Every hour on the hour, I'm saved by the bells. I'm reminded to take a deep breath and to be grateful for all things, even for the assignment I may be working on that is frustrating the hell out of me (leave it to church bells to knock that out!). I welcome this peaceful prompt throughout the day to stay centered. What noisemakers are in your world that can help you not act or think like a ding-dong? (Not that you ever would, but being prepared just in case is always a good idea).

EGG #12: WEAR A TIARA

Concert Chicks love their tiaras! Do I dare say even more than our shoe collections? Very close. Which is why it warrants its own egg, the Faberge of your nest. It's a known fact among Concert Chicks that when you tiara top, you terror stop. In other words, it's practically impossible to be fearful and worried with a tiara on.

Tiara on = stress off. The moment it's anchored on my head, I'm telling the world that I'm in "all about me" mode and am not to be bothered. It's classier than a standard issue "do not disturb" doorknob hanger from some cheesy motel or a snarl and growl when someone approaches. There's more tiara talk in the next chapter. Tiaras are both inner bling and outer bling things!

And you don't even have to actually wear one physically to experience the profound positive effects, though there is nothing better than sporting the real thing. But still, it isn't always the time or place, even for those of us who march to our own drummers. Perhaps one day, when the whole world lightens up, tiaras will be staples like baseball caps. But until that glorious day, sometimes you have to leave your head bling home and work it as if you are tiara'd (yes, it's a verb where we're from) nonetheless, once again tapping into your active imagination. Shoulders back, head up (don't let the tiara topple!), standing tall, not small. While a virtual tiara is your little secret, "seen" only by you, the minute it's imagined to be on your head, the world sees something. Perhaps it's that serene glow or the sparkles swirling around you. A tiara is magical, mystical, and princess powerful! Wear one, real or virtual, every day of your life. Of course, the Swag Lounge will let you know where to find your crown.

Now that your inner bling is flashing brilliantly, the spotlight is now shining on your boudoir, where you'll learn how to super-sparkle your external bling.

Chapter 7

Sparkles Out: That Outer Bling Thing

Everyone is a star and deserves the right to twinkle.
~Marilyn Monroe

In Chapter 2 you adjusted your attitude, and in Chapter 6 you learned how to super-shine your inner bling. You prayed, meditated, lit up, slowed down, got stoned, lived in the now, hallucinated, cut and pasted, and otherwise nurtured your mind, heart, and soul. It's now time to shower sparkles on your material world, and flip the Barbie switch to the on position!

First, you'll remove all the physical stuff that blocks your light, creating a new playground where the sun always shines. You'll give yourself some breathing room. And then you'll hook up with your stylist in rehab's wardrobe and makeup department to play dress-up and head-to-toe pamper princess to enhance your natural beauty. The intention is to surround and adorn yourself with stuff that makes you smile, that inspires you to be your best, and that supports who you are authentically. In other words, you'll be decorating your space and your face+!

ENOUGH WITH THE STUFF ALREADY!

Your perfect nature is all sparkly and twinkly without stuff. Material things are nice, very very nice. It's simply that things don't make you who you are. You're fabulous with or without your fabulous shoes, and your shoes are fabulous with or without fabulous you. Likes attract. That's all. I'm in no way suggesting that you stop shopping. Some things are essential like water and air, especially things that sparkle! To cut off your shoe supply is akin to blocking your air supply. We want you breathing deeply and beautifully, *ma belle*.

There's nothing more to it if you're acquiring items for the right reason. Your outer bling things are decorations (sparkly reflections of your inner light) that emphasize your declarations (of red carpet living for life). That "it" Thakoon clutch will be yesterday's news in a flash. But you? You're perpetually on the "it" list when your body+mind+heart+soul are sparkling in unison.

Since more stuff means less you, stuffing your closets, drawers, and every nook and cranny in your nest is right up there with stuffing your face. Don't go there! Well, do go there, but only to get it outta there. This is a very important part of the Rox Detox. Physical excess of anything causes *stuff*ocation, which can be just as breathtaking as suffocation, and not in the beautiful, breathtaking way.

It's truly amazing what happens when you declutter. While you may be tempted to turn your entire nest inside out and upside down, I'd suggest picking one area to focus on while you're in rehab, preferably a place where you spend much time so you can experience up close and personal the miracles that will fill the gap created when there's no more crap.

Without the clutter, you'll have lots of room to do the happy dance, dance, dance in your skinny pants, pants, pants, without bumping into stuff that does nothing more than take up valuable real estate in your life. The Rox Detox creates the space for your soul's wings to spread wide and really flutter. You must clear it all out without a pout, sparkletart! And when you do, and *you will,* nothing will be the same.

Go ahead and donate clothes that are too big, too small, or just not you at all, even if they still have obscenely high price tags dangling from their sleeves and waistbands. And it's more than okey-dokey to consign that not-so-cheepo "must have" handbag that you spent a fortune on last season but carried only once because, truth be told, it ain't all that. You have the guilt-free green light to pawn jewelry your ex or even your grandmother gave to you because you don't do gold. If you can't bring yourself to say good-bye yet, relocate all to a box, seal with packing tape, write the date on the outside, and stow. If you haven't paid it a visit—as in unsealing, removing, and actually wearing any of its contents—by the one year anniversary of the stow, bring it to Goodwill without a peek or a second thought. Or ship the goods off to any one of the charities noted in the Swag Lounge. Poof! More space created. Your prescription contains a "purge" reminder to make sure you do your daily dump.

When all the heaviness is lifted, you *will* soar because you'll be rid of all that extra baggage and garbage that clings to you, weighs you down, and holds you back. Besides, let's face it, the weight of the world does nothing for your posture! Time to say buh-bye, sweetie pie!

As you detox your nest, filter everything through these questions:

- ♦ Do I love this? If it's less than love, get rid of it!

- ♦ Does it make me smile? If it does, it's a keeper. If not, out followed by a big grin.

- ♦ Do I use/wear it? And not just once a year. Let it go if the answer is no.

- ♦ Will a photo hold the memory of the stuff cluttering my room? I collected teddy bears for a long time. I finally had too many and no idea what to do with them. I snapped a farewell group photo before I donated them to a charity that helped children cope with the death of loved ones. The bears found new homes and I created a lot of space. I smile when I see the photo and I hope the children smile when they hold their new friends.

- Do I really need all those love letters, drawings, documents, cancelled checks, and photos? If not, destroy 'em! Putting documents through a shredder is therapeutic. If you must keep, are originals required or can you scan and save all electronically?

- Do I need more than one (or four or more)? Keep your fave and share the spare(s).

- Who can I surprise with this? One December, in the spirit of the season, I recalled items of mine that people admired such as a necklace or even shoes. I then "gifted" them out of the blue. Do this any time of the year for some good cheer. My friend Kelley put a bow on a bag of hers that I liked and handed it to me. The fact that she noticed, remembered, and then parted with the purse meant a lot to me on many levels.

- Is it broken? Any future solid plans to fix? If yes, and then no, it's gotta go!

- Does that souvenir still serve as a fun reminder of your travels? If not, send it off.

- Are you holding onto something out of guilt? Donate it to your church's thrift shop and be done with it already. Surely if a church accepts your donation, you're absolved of any bad anything. Still not convinced? Go to confession while you're there and do the prescribed penance.

- Are you going to read all those magazines and books piled next to and under your bed? Be smart and get 'em out. Share the knowledge!

- What about all those framed photos? Dust collectors or smile inducers?

- Are you spritzing yourself with all that perfume? If not, go for one final spray and send it on its way.

- Is all that makeup doing anything for you? If it's old, toss it (more on this later). If new or slightly used and just not you, pass it on to someone that looks awesome in baby blue shadow and Day-Glo lips.

- How many items in your closets are still wearing price tags? How many garments have never been worn? Either wear, return, consign, or donate.

- Do you have "fat" clothes just in case? Dump the "cover the flab" and keep only garments that are "oh-so-you fab."

Rehab is a great time to clear out your bathroom cabinets, drawers, and shelves. Dump stuff you don't use, that has expired, or otherwise turned color or has a funky smell. Chuck old toothbrushes, soap slivers, rusty razors, near empty, perhaps even full but never gonna be used, bottles of shampoo, conditioner, and other products and everything else that not only takes up space, but could do more harm than good. Toss them out of your nest.

Here's a "when to chuck" guideline to keep in mind as you detox your makeup drawers, bags, kits, and bins:[26]

- Oil-free foundation: 1 year
- Cream or compact foundation: 18 months
- Concealer: 12–18 months
- Powder: 2 years
- Blush and bronzer: 2 years
- Cream blush: 12-18 months
- Powder eye shadow: 2 years
- Cream eye shadow: 12-18 months
- Eyeliner: 2 years

---

[26] Thank you to iVillage for the article "*Are your cosmetics past their use-by date?*" by Eva Gizowska.

- Liquid eyeliner: 3-6 months
- Mascara: 3 months
- Lipstick: 2 years
- Lip liner: 2 years
- Lip gloss: 18-24 months
- Nail color: 1 year

And while you're at it, clean your makeup brushes. Wash the bristles with a mild detergent and warm water. Blot excess liquid and set to dry flat on a terry towel. There are also spray-ons such as Brush Off that make cleaning up a breeze. Spritz, wipe, dry, and reapply rosy cheeks.

Dumping dated doodads doesn't have to be dull or a drag. Do you remember the song by The Clash, "Should I Stay or Should I Go?" Download this hit and make it your purge theme song with a slight tweak of words. "Should this stay or should it go?" You'll be rockin' and rollin' while purgin' and it will feel good! And if you dance as you dump, you'll score Chapter 5 play points—the ultimate in multitasking. Don a tiara, add a wiggle and a giggle, and you'll be a dancing domestic detox diva for life!

WARDROBE CALL!
DRESS REHEARSAL—HAVE A BALL!

When you are pretty sure that an Adventure is going to happen, brush the honey off your nose and spruce yourself up as best you can, so as to look Ready for Anything.
~Pooh's Little Instruction Book

Now that you've cleared out all that isn't you and made space for all that is, it's time to embrace what's left, to express your signature style through clothing, accessories, makeup, and hair. What you put on your body and on your face sends strong messages to the world about who you are, what you think of yourself, essentially how you show up in the world.

Say "Hello" To Your Stylist: While it would be really cool to hang out with Rachel Zoe for a day to chat about the latest "its," tips, trends, and to take a peek at her enormous, infamous Chanel accessory collection, ultimately you are your own best stylist. If you don't have the confidence to pull your look together yet, by all means seek some professional help. But at the end of the runway, it's all about how you feel. The Bobbi Brown artist may think that the "Peony" blush creates an angelic aura about your face, but if you feel clownish and your gut responds with a "she has got to be kidding, they must have an overstock of this product," kindly say "no thanks" with a smile. On the other hand, if "hmmmmmm...wow! I look great but this is so not me" pops into your pretty head, buy the blush, because if you look and feel great about what you see in the mirror but the comfort zone chokehold is on, get the heck out of your way, release the grip, and gracefully (yet boldly) embrace that angelic aura.

Always show up your best. What you project to the world on the outside is a reflection of how you feel on the inside. You never know who you're going to bump into. Your next husband, boss, publisher for your book, Bradley Cooper. Why would tattered bottoms and stained tops be in your closet and—shudder—on your body? Ewwwwww—so not you.

If you don't like how you look, do something about it. Chop off your hair and/or hemlines, soak off your acrylic talons or attach a set. Shake things up a bit. That's what the Rox Detox is all about. Out with the old heavy and in with the new light. Let rehab push you out of your comfort zone and into your own.

> *How many utterly drab and uninteresting people are there in the world who might have developed real personalities if they had only had the courage to do something and be something different from the crowd?*
> ~UNKNOWN

Make the most of what you've got. Feel free to look to others for inspiration and motivation, but don't try to be someone else. Do things, wear things, buy things because they are in line with your style as defined by you. Pastel pink may be the color of the season on every catwalk, but if your skin tone screams sallow within a mile of that hue, please don't add that "rose petal" cardigan to your collection even if it is cashmere and Gucci and on sale. *Very* on sale. We're talking 75 percent off the already reduced price. Matters not, hotcakes. Put. It. Down.

Register Your Trademark: Now's the perfect time to develop your own signature style if you don't already have one. Express yourself not only through your voice and actions, but also in how you decorate your body. What body+mind+heart+soul trademark have you registered? Are you a glamour puss? Sassy fancy? Smart flirty? Tutu'd tomboy? Power Princess? What effects reflect your inner light? Rock it!

> *Why not be one's self? That is the whole secret of a successful appearance. If one is a greyhound, why try to look like a Pekingese?*
> ~Edith Sitwell

I'm a "sunglass whore" according to my friend Dari, and she should know, because she is one, too. I have more pairs than I will ever admit to. All I know is that if I put them on eBay, I might be able to put a decent dent in our mortgage. OK, perhaps not that bad. Do you remember Carrie Bradshaw's shoe calculation in *Sex and the City?* Maybe that bad. Anyhow, they're my trademark. I wear shades on top of my head like a headband, rain or shine. I also wear sparkles during the day, especially chandelier earrings and huge chicktail rings that would normally be flashed only at night but who wants normal? What is normal, anyway? Nonbling = bo-ring! Concert Chicks are anything but.

What is your favorite color? Do you love purple? Make it yours! Lilac polish on your toes, a stunning amethyst superhero ring on your finger, an orchid yoga mat. What is your best feature? Bright green eyes? Cherub bowed lips? A tiny waist (but not like Barbie's)? A nice bum? Whatever it is, work it, girl. As I shared earlier, Coco Chanel has been my muse for many moons. As a kid, I'd pedal my bike to the library and while other girls my age were checking out Nancy Drew books, I was in the biography section loading my arms with Coco. She was an amazing, independent woman who discovered the little black dress, slacks, and suntans. She also gave *très chic* status to costume jewelry, encouraging women to drape ropes of *faux* pearls around their necks. She did her own thing, her own way, and was a huge success. I found myself asking not WWJD (though I do love Jesus) but WWCD? I was the girl on the block draped in pearls playing flag football in the street with my four brothers after ballet class. Nothing *faux* about that! And I have the tutus, toe shoes, strands, and scars to prove it.

Be inspired by these Coco pearls of wisdom:

> *Beauty is the charm which has nothing to do with looks; and it is physical proportion —nothing too much, everything in balance.*
>
> *You can be gorgeous at twenty, charming at forty, and irresistible the rest of your life.*
>
> *Nothing is ugly, so long as it is alive.*
>
> *Whatever you put on your body, or do to your hair, or do to your face, should be some sort of extension of yourself, not some trend that someone wants you to follow.*

Gift Wrap: This chapter is more about adding some extra oomph and ooh la la to your body before and after the package is wrapped in gorgeous garb. You know, sparkly scrubs and shimmers and frilly bows. So I'll leave the actual wrapping to someone else. But I must say this:

We come in all shapes and sizes[27] and colors and textures. No one "design" is best. Enjoy what you have and flaunt it. There are just as many unhealthy, miserable size 2s out there as there are size 22s who are living life large in all ways. What matters is that you're healthy and happy, and that your body+mind+heart+soul are in harmony, whether the gift of life you are blessed with is wrapped in a size 4 or 24 skin.

> *The body is a sacred garment. It's your first and last garment, it is what you enter life in and what you depart life with, and it should be treated with honor.*
> ~Martha Graham

OUTER BLING THINGS TO BE TO JAZZ IT UP A BIT

It's all about the accessories, girls! You can easily transform any look with a zing of bling, because not all the bells and whistles are sparkly in and of themselves. But rest assured, the collective whole of your external body, just like your inner self, is naturally extraordinarily sparkly and twinkly. Having said that, tangible sparkles are nonnegotiable. Inconsistent? I suppose. Even if you insist that rhinestones are "not you," find one little piece of bling to wear. That tiny crystal in the middle of your bra bow counts. It's a fact that wearing something sparkly activates pleasure centers in the brain, making happiness happen in a hurry. Nothing better than a scientifically supported mandate to wear sequins.

What you'll find below are random musings, thoughts, and tips, tried-and-true strings of outer bling to inspire you. The Swag Lounge has many specifics for your exploration and transformation. For now, take note of what attracts you.

---

27 And this is why Concert Chick tees are not sized S, M, L, or XL, but rather Stunning! Magnificent! Luscious! Extra-Lovely!

Be a Flasher: You are never fully dressed until you put on a smile. A smile is *the* best accessory in the universe. And no *faux* flashes. Those "plastic" grins are rude at best, condescending at worst. Flash genuinely and generously. Keep it bright. Use Crest Whitestrips and frame with glittery lip gloss. If your smile morphs into a laugh, all the better.

> *Good humor is one of the best articles of dress one can wear in society.*
> ~THACKERAY

Be a Shady Character: As I mentioned previously, sunglasses are my thing. Ray-Bans, Chanel, and Juicy Couture—classic or loaded with bling—dominate my sunglass drawers (yes, plural, as in *deux*, going on *trois*). As much as I favor rose-colored, I am very aware that I have to keep it real and make sure the lenses offer UVB/UVA protection. Sunnies—surprise-surprise—should be sported only outdoors in the sun. Don't hide behind your shades unless you have a serious eye condition, are eye-doc dilated, or wake up as Jennifer Aniston one morning and need to go incognito. Eye contact is important. And if you have any glasses that no longer work for you, please donate them to charity. See the Swag Lounge for the info.

Be a Bijoux Babe: Your inside light desires an outside partner in "shine" and *bijoux* bliss is where it's at. Real or (my weakness) costume. Necklaces, bracelets, rings, trinkets—all sorts of dangly, jingly-jangly thangs. Decorate your miraculous body with crystals, natural stones, rhinestones, precious gems, pearls, and other assorted baubles. Gold, silver, platinum, rose, copper, brass. Hoops, tassels, studs. There's nothing like a couple of chandeliers swinging from each lobe for some light bright fun. Wing bling—bracelets and rings—make me sing. Don't be afraid to layer, stack, and mismatch. A black leather-wrapped bangle coupled with a pearl bracelet is hot.

Be a Bag Lady: Hobo, clutch, tote, messenger, evening, supersized, wristlet, pouchette, satchel, designer monogrammed or not. Leather, vinyl, sateen, straw, metallic, crystallized. No matter what, they're all handy ways to express yourself and carry your keys, a credit card, valet cash, and some Chanel Rouge Coco Shine in "Boy." The purse you carry speaks volumes about who you are. Kathryn Eisman explains all in her fabulous book, *How to Tell a Woman by Her Handbag.* As an aside, did you know that it's bad feng shui to place your purse on the floor? As they say, "a purse on the floor is money out the door." Keep your handbag clutter-free, too, by using one of those purse organizers that you can move from bag to bag.

Be a Hip-Hot Wrap Star: Hug yourself with a boa, pashmina, stole, scarf, poncho, or cape. Silk, cotton, wool, fur (faux or not), angora, suede, organza, cashmere, chiffon. Encrusted, pompommed, fringed, embroidered. Scarves are the equivalent of a man's tie, only better, because not only do they completely change the same outfit with their colors, designs, patterns, and fabrics, they come in many sizes for assorted uses. Tie one in your hair or on your handbag strap, wrap one around your waist, your head, your wrist, or your shoulders. A fashion statement, outfit converter, and shoulder warmer all in one!

Be a Shoe Slut: May as well go for the whole shebang. Stilettos, platforms, wedges, sandals, thongs, ballerina flats, penny loafers, flip-flops, mules, clogs, boots, booties, slippers, gladiators, and more. Suede, patent leather, vegan pleather, satin, *peau de soir,* metallic, rubber, mesh. Strappy, buckled, laced, bow-tied, beaded, studded, crystallized. You know what to do when it comes to anything "shoe." Maybe I should be suggesting that you zap Zappos—this is a purge program after all—but alas, I cannot. Make sure you get regular pedicures (more on this later). I gotta run... out of this section, and fast, before I switch over to Nordstrom's Web site for a little between-sentence shopping or perhaps a lap around Saks Fifth Avenue's spectacular shoe salon.

> *When you see someone putting on his Big Boots, you can be pretty sure that an Adventure is going to happen.*
> ~Pooh's Little Instruction Book

Be an Undercover Agent: Nothing puts the "girlie" in front of "girl" better than ruffles, lace, and other frilly fancy things with or without marabou. Hooray for lingerie! Jammies and pj toppers, too! Robes, peignoirs, flannels, chemises, and those adorable Dr. Denton's with the convenient flap. And then there's all those sneaky perker-uppers and other secret weapons that do a garment good. Push-ups, squish-togethers, minimizers, maximizers, demi-cups, sporty. Cotton, silk, satin, velvet. Bra cutlets and headlight covers. Boxers, boyshorts, thongs, g-strings, granny pants. Leggings, thigh-highs, fishnets, opaque tights, anklets, knee-hi socks. SPANX! Lots of undercover top and bottom secret stuff here to play around with. Think pin-striped business suit with a silk camisole, a garter belt, and stockings. Who knows? Only you and whomever else you show them to. That Victoria was definitely onto something! Did I just hear you say that you're off to find your trench coat?

THE LOWDOWN ON MAKEUP

Makeup in Concert Chick land is a colorfully fun way to enhance your natural beauty and to transform your look just because you can—not hiding from anything, but rather showing up playfully confident, with ultra-long lashes and silver glitter liner to prove it. It's a risk-free, wash-it-off way to play. While you're in rehab, I'd encourage you to drop by a makeup counter and get a makeover or makeunder, as the face case may be.

Whether you want sparkle or are having one of those "need spackle" moments, make it up. Some days a swipe of baby pink lip balm is all you want (in rehab). Other days, vixen *rouge* lipstick is what you need (on the red carpet). And then there are *those* days where nothing less than the whole chick warrior package will do. My friend had a tough meeting one morning. She told me that she was more than ready because she had her "war paint" on—dark smokey eyes, power red lips, everything—with a black outfit to match. She's a very confident, smart, beautiful woman but she wanted some extra oomph to take care of business. And she did. Oh, yeah, she did.

Before you get all dolled up, it's imperative that you start with a clean slate. Facials, masques (at home and professional), steam, deep clean, pore uncloggers and minimizers, exfoliants, peels, AM/PM moisturizers, under eye gels, wrinkle zappers and crinkle wrappers, and more for you to explore. And make sure you always remove your makeup before you go to bed. There are many wipes you can use such as Soap & Glory's "Off Your Face" in case you're ready to crash. A couple of swipes leave your skin clean, and breathing in health while you're dreaming. Otherwise, you could wake up with a huge zit on your chin. A nightmare! Check out the "face the music" in *chez moi* spa below for some skincare ideas.

Here are some more Rox Detox random flow musings to inspire your makeup adventures:

Let's Face It: Now that your canvas is bare, have fun putting color everywhere starting with a skin primer and then moving on to foundation, illuminating and bronzing powders, highlighters and face brighteners, blush, rouge, and more. Two musts: sunscreen and no fear of glitter.

Window Dressing: Eyes truly are the windows to the soul. Don't be afraid to frame yours to enhance the peepshow. Golly jeepers, where'd you get those peepers? Beauty truly is in the eye of the beholder. What do you see? Play peek-a-boo with flirty, lush lashes that you create with falsies or super-volume-length mascara. Try lash and brow enhancing serums. Revitalash rocks! Tweeze, wax, pencil 'em in, arched perfection. Line, color, smokey, or *au naturel*. Brow fixatives, powders, creams, glosses, under eye-concealer, upper lid base, pencils. Visine to get the red out. Innoxa French Blue Eye Drops to bring out the blue. Cucumber slices to depuff. Do you have crinkles under your twinkles? Big deal and so what!

Twinkles trump crinkles all day and night. Remember to get some shut-eye—Concert Chicks treasure their beauty sleep.

Mwaaaah!: Pucker up, baby! It's double air kisses and super smooches time. Apply a glossy, matte, shiny, glittery, sparkly, sexy frame around your smile. Tubes, sticks, pots. Lips scrubs, balms, Chapstick, plumpers, liners. Keep what goes on your lips juicy and what comes out of your lips not so juicy, if the juice is at the expense of some other chick. Brush, floss, pop Altoids religiously. And no ass-kissing—so not Concert Chick.

Body Bare + Care: The rest of your skin needs some decoration, too. Self tanners, luminescent powders, moisturizers, body lotions, oils and other potions, glitter spray, hair removal—wax, cream, razor—cellulite delumpers. And the non-negotiable *s* words: sunscreen, sunblock, and shimmer!

THE MANE ATTRACTION

Step right up! Hair is the easiest way to experiment with a new look because it grows back and the color can be changed again and again and yes, even one more time. The state of your hair dictates the tone of your day. Good hair day—hooray! Bad hair day—get outta my way! Good or bad, it's a fact. Hairy scary? No need to commit hara-kiri.

Sometimes being hairless seems appealing. No maintenance, just a quick powder puff of shimmer all over. And it sure would free up much time and money, but then I think about my tiara. Affixing it with the assist of a chinstrap or glue gun is definitely not Concert Chickish so forget that! Here's how to make every day (most) a good hair day.

A good cut is key. Long hair is sexy and versatile, but if it isn't healthy, chop it off or "dust" the ends diligently to eventually phase in luscious locks. This is the approach my stylin' sista, Donetta, took with my tresses and it worked. Snip snip for about a year and no more dead or split ends for *moi*.

Browse the hair-care aisle at your neighborhood drugstore and pick up a few styling products and tools to experiment with. Play with volumizers (big, thick), conditioners (leave in, deep, daily, spray on, rinse off), serums (gloss, shine), sprays (glitter, extra hold, fine mist, aerosol, pump), shampoo (wet and dry), detanglers and excess buildup stranglers, hair color in every shade (permanent, semi-permanent, henna, rinse), and much more. And don't forget to take a peek at all the elastics, headbands, barrettes, curlers, brushes (paddle, round, synthetic, or boar bristle), and combs (wide tooth, teasing).

QUICKIES

Get Banged: If you're into quickies, listen up! Snipping bangs is a cheep but not cheap way to instantly change your look. They're very youthful and flirty. Bangs not only frame your eyes, they cover wrinkled foreheads, thus alleviating the need for Botox (not that any of us have any of *those* or need any of *that*). If you hesitate to snip, try clip-ons.

Be a Tease: Every chick should know how to backcomb. Big hair, high hair, hair all the way to over *there*. Very '60s. Beehives and bouffants. Tease for behind-headband height or a ponytail push-up. A little teasing takes you from ordinary to extraordinary in a few flicks of the wrist. Here's how to do it:[28]

1. Separate a strand of hair about one to two inches wide at the crown of the head and comb to make sure it is smooth and tangle-free.
2. Comb the section straight up and then forward to about a 145-degree angle. Hold it taut while you work.

---

[28] How to Back-Comb Hair | eHow.com http://www.ehow.com/how_2274622_back-comb-hair.html#ixzz1KQBBU3so

3. Use a rat-tail comb or teasing brush (my preference) to backcomb the hair near the root area. Comb down three to four inches lightly and quickly, about three times. This is enough to give the hair a damage-free lift.
4. Spritz the backcombed section of hair with hair spray, and let it fall forward over the face. Continue to section and backcomb the hair until the entire area is completed.
5. Flip the hair back and brush the top of the hair into place very carefully. Use the tail of the rat-tail comb or teasing brush to lift the backcombed area, pushing up lightly with your hands.
6. Spray the completed hairdo to help keep it in place.

Be Not Afraid of The Braid + Hail to the Ponytail: Whether Pippi Longstocking style sticking straight out of both sides of your head or Pocahontas down your back or to one side, braids are sporty and sassy. They can even be sexy and sophisticated. They're adorable dangling out from under a cowboy hat or a baseball cap. They're beautiful when swirled and pinned into a ballerina bun. Add ribbons or crystal elastics for extra bling. Braid your hair when it's wet (loose or tight depending on the style you want) for a casual daytime look. When you've rocked the braid enough (and when it's dry), undo and fluff for some sexy beach hair waves. Braid praise applies to ponytails, too. Wear them high, low, to the side, or out of each side. Backcomb your crown, side sweep your bangs, pull your hair back, add a headband or not. Giddy up! Hair not long enough to braid or tail? Move on to the next tip and clip.

Clip-Ons + Extenders: Tressed to the max or not—your call, you can have it all! Extensions, wigs, and clip-on pieces (bangs, braids, ponytails, buns, full-on falls) including feathers allow you to change your color, style, texture, and length instantly. Go fuchsia, go afro, add a row, just go. And don't forget a Lady Gaga bow!

The Ultimate Headdress: The all-time Concert Chick staple that deserves its own section (again) is the tiara. No matter what your hair looks like, don a tiara and you are a pretty, poised, powerful princess. Every chick should own one or more and not only own, but wear! Tiaras are the external radiance of your internal brilliance. You're confident enough to possibly look silly, but you don't care; you're having fun and you're shining your inside light out. I'm tiara'd as I'm writing. And I must say I look quite regal and it keeps me in perfect posture, which is good, especially since I'm parked at my computer for hours on end. It's impossible to slouch when one has a tiara on one's head. Besides, a tiara topple is quite traumatic. You definitely don't want to experience one.

When All Else Fails...Be a Head Case! Every day is a good hair day if you cover up your bad hair with good hair (we've already had our wig chat) or a hat, something to encase the hair on your head. Go crazy! Cowboy, bowler, baseball cap, beret, sombrero, or a scarf make perfect head cases. Some days you just have to say "f&^$ it!" and pop on a bucket (as in cute hat, not pail, though a sand pail would work and could be cute under the right circumstances) or some other topper (though never a lampshade). If you don't need a complete cover-up, but you do want a little distraction or sparkly attraction, stock up on barrettes, clips, silk flowers, and headbands, or wear the aforementioned tiara.

THE RED CARPET OOH LA LA SPAAAAAHHHHH
A.K.A. CHEZ MOI SPA

Hi. My name is Denise and I am an addict. A spa addict that is. There, I said it. And I feel much better. And I'll feel even better after I finish this chapter so I can soak in a honey almond candlelit bath with a *Life & Style* magazine. No matter what happens during my day, all tension is stripped from my body and escorted down the drain whenever I indulge in bubbles (as in soapy, not sippy—that'll happen on debut day, for sure).

My first hit took place at the Elizabeth Arden Red Door Spa on Worth Avenue in Palm Beach. It's no longer there, but the memories of it will remain forever. I couldn't afford the full day I treated myself to (it was my birthday!). I handed over my credit card feeling all grown-up. I was hooked (and in debt but pampered nonetheless). Fast forward twenty plus years and spas are on every corner, just like Walgreens.

Even though spas are all over, your nest can be the best place to truly pamper yourself, which is why the red carpet spa is also known as "*chez moi* spa." At-home spa products can be found everywhere, so it's a breeze to pamper yourself head to toe without leaving your castle. Here are some *chez moi* spa ideas, focusing on body+mind+heart+soul detoxification—you are in rehab, after all—that are formulated to draw impurities out of your body, allowing your outer glow to shine brighter than ever. Head to *chez moi* spa and say ahhhhhhhhh.

It's a Wrap!

Here are two awesome detoxifying bundles for you to get all wrapped up in during rehab. Do one the first week and the other the next.

This Brew's for You!: First up is a coffee body wrap that will help remove toxins from your lower body. Even though I've never tasted coffee, I have been wrapped in it, and it's yummy. The stimulating caffeine helps release harmful toxins and encourages blood circulation. Here's how to serve one up. Put about 1 cup of used coffee grounds into a bowl. Add 1 tablespoon each of seaweed oil, olive oil, and eucalyptus oil. Mix to form a nice paste. Zap for 20 seconds in the microwave. Grab a roll of plastic wrap, such as Saran. Starting at your ankles, apply the paste and wrap with plastic as you move up to your hips. When your lower body is sealed, relax for about 30 minutes and then hop in the shower. Remove the wrap and the toxic crap to reveal your beautiful skin. Finish with a good lather of a moisturizing liquid soap followed by a warm-then-cold water rinse. Pat dry and apply a nice hydrating oil, such as sesame or almond.

Play with Clay: Boil 2 cups of water in a medium-sized pot. Add 1 cup of bentonite clay, one-quarter cup of sea salt, 2 tablespoons of olive oil, and 4 drops of grapefruit essential oil to detoxify your liver. Mix all well. Remove from the stovetop and allow to cool for 10-15 minutes. In the meantime, exfoliate your skin with a dry brush. Once the clay is cool, apply all over your body, starting at your ankles and working your way up. Recruit a helper for this to make sure you cover all areas. Wrap yourself with large towels. Lie in a warm room for 45-60 minutes. Carefully remove the towels. Rinse the clay off in the shower using warm water. Pat dry and moisturize.

Get Stoked with a Soak

If you polled the women of the world about their favorite place to escape and unwind, odds are great that "the tub" would rank right up there next to a wine bar or Target. Add bubbly magical potions and elixirs to your bath water, light a candle, put on some relaxing tunes, enter, and melt. To make your tub time extra playful, float a little yellow rubber duckie, toss on a tiara, and splish-splash. Have a good long soak and think about how great life is. If anything negative pops up, know that as the water swirls down the drain, the psychic crud leaves with it.

Epsom salt and baking soda baths[29] have been around for many generations. Epsom salt draws out, while baking soda helps absorb. Quite the combo! This duet, in addition to deep cleaning and purifying the body, is a proven joint pain reliever and aging slower downer, which is an upper if I ever saw one! Epsom salt is not actually a salt at all. It's a natural mineral compound called magnesium sulfate. Magnesium is a valuable mineral that many people lack. It's required for the metabolism of other minerals, efficient muscle

---

29 Because this type of bath can be so powerful, it may not be beneficial for everyone. Pregnant women and people with heart problems and high blood pressure should consult a doctor before getting stoked with this soak.

and nerve function, and for restful sleep. It also disinfects blood and flushes toxins from cells. Sulfates are necessary for the synthesis of new collagen, which is needed for healthy, young-looking skin. This factoid alone makes me want to stop typing and start Epsom salt soaking.

Baking soda bears its own gifts. The typical Western diet is filled with red meat, cheese, sugar, and refined foods that are acid-forming. Baking soda has an alkalizing effect on the body, neutralizing the consequences of an acidic diet. It also helps detoxify the body after too much alcohol, caffeine, medication, and nicotine, all the while making your skin soft and supple.

Here are some soaks to savor, preferably every other day for the entire time you're in rehab:

Rox Detox Get Stoked Soak: Add 2 cups Epsom salts, 1 cup baking powder, 11 drops of essential oil (jasmine or rose for a peaceful soak, or chamomile or lavender for a relaxing one), and 1 tablespoon of dried seaweed to a tub filled with the hottest temperature water you can stand (within reason—no scalding!). Simmer to shimmer for about 20 minutes. After stewing, wrap yourself in a thick terry robe and allow the sweat to continue. After you've had enough, shower and finish with a cool rinse. For some added oomph, drink a cup of peppermint tea before taking the bath, or add a cup of brewed peppermint tea to the bath. This will promote the release of toxins through the skin even more.

If you don't want to deal with gathering, measuring, and mixing ingredients, I highly recommend Fresh Rice Sake Bath. As stated on the label, it's a "potent healing therapy for the body... detoxifying, curative and warming." It contains 50 percent real sake to "help remove impurities from the body." This stuff is OMG + WOW! After a 20-minute soak with a good book (if you can keep the sweat out of your eyes), rinse off in a cool shower, apply Sake Rice Oil, cuddle in a fluffy terry robe, and get back to that book (if you can keep your eyes open).

I also highly recommend White Gold Detoxifying Crystal Salt INA (Inner Nutritional Alchemy) Crystals. According to the package: "This deep penetrating detox bath contains minerals small enough to penetrate the cells and be absorbed to help the body expel internal toxins accumulated over time through pollutants in the air, alcohol and processed foods. The White Gold Crystal and the detoxifying essential oils of basil, fennel and juniper cleanse deeply whilst improving the sense of well-being." It claims to be the equivalent of a 3-day detox diet and I don't doubt it one bit.

Shower Power

OK, superstar Concert Chick, it's time for some singing in the rain! If you're not a bath babe or are on the run, turn your shower into a mini-spa chamber with all the wondrous gels, scrubs, soaps, body treatments, loofahs, sponges, and mitts on the market today. It's like a bubble bath in a booth! Shower perks, besides quick and "get clean", are good and plenty. The spray acts as a massage (even if you don't have one of those fancy shower heads). And because you're standing, gravity causes fluids to drain from your face, joints, and upper body, decreasing puffiness and bloating. And a shower is less drying than a bath because you're not soaking in the water.

Always finish with a cool rinse to energize your body. Or rev things up a bit with an alternating hot and cold shower. Take a hot shower for a few minutes then switch to thirty seconds of a cold spray. Repeat the hot/cold swap three times. This practice gets your blood flowing, increases lymph drainage, discharges toxins, tones muscles and skin, and stimulates metabolic energy. Hot water dilates your blood and lymphatic vessels and cold water constricts them, creating a pumping action that massages your cells' nutrition and detoxification pathways. By the way, this is the only time running hot and cold regularly is acceptable for a Concert Chick.

Spaaaaahhhhh'ing with Wine is Divine

Even though we can't savor sips while we soak until grape and debut days, we can still stay connected to the vine. If you have any leftover cheep wine, pour it into your bath water and soak for thirty minutes to detoxify your body and rev up your circulation. Enjoy the many amazing wine-based and inspired scrubs, facials, baths, gels, and lotions. See? You don't need to drink the stuff to be incredibly intoxicating.

Polish it Off

And no, I'm not talking about the rest of the cookies you didn't toss during your prep days, but rather, the rough spots on your body and in your life. If you're crusty and scaly or simply not as silky as you'd like to be, it's time to polish the skin that you're in. Nothing zaps dead skin like a good ol' salt scrub. Salt fights bacteria and unclogs pores. If you want to create your own, try our *"gommage the garbage, a.k.a. take out the trash"*. Here's what you'll need and what to do with it:

> 2 cups coarsely ground sea salt
> 1 cup light oil such as sesame or almond
> a few drops of essential oil
>
> Mix the salt and the oil to form a paste. Add the essential oil drops. While in the tub or shower, take a handful of the mix and massage into damp skin all over your body. Rinse with warm water and pat dry. Don't use soap—it'll remove the oil that makes you one slick chick.

For the rough spots in your life, turn your exfoliation time into a mini therapy session. While you're physically shedding dead skin, set an intention to also emotionally scrub away thoughts, feelings, behaviors, and habits that bump into and lump up your smooth sailing path. Visualize waste leaving your head (incessant chatter and negative self-talk), heart (blockages and walls), and soul (feelings of worthlessness and non-acceptance). Imagine that whatever has been clinging to you is released (with love) and visualize (with joy) all going down the drain. You emerge from the water light, bright, and silky smooth. Though technically not a scrub, but since I included "head" in the visual, I must mention LUSH's Big shampoo. As they say, this salt and lime shampoo inspires mermaid locks. Must get.

Give 'em the ol' Brush-Off

Another approach to sloughing is a little dry brushing before you take your morning shower or bath. Consider brushing your skin as important as brushing your teeth. Take a natural bristle brush (you can find one at a health food store) and, starting with the soles of your feet, brush your dry skin using smooth, gentle circular strokes. Move up your legs, then on to your hands and arms, moving clockwise on your abdomen, and finishing with a brisk butt brushing. Don't brush your face or breasts. You may feel a tad tingly afterward, which is a good thing. It may take a few days for your skin to get used to this because you're brushing dry bristles on dry skin. This simple practice not only feels great, it does great. Dry brushing your skin assists with lymph flow, removes dead cells, makes your skin soft and supple, excretes waste and excess fluid, and can help reduce the appearance of cellulite. So please, do rush to brush!

Face the Music

Your skin is your "taking toll" booth. Stress, strife, sugar, and other toxins can make you look many years beyond your years. Your skin's condition is an indicator of what's going on in your life, what's taking its toll on you—too much of this, too little of that, not enough sleep, way too many sweets. You have to care for the skin you're in. The good news is that your skin responds rapidly to any goodness you send its way.

One of the ways to put your best face forward is to get bzzzzzzz'd on some honey, which has astonishing antiseptic, antioxidant, and cleansing properties. Plus, Winnie the Pooh was a huge fan, so how can it not be good for you? Soak a washcloth in warm water and place it on your face to open your pores. Smear honey all over and leave on for fifteen to thirty minutes. Rinse off with warm water, then splash with cold *l'eau* to close pores. Do this once a week for delicious skin. By the way, it's OK to lick your fingers after the smear as long as you're getting bzzzzzzz'd post rehab.

GET NAILED!

Nothing squeals "trailer trash" louder than chipped filthy nails with ragged cuticles on your fingers and the same plus caked-on crud and scales on your feet. Dirty girls are one thing. Scaly, another. Your hands do talk (what are yours saying?) and your feet do walk (where are they taking you?). Treat yourself regularly to a manicure/pedicure, especially for your red carpet debut. DIY with the tips below or let a salon do you.

Facts for Fancy Fingers + Tips Toward Twinkly Toes

You can do a number of things to treat your hands and feet regularly to keep them kissable (hands, for most) and strappy sandal ready (feet).

Dreamy Creamy: Slather moisturizing cream generously on your hands and slip on some cotton gloves to create velvety skin while you're in lala land. Do the same for your tootsies, only using a pair of socks instead, unless gloves work, in which case, a toast to you for being extra unique.

Applause for Your Paws, A.K.A. A Hand Job: Stash hand cream in your car, purse, and desk drawer to apply throughout the day. Don't forget to apply sunscreen to the back of your hands as well.

Play Footies: Apply a thick moisturizer to your feet before you move it, move it. Slip on heavy cotton socks and your sneakers to treat your feet to a heated moisturizing treatment while you're playing.

Get Wild: Don't be shy with nail color. Let your wild child come out to play with glittery, glossy, and frosty hues that you felt were too out there.

This File Takes the Cake: Diamancel foot buffers are a must!

"Chez Moi Spa" Get Nailed Menu

Concert Chick "twinkle toes dance" pedi + "fancy fingers prance" mani: Feet first! Fill a tub or big bowl with warm water and add a cup of sea salt. Drop in a tablespoon of olive oil and soak for 10 minutes. Take a pumice stone and scrub gently to remove dead skin cells. Wash and dry your feet. Apply foot lotion and massage feet and then legs using long, upward strokes. Mix a ½ cup of sugar with ¾ cup of sesame oil and apply to feet. Wait 10 minutes, and then slowly rub off the hardened masque in a gentle circular motion. Rinse with warm water and massage in a rich moisture cream. Do the same steps for the manicure only skip the pumice filing and massage your wings instead of your legs.

Chickarita Pedirita + Manirita: First off, concoct a strong margarita mix with ½ cup tequila to deep cleanse nails and skin, sea salt to exfoliate (use enough to thicken mixture), and 2 tablespoons fresh lime juice to even skin tone and bleach away yellowish polish stains. Slice a lime into 8 wedges. Fill a large bowl with water. Soak one foot at a time while massaging the margarita mix into the skin and nails of the other for 5 minutes, targeting any rough spots. Switch feet. You should feel some tingling—terrific! Rinse and dry your tootsies. Place a lime slice between your toes to separate them and then polish your nails as usual. Repeat for manicure minus the lime wedge separators. If you're enjoying this *muy bueno* treat on debut day or afterward, sip a Chickarita[30] while you soak.

GRAB A ROADIE

Chez Moi Spa Goes on Tour! If you find yourself in hotel rooms often, you're a lucky chickie! In addition to 24-hour room service, a pool bar, and someone else to make your bed, hotels can be the perfect setting for some "all about *moi*" spa time. Here are some on-the-go tricks and treats to enjoy on the road:

Sweet 'n' Glow: If you're enjoying a meal out, take some sugar packets back to your room (no, this doesn't set you up to be one of those blue hair, Sweet'N Low snatchers unless you do this every day and only order a cup of coffee). Suds up with the hotel soap and then sprinkle sugar granules in your hands. Scrub lightly and rinse to create a sweet hand softener.

Teabag Debag: Lounge in your bed with wet tea bags on your eyelids for an instant booster.

Leftover Makeover: Room service can also provide the goods for more spa opportunities depending on what you order. Use leftover condiments in the bathroom. Massage mayo into your hair and scalp and cover with a shower cap. Shampoo out after twenty minutes. If a small jar of honey comes with your tea service, treat your freshly washed face to some super hydration by enjoying the honey facial described above in the "let's face it" section.

Make it Yours: Pack a small bottle of your favorite scented essential oil to add to hotel-provided shampoo, conditioner, and body lotion for a custom blend.

---

30 Your fave margarita recipe using lemon juice instead of lime, sipped while wearing tart shoes.

Now that you're supersonic sparkly on the inside *and* on the outside, armed with loads of luminosity and brilliant power, it's time to learn how to protect your light and brilliance from the dark, including your own stash.

Chapter 8

How to Cope with the Dope + the Mope

In our world of many melodies, let us bring harmony.
~Sanjay Chakraborty

OK, so name-calling is childish and so not Concert Chick, but sometimes you just gotta call them as you see them. We've already spent a lot of time purging material things. Now we move onto human beings. Mopes and dopes, plain and simple, are the folks who fizzle our sizzle. They include, but certainly are not limited to, mean chicks, critics, other start-with-"c" words, know-it-alls, whiners, naysayers, holier-than-thous, too much winers, saboteurs, party poopers, backstabbers, and yakkers.

You know who they are. They're all over the place. You might even be one yourself, or at least used to be, so you'll also find a prescription for an in-depth examination of your own mopiness and dopiness. If you do anything in rehab, please purge these energy suckers (after working on your own like behavior if the shoe fits). You can't do anything about how others show up, but you can control who you give your time and energy to and, most important, how you react to them. This was discussed extensively in Chapter 6 but bears repeating, often. Dumping dimmers is by far the most significant, positive thing you can do for your body+mind+heart+soul light.

You must reflect on all the relationships in your life to see who weighs you down and who lifts you up. The universe puts certain people on your path to teach you lessons you must learn to be able to move to the next level of your evolution. As Alan Cohen, the great spiritual teacher and author says, "Life is like photography. We use the negative to develop." The same kind of folks will keep showing up in your life over and over again until you get it. The sooner you realize this to be true and do what you have to do, the sooner peace will find its way to you.

The heaviness of toxic relationships can burden your body+mind+heart+soul more than a daily dose of In-N-Out Burger's Double-Double. Forget the extra twenty pounds of padding you're waddling around with. Much of that might have to do with others pushing your buttons, and since you haven't quite yet figured out how to deal with the feelings that surface, you reach for Poppycock Glazed Popcorn to crunch away the tension. When a desire to dial "m" for murder pops into your head, you need to stay far, far away from the trigger (as in the person who pushes your buttons), if you can help it. But sometime you can't. That person either signs your paycheck or is sitting across from you at the family dinner table. This is why it's essential for you to master nonreactivity to the extent you humanly can.

There's a time and place for everyone you cross paths with, and at times that place is as far away from you as possible, with no time to spare. Friendships and other relationships should stimulate, enhance, inspire, and support your experience on this planet, help you become the person you were meant to be, and otherwise bring you up, not down. And remember, the paths we take are two-way streets. Chances are good that if someone isn't enhancing your life, you probably aren't doing much for theirs either. As they say, it takes two to tango.

We'll start with a review of you and then move on to *them*. After familiarizing yourself with the general mopes and dopes, a.k.a.

"tools," you'll be asked to get specific and start naming names. You'll then open your Detox "Tool" Box and learn how to cope with any "tools" you have in your life. Under its lid you'll find an array of tools to deal with people who sabotage, criticize, minimize, block, or otherwise dampen your efforts and darken you. The box closes with a discussion about cultivating and nourishing the healthy relationships you have or want in your life.

YOU FIRST

Yeah, you. And me. And everyone else individually. All of us are dopes and mopes at times and the sooner we embrace this fact the better. You could very well be the biggest mope and dope in your world, and that's why we're starting at home, because you can at least do something about it. When someone upsets you, look at yourself first, especially if your reaction is an overreaction. Triggers point to something in you, not around you. As you learned in Chapter 6, rehab requires you to practice as a "souloist" and then moves you onto duets, trios, quartets, and even orchestras, all of which play a role in the reality show called your life. Chapters 2 and 6 must be integrated in order for you to come from a secure place before tackling (not attacking!) others. You may find that Little. Ms. Know. It. All. does, in fact, know a lot and yes, she's still freakin' annoying, but no longer does she push you over the edge. Yay!

So the next time someone gets in your face, make sure to look at your own face in the mirror first and see if anything about that person is a part of you that could use some adjusting. You may be shocked and ultimately grateful for and to that pain in the *derrière*.

Bear in mind that the way you show up in others' lives influences how others respond to and treat you. If you've played the doormat role for years, don't be upset if you're stepped on. If you had an epiphany and it's time to roll up the mat for good to make way for the red carpet, by all means redefine or release those relationships that knew you as the mat. If they have a problem with your authentic self, open your "tool" box and do what you must.

> *How others treat me is their path. How I react is mine.*
> ~ UNKNOWN

NOW OTHERS

All right then, here you are in your non-reactionary, confident glory. The coast is now clear to move on to others. Have you ever felt bad vibes from someone you've never met or even seen before? Do you get goose bumps or a tug in your gut when *she* comes within your range? Do you feel the life being drained from your fabulous self when you are around *him*? What is it about some people, known or not, that rubs you the wrong way and makes you want to run the other way, and fast? That's energy swapping in action.

And you'll be swapping energy for the rest of your life. The goal is to do so as positively charged as you possibly can be. The world is an interesting place because of the mix of folks. We're designed to interact and connect. It does take two to tango, three to musketeer, and a whole team to bring food to your table and shoes to your feet. There are the "cools" and the "tools." We'll focus on the latter in this section because tools are indeed toxic, and then wrap up with the cool peeps before we head to our celebration.

It's delusional to think that the strength of Chapters 2 and 6 enables you to embrace everyone as your new BFF. And it's just as insane to believe that even if you show up with your best self, everyone will give you loving hugs and positive plugs. Just remember as you ponder others that you deserve to be treated with respect and kindness, and are not to be dissed and dismissed. As humans, love is universal on the most fundamental level, but outside of heavenly delight living—we are earthly beings and as such, we just ain't gonna love, or even like a little, everyone no matter how much of an angel we may be.

We're all here to inspire and motivate in our own special way. Some people haven't realized this yet, but even through their venom, we learn something priceless. Like how not to choke someone. Like it or not, we're all connected on some level. Yes, it's difficult to accept that the catty chick is somehow one with you, but she is. And yes, the jackass in the office down the hall is one with you, too. The most toxic obnoxious people in my life have made me stronger, more compassionate, patient, accepting, forgiving, understanding, and aware of my own good and the good in others. Every single person you interact with, even if just passing each other down the street, affects you in some way, fine-tuning how you show up. We're always learning. What we have to master after accepting this truth is to know when to let go. Do you have any toxic obnoxics in your life? What have they taught you?

THE DOPES + THE MOPES, A.K.A. THE "TOOLS"

Let's start with an overview of the types of light dimmers that you may encounter from time to time or always. Keep in mind that this list is compiled based on my experiences. Some of the types mentioned might not annoy you at all, and others that do who aren't mentioned are people that haven't entered my world yet or they don't negatively impact me for some reason. We're all very different and have varying degrees and breaking points of sensitivity, security, and exposure to more of one than another, depending on our line of work, our tolerance levels, culture, gender, life experiences, and many other factors. Simply be aware of how blessed you are to not have crossed paths with some tools, and acknowledge your ability to cope with the tools that I still struggle with. No matter what you call them, they're all light dimmers and energy drainers—toxic!

As I mentioned during our meet + greet, I believe that everyone is born inherently good and kind. But for many reasons, as soon as we're hatched things start changing. Be it the environment, our parents, the media, and/or other people, life is an uphill battle if you don't want to go downhill. Your life will be peaceful and balanced if you understand and accept this fact.

I tried to separate types of folks into neat little packs of peeps that behave in certain like ways, but life isn't compartmentalized like that, especially when people are involved. By the way, as mentioned in the legal c.r.a.p. section of this book, any similarity you have to any one or more of the tools set forth below or anywhere else in this book is purely coincidental, but please feel free to step into that tool's shoes and excavate further. You just might find a hidden treasure.

> *For one human being to love another is the most difficult task, the ultimate, the last test and proof. It's the work for which all other work is mere preparation.*
> ~RAINER MARIA RILKE

The One-Upper/Party Scooper/Rain on Your Parader/All About Themsters

These people always do what you do, only bigger and better. You share tidbits of your wonderful Grand Canyon hike—the adventure that you had been looking forward to for years and finally experienced. Even before you get to the bit about the donkey ride, this tool starts wagging his tongue about the time *he* hiked the Grand Canyon *and* the entire Great Himalaya Trail as well as every other range known to humankind in the universe. Moon included, *fer sure*. They're the blowhards, full of hot airheads, who blow you and others off as they steer the convo back to their favorite subject—them! Do you know anyone who thinks the world revolves and evolves around him or her? I've had "friends" in my life for many years who never ask me how I am. But I can tell you how they're doing because that's all they talk about: themselves. Everyone should have a moment to shine and share. Recognize and appreciate others' value and be willing to give them equal billing. And really listen when others talk.

The Whiner/The Party Pooper/The Crybaby

Wine is one thing. But drop an "h" as in "hellacious" into that delicious word and you end up with "whine," and when *that* pours from someone's spout, I want to poke sharp pencils in my ears for a less-painful experience. Bitching and moaning does not improve with age like a fine wine does. At all. Ever. To whine is not to shine. The takeaway here is that complainers are drainers. Do not let them spew their toxic waste on you. Something is always wrong in a whiner's life, be it their health, the meal in front of them, the weather—you name it, big or small they're hardly ever having a ball. Too hot, too cold, too much, too little, too loose, too tight. Never enough, never OK, never right. They're usually victims and martyrs, too. Oh, my. It's getting really dark in here. What I find particularly irritating is the need to constantly gripe about the same ol' thing. I suppose I can put this type in a separate category called "broken record." Venting is OK, necessary even, but there comes a point where it's time to shit or get off the pot. Or at least don't tell me what the problem is for the tenth time.

The Drama Queen + King

It's all about theatre! This type has a knack for making everything larger than life. He or she will barge into your office, exasperated and flustered, with yet another recitation of a big-deal problem (not). She works herself into such a frenzy that I swear I see froth at her mouth. By the way, mouth frothing completely destroys lipstick; so for that reason alone, don't go there unless you want to constantly reapply. While deaths are sad, the drama queen will need weeks out of the office to grieve and visit the grave every day to bring the dearly departed his or her favorite treats. All this just for her hamster. Imagine if her third cousin died. The constant crisis mode and neediness of this type is exhausting. The sniffles this morning are sure to be the swine flu by dinnertime. There's always something. Always.

The Grand Opposition

Included in this lineup are naysayers and critics. Do you know anyone who always says no? Someone who incessantly finds a flaw in everything, everyone? The naysayer, which I like to call a no-er since he's the opposite of a doer, is the most challenging, because you can't get past go. It's "no, no, and *no!*" for any one of a number of bogus reasons. I worked with a "Mr. No." He opposed, objected, and denied everything we asked for or questioned. No-ers obstruct, resist, and thwart. It got to the point where we'd make stuff up and have fun with the *no!* The interesting, frustrating thing was that the "no" became a "yes" after some time passed, because by then it was his idea. Too funny. Do you know someone like this? When people sow the no, it's their own insecurities that are doing the gardening. Sometimes they say "no!" because a "yes" means work. While critics aren't always "no" people, they tend to judge, usually harshly, and find fault or place blame. They can do better. Always. There's forever something that has to be tweaked, be it one word or a sofa push two inches to the left. At times I'd wish the cynic would just say "no" without the bullshit because the judgment wasn't worth getting to "yes" on.

The Know-It-All

Or, more accurately, the no-grow-at-all. These are the bombastic individuals in your life who summarily dismiss with a wave of a hand or reject with a roll of the eyes any advice, information, or ideas others may have, if they're even listening. Information exchange is essential, for we all have something of value to say. Intelligence and knowing exist on many levels. Knowledge we glean from others helps all of us grow into our best selves. No one person walks this planet knowing all. Another characteristic of this type is saying the exact thing you said a few minutes after you did, as if it was the first time and it was that person's brilliant idea all of a sudden. Great minds can think alike, but people who do *that* usually don't want to believe that you could know something they don't. I bet they devour pink-iced cupcakes in secret.

> *When conversing with owls, remember that they think it is rather beneath them to talk about little cake things with pink sugar icing.*
> ~Pooh's Little Instruction Book

> *Do not argue with an idiot. He will drag you down to his level and beat you with experience.*
> ~Unknown

The Holier-Than-Thou

This type is a legend in their own mind. They view themselves as far superior to the mere mortals they are forced to share the planet with. These self-righteous folks who think they are God need to be reminded that the real one-and-only God created all people good and equal, with no one being better than another. Amen!

The Saboteur/The Heckler

These are the people who try to sabotage your rehab or any other efforts because your looking and feeling good pisses them off. Why? Because they're threatened by your resolve to take care of yourself. They wish they could do what you're doing, but it's too hard. It's easier to sit back and heckle or try to trip you up. Hecklers are included here because they come to your show, and even though they have the ability to leave at any time, they stay and oft return for another performance. Go figure. The great torturer has a need to put you down to build himself up. Very sick this one is. Be prepared, princess. As your arse shrinks, as your heart opens and gushes joy, as your mind expands to learn the new and exciting every day, as your soul soars and sparkles, and as you follow your bliss, some of your relationships will likely suffer. Miserable people usually can't stand to be around happy. And that's OK, because the happy campers surely don't need their good energy sucked out by viral vampires. Sabotage can take form in many ways. Love fresh-baked Toll House cookies but you're eating healthier and don't want to go there now? Tada! There sits a fresh-from-the-oven, chocolate-oozing dozen smack dab in the middle of your desk just for you. Geez, thanks.

The Mean, The Catty, The Drunk, The Green + Everything In Between

Green is toxic to the environment no matter where you are when we're talking about green as in jealousy, the green-eyed monster. This type wants what you have. They don't appreciate that there's enough to go around for all, so they'll do what they can to portray you in a bad light to make them look good. Troublemakers, mischief-makers, tattletales, scandalmongers, call them what you will, they're all the same—lame! They diminish. Ridicule. Point out flaws and weaknesses. As my dear friend Russell would say, "Just another star out of work." Sarcastic little remarks are these cacklers' calling cards.

There was this mean chick who seemed to single me out for her venom. One day I asked her why she felt the need to be so snippy. She blamed it on hormones. While I'm sure there are moments when chemicals get out of whack and nudge someone to attack, I usually call BS on the PMS and other shifts that come later in life. I'm sure there are legitimate affects, but this morph into psycho bitch every 28 or so days is highly suspect. Why is it so difficult for women to support other women? Growing up with four younger brothers and my father without a female presence for most of my life made me less tolerant of typical mean girl behavior.

Before I leave this category, I have to bring up the drunk chicks. This is a tough one because the prior-to-the-third-cosmo girl is fun and sweet, but transmogrifies right before your eyes. I call this a case of the *vin* din—the wine noise. Drink up and shut up, honey!

The Back Yakker + Stabber

We're talking the big *g* word here, girls, and it ain't Gucci or anything to do with a spot. Yep, *gossip*. I know it can be quite entertaining and amusing but it is cruel and destructive. Entire industries are built and thrive mightily on sharing the scoop about others. Most often, the talk isn't about how awesome someone is but more along the lines of how that person is a big, fat, lying/laying tart who is sleeping with her boss, or the typical catty crap about someone's appearance and the like.

> *Intelligent people talk about ideas. Average folks talk about things and events. Dumb, small people talk about others.*
> ~Unknown

I'd much rather have someone tell me to my face exactly what's on her mind than have that person scurry around and yak to twenty people behind my back. What am I missing? I'm not talking about "Hey there, is Penelope on vacation?" It's more like, "Heeyyyyyyyyy, did you hear that Penelope is shagging Peter?" Why is this anyone's business unless you're either of their respective spouses? Given the choice, I'd say that the direct expression of interest and concern is less intrusive, if at all. People want to know that people are interested in and care about them.

Worse than this is a chick acting as if she's your BFF (frenemy is more like it) and then doing the yak attack thing (not to be confused with the "crack attack" mentioned in Chapter 3—one requires a muzzle, the other, a diaper or a plug. One has diarrhea of the mouth, the other from a part more south. Either way, it stinks).

Remember, if they're talking to you about someone besides themselves, you know that as soon as you turn your back, they'll be talking about you behind it, stabbing it even. Run away from this type as fast as you can. Before the knife hits.

Don't let your tongue cut your throat.
~UNKNOWN

*Violence of the tongue is very real—
sharper than any knife.*
~MOTHER TERESA

I'll leave this section with this dirty dirt exchange. A gossip was complaining about her neighbor to a visiting guest, telling her that the woman was so dirty and a disgrace to the neighborhood. To back up her point, she cackled, "Just look at the sheets and pillowcases hanging on her clothesline. They have black streaks up and down them." Her guest replied, "It appears, my dear, that the linens are clean; the streaks you see are on your windows." Are your windows clean?

The Simple Yakker

This is the person who has fallen and can't shut up. She isn't a malicious troublemaker, intentionally throwing barbs with her blabs like the back yakkers and stabbers. She really isn't mean-spirited at all. It's just that she doesn't know when to shut up. Even nice words, if too numerous, can be exhausting. She can easily frazzle your dazzle. This one repeats what she hears without discernment. She constantly puts her foot in her mouth, notwithstanding the fabulous studded Dior wedges she wears. I'll never figure out how she manages to do that. In any event, just don't tell her anything big or small that you don't want the entire world to know. She may not qualify for a muzzle yet, but surely a zipper or a really heavy piece of tape.

Never use a gallon of words to express a spoonful of thought.
~ANONYMOUS

The Users + The Takers

I know a lot of people who want to meet and hang out with the movers and the shakers. Not me. I pay more attention to the givers and the takers. For many people, it's all about them and what you can do to enhance their lives. To give and receive is the natural flow of a healthy universe. We should do things for others out of the kindness of our hearts and not for anything in return. However, if it's constantly take, take, take from you, it's time to make new friends. Pay attention to how the energy is exchanging between you and the people in your life. An even exchange of energy makes the world go around.

The Yes-Actor No-Acter

This type annoys and frustrates me tons. It's the all-talk (the yes-actor) and no-action (no-acter) person. This is the guy or gal who says they're going to do something and never follows through even when they bring it up in the first place. Why would anyone commit to something and have no intention of doing it? This type of behavior perplexes me because all the person had to do was keep his or her mouth shut. Why not keep life simple and say what you mean, mean what you say? As I said, just shut the f@$k up!

IT'S TIME TO NAME NAMES...
...IF YOU WANT TO END THE GAMES

Now that you've met the "tools", let's delve into the specific relationships in your life and see if any of these caustic culprits or others known by you and not mentioned above show up in your world. You may have already created such a list during your prep days. If so, pull it out and see if any updating is called for. Here's a little exercise to see who's on your team. These are the relationships to be explored and perhaps redefined or cut. Who do you need to kick (politely and not that hard unless absolutely necessary but with grace nonetheless) to the curb? Write down the names of the people you deal with regularly—co-workers, social friends, acquaintances, hair stylist, nail girl, dry cleaner, anyone and everyone. Now, look at each name and ask yourself these questions:

- Am I relaxed and at ease when I am with this person?
- Is this person critical of me?
- Is this a give-and-take relationship or just take, take, take—with me doing the give, give, give?
- Do I feel tired or inspired when I am with this person?
- Does this person share common goals and interests with me?
- Do we share the same values?
- Do I feel as if I must take a shower after being in the company of this person?
- Does this person fill or deplete my energy tank?
- Do I look forward to seeing this person? Spending time with him or her?
- Does this person call me only when he or she wants something?
- Does being with this person stir feelings of frustration or guilt?
- Does this person ask me about my life, my family, my work, or is it truly all about them?
- Does this person take me for granted?
- Do I trust this person?
- Does this person regularly dump on me?

- How do I feel after talking with this person on the phone or in person?

- Do I walk on eggshells when around this person?

- How much of what I feel when I'm around this person is about me and my own insecurities?

Some other provocative questions to ask yourself about the people in your life come from my friend Jana Fleming who is a healing coach, retreat leader, and meditation instructor. She shared these perspective inducers, adapted from *The Spiritual Rules of Engagement,* by Yehuda Berg, during one of her fabulous yoga and meditation weekends:

- Are we headed in the right direction? If not, a collision could happen!

- Are we at the same altitude? If not, one will be spending lots of time pulling the other up, while the other is pulling the other down.

- Are we at the same speed? If not, we may outgrow each other.

Is it time to ditch the b+%#$ and chuck the big cluck? Concert Chicks don't naturally click with turkeys, buzzards, dodo birds, vultures, cuckoos, and vampires (*oui*, not a bird, but winged, flies, and bites thus relevant). Friendships should be nurturing opportunities for growth, a joy in your life, not another job. If any relationship is too much work and drains you, rethink it. You are not stuck with any one person forever. Let the friendship go with love, acceptance, and appreciation for what it brought and taught you. Some folks are just plain ol' too much work. Maybe, just maybe, you have simply outgrown each other and you are off on separate paths, journeys, and missions.

Is your friend low maintenance or high maintenance? If the "friend" is too much work or otherwise zaps your energy, she falls into the high-maintenance category and you need to revisit your relationship with that person. Low-maintenance friends, on the other hand, love you for who you are, whether you get together once a month or every six years. They go with the flow, are usually on the same growth path, share the same interests, and they love, appreciate, and respect you as a unique soul. Don't get me wrong. They'll let you know when you're out of line or out of your mind. They share their honest opinions and ideas because they truly care about you, not putting their own interests first. They inspire and support you as you realize your potential and make your dreams come true. And you do the same for them from your heart. Dreams manifest swiftly when you share them with people who truly care....about you and not about what you do...for them.

> *Happiness is having a large, loving, caring, close-knit family in another city*
> ~GEORGE BURNS

As you make a list of the toxic people in your life, don't skip over your blood relatives. Just because you were born or married into a certain clan, doesn't mean that God intended for you to suffer. The universe wants you to be happy. *Really* happy. The tools mentioned in this chapter can yank you from family hell as well. Go through your own pack and see who's who and what's what. Who are your peeps? Your tribe?

Go over the list of the people in your life in light of the questions above and identify those who are toxic (tools that gotta go), toxic-lite (teetering on full tool if can't be redefined), and nontoxic (not a tool—cool!). Slash a big red "X" through any that gotta go, a checkmark next to every teeterer (stirs up drama once in a while but still brings something to the table), and hitch a star to every peep who plays a supporting, loving role in your life.

DISCONNECT: WHAT TO DO WITH THE "TOOL"
THE DETOX "TOOL" BOX

Finally, the cope part. Now that you know who the "tools" are in your life, and even how you might show up as one, it's time to do something about it with the help of your Detox "Tool" Box. It contains some tried-and-true ways to energetically dump the toxic obnoxics.

Open your journal to a fresh page and add this heading: "ways to cope with the mopes and dopes in my life." As you discover the coping tools introduced below, note the ones that you can put to good use to rebuild, redefine, or remove relationships. You're basically creating a custom toolbox to assist in your personal relationship purge. No matter what "tool" you're dealing with and no matter what tool you use, ask your higher self to release you from the prison of holding onto any resentments or grudges. This is an important component to successfully moving forward because, once again, we can't control others, including how they are going to respond to us, if at all.

> *Holding resentment is like eating poison and waiting for the other person to keel over.*
> ~UNKNOWN

Here are the tools for your "tools" to place in your box as needed:

TOOL #1: NON-REACTIVITY

Hands down, this is the primo-supremo dope and mope repellant. Return to Chapter 6 to reread the reactivity portion. Master this and you will harness unbridled happiness. When you return, the bouncer has already been told to let you past the red velvet rope in tool #2.

TOOL #2: A RED VELVET ROPE

Entre, s'il vous plaît! You're welcome to stay in the VIP area for as long as you'd like. The only catch is that once you enter, you can't leave until you adopt something. No worries, not another mouth to feed, but rather, a policy to heed. A life-changing policy. As years pass, I have less patience for *connerie*.[31] I don't have room in my nest

---
31 "Bullshit" in French.

for negative twigs, twits, or turds. As soon as I instituted the policy, I was able to bid *adieu* with love to the people who dimmed my light.

Not only should every Concert Chick have a red carpet under her feet, she should have a red velvet rope to block toxic people from her light. While a physical barrier would be nice, an energetic one is more practical and less obvious. It's time to adopt the "red velvet rope" policy. Essentially, it's your personal supersensory filtration system. Your body+mind+heart+soul is housed in the most exclusive club in the world. Membership should be highly selective and cherished once attained. You are the manager of this club—your life—as well as the caterer, bartender, valet, and everyone else who keeps the club open and thriving, including the very powerful bouncer.

Through your inner knowing—your gut instinct—your bouncer self chooses who comes into your life—who has access behind your red velvet rope. This isn't about judgment; it's about discernment. We're all vibrating at different frequencies and we won't all get along. We've touched upon this earlier. The people who don't make the cut in your life are superstars in others. Don't hold them back. There's nothing wrong with them or you. You just don't jive. You want to give your peeps the full-strength version of you, not some diluted, exhausted being that shows up when you spread yourself too thin by saying "yes" to everyone.

Commit to the red velvet rope policy while you're in rehab so when you exit, you can start deciding who receives an all-access VIP (Very Important Peep) pass. Tie a red velvet cord around your wrist to remind you of your commitment to this critical policy. If you're really into this, visit the Chapter 8 section in the Swag Lounge to find out where to buy a real life-size red velvet rope. And while you're there, you may as well pick up a red carpet, too.

TOOL #3: CIRCUMCISION

I'm assuming that you're a chick reading this, so when you saw the name of this tool you most likely didn't squirm and cross your legs reflexively. If you're a Concert Chuck, I'm so sorry. Since we're dealing with the "tools" in our life, I felt it a highly accurate term to use since this tool deals with cut and release like no other. Grab (but don't run with) a pair of scissors, a pen, some paper, and a desire to cut loose whoever weighs you down. Sketch a depiction of your body+mind+heart+soul or use a full-length photo of yourself. Draw a large heart in the center of your body and color it red. Next, pen lines from your heart center to the ground, each representing a person you need to let go of. If you want to get really creative you could use string instead of pen lines. Whatever you use, write a name next to each line.

Reflect on each person and journal what comes up. What has this person taught you? Express gratitude for the lesson. What do you love about them? Why isn't it healthy to continue the relationship? Ponder these queries a bit for that person, and then pick up the scissors and snip, snip the string or across the line on the paper (set the parts aside for later use). You are symbolically and energetically releasing the tie you have to that toxic person—the one that holds you back and weighs you down. Even if that person is still in your life, the relationship will shift. It will either be redefined, fade away, or completely cut in the future when the time is right. Move on to the next person and go through the same questions, reflections, and—*ahem*—circumcisions until you've operated your way through your relationships. With each snip, snip you become lighter and brighter. Cut, cut, snip, snip, oh what a relief it is! Gather the strands or strings you snipped and cut them into tinier pieces. Place the snippets in the palm of your hand, whisper *au revoir,* and toss like confetti in celebration of another brave move by you. You're really letting go to grow now. Carry on!

You can also circumcise toxic peeps from your address book, phone and e-mail contact list, and Rolodex, electronic and paper. Ask yourself the same questions you did in the previous snip snip practice, only here, the procedure involves erasing, whiting out, and pressing the delete button.

> *Some cause happiness wherever they go;*
> *others, whenever they go.*
> ~Oscar Wilde

If the relationship is worth saving, having a heart-to-heart in person is the best way to initiate redefining. I know this isn't always necessary, appropriate, or even desirable, depending on the circumstances. A letter may be a better way to bring to light your feelings with an invitation to discuss face-to-face. This way, you can spend more time composing and organizing your thoughts and the recipient can sit with your words a bit.

By the way, confrontation is very different from communication. Many people don't seem to get this. For some reason, there's a preference for pussyfooting around an issue, talking to everyone else about what someone said or did instead of going to the person directly, which would be the most constructive thing to do, not to mention considerate and professional. Instead, toxic drama has been spread that wastes everyone's time and energy. It isn't productive under any scenario, at any level; in fact, it's downright destructive. I'm constantly challenged and frustrated by this immature behavior. I already mentioned this under the "backstabber" and "yakker" section but it's a good one to come back to since these "tools" are ubiquitous.

And when you reach out—no matter how you do it—let go of any expectations you may have of the outcome. I learned this lesson up close and personal after accidently hitting the send button on an e-mail I thought I saved as a draft. I very pointedly told this person who I held in my heart as my closest friend how I really felt. I held nothing back. At first I was mortified that it was in her inbox at that very moment. But then I quickly felt relieved. I finally released what had been on my mind and hoped that my words would bring us back to where we were around the time we first met. No such luck. When I saw a response pop up later that night, it took me awhile to build up the courage to open it because I truly believed that I'd find an equally encompassing heartfelt outpouring. But it wasn't there. Not even close. OK! At least everything was placed in perspective and my feelings confirmed. The email was never mentioned by either of us, but it definitely changed our relationship. The bottom line: Let go without expectation of any specific outcome. I still simmer about this at times when we're together because of what hasn't been said but for the most part, I'm over it, slowly fading away into the depth of genuine connections, emerging to the surface if it benefits me.

Occasionally it becomes necessary to end a long-term relationship with an energy vampire. Under such circumstances there is no need to back up with a U-Haul, pack up all the memories, and tear off into the future in a cloud of dust. It is better to slowly but surely extricate yourself from the relationship. You can reduce residual guilt or dread experienced at a chance meeting with the emotional mugger by planning an occasional get-together (you define what that means). Perhaps that event can include other people to diffuse the situation (and you can wave from across the room). Gaining an enemy for life has no upside.
KRISTA MARX, ASPIRING TO KEEP IT REAL + TO MAINTAIN A SENSE OF HUMOR IN THE FOLLOWING ROLES: MOTHER, WIFE, DAUGHTER, SISTER, JUDGE + FRIEND

There may be some highly toxic peeps that you're finding difficult to release. These things take time, years even. Being aware of who drains you and slowly but surely starting to establish boundaries is a huge step in the right direction. Allow the redefining and reframing to unfold in its own time. Practice patience, forgiveness, and acceptance. Most of all, don't be hard on yourself.

TOOL #4: EXORCISM

Hello, Linda Blair! Your purge doesn't have to be as dramatic or projectile, but a little exorcism here and there works wonders to expel any demons you may have in your world. Exorcism is a bonus sub tool for those who don't like sharp objects and get queasy at the thought of snip-snipping. It's a very simple method. Just pray about the relationship. For the relationship. No need to cast spells or go into complex incantations. Just pray, and one day you may say hooray because they'll either be out of your way or you'll both be going out to play. With each other. Nicely.

TOOL #5: FLIP 'EM A WING, FLASH 'EM A SMILE

While we believe that flipping 'em off to flash your new sparkly chicktail ring is not only acceptable but highly desirable and certainly preferable over flipping 'em a wing, we know that sometimes a straight-up flip is what's called for, especially when rude mutter/mudder cluckers show up.

But better yet and way more effective, not to mention polite—but I will anyway because one can never have too many manner reminders—if you really want to piss off a grouch, flash him, and not in the way he'd like you to (keep your skirts down, girls!). Flash that killer smile of yours. That ol' "kill 'em with kindness" really works, and it isn't illegal, unladylike, or messy. This doesn't make you a pushover. Instead, it makes you powerful. You completely disarm the dope/mope. A smile is not only your best weapon, it's also your finest accessory. That flash completely disarms your tormenter, who is most likely expecting a defensive confrontation since that's what they know. Take 'em out of their comfort zone in a flash.

The only right time to look down on others is when you're helping them up.
~William Arthur Ward

SPARKLY CHICKS' TIPS + TRICKS

Remember some of my like-minded soul friends that I acknowledged earlier? Well, here they are and more. In the "cope" section of your journal, jot down any of these sparkly chicks' ideas that you want to practice in your life.

I read this: "Don't make someone a priority if they only make you an option." It is such a waste of time to try to get someone to do/feel/think something they are not inclined to do. Learn to move on.
~KATHRYN WONG, TANGUERA, DECORATIVE PAINTER, COLOR SPECIALIST, GRAPHIC DESIGNER, DOG LOVER

Constantly remind yourself that "Emotions Are Contagious", whether positive or negative. Let's call them dimmers and shimmers. If you are around a dimmer, pull out the hand sanitizer immediately and prevent infection. If you are basking in the glittery vibes of one who shimmers, pour it into a martini glass and drink up. Your soul will thank you.
~CATHERINE WALLACE, RETIRED + SUPER INSPIRED TO LIVE SPARKLY, FRANCOPHILE, WORLD TRAVELER

"Surround yourself with only people who are going to lift you higher." (Oprah). This is my mantra, helping me then, now and forever to make the conscious decision to avoid those people who are the dimmers of my joy and light within!
~KATHLEEN FOX, BELIEVER IN MAGIC AND THE POSITIVE POWER AND INSPIRATION OF GIRLFRIENDS, LOVER OF NATURE'S BEAUTIFUL GIFTS, MOTHER OF TWO ADORABLE, FURRY, FOUR-LEGGED BOYS, SOMEDAY WRITER

When people are 'dimmers' I try to remember that they are not allowed to steal my joy. It's not always that simple but I TRY. When I am really down and the dimmer is a circumstance, I remember that Psalms 30 says that "weeping may last for a night, but Joy cometh in the morning". Bottom line is that God is what allows me to let my light continue to shine.
~ BARBARA CHEIVES, TRAINER + CONSULTANT AS CONVERGE & ASSOCIATES, FIBER ARTIST AS AFRASIA DESIGN STUDIO, LONGTIME COMMUNITY VOLUNTEER LEADER + RECURRING GUEST HOST AT WXEL'S SOUTH FLORIDA ARTSVIEW

I always say, "everyone is doing their best (even if that best is lousy right now)" - it's a great reminder and helps me reframe anger into compassion.
~ HALLE EAVELYN, JULIE THE CRUISE DIRECTOR FOR
SPIRIT QUEST TOURS

I go in to a standing forward hang and open an imaginary door in the crown of my head and let all the junk and garbage fall in to the floor and say bye-bye to it forever. Then, I round up slowly to stand with a fresh new perspective as well as a stretched out spine, back, hamstrings, hips, neck and shoulders. I love forward bends in yoga.
~ KRISTIN MCGEE, YOGA/PILATES/FITNESS CELEBRITY, WRITER, FILA'S YOGA AMBASSADOR, IDAHO GAL, SKI BUNNY, THEATER GOING, NEW YORK CITY GIRL, SEX IN THE CITY + 30 ROCK GUEST SPOTS + MORE, OH MY!
WWW.KRISTINMCGEE.COM

I realized that just like when the plane you're taking is late to depart and you're going to miss your connection, there was nothing I could do to get him to change. When your plane is late, you can't do anything to make it fly faster. Yelling at the pilot or the flight attendant won't make the plane fly faster, you can't get out and push the plane to a higher speed, and sitting in your seat stewing about tardiness and missed flights does nothing to speed you to your destination. All you can do is deal with whatever has to be dealt with when you get where you're going. Adopt the "late plane" philosophy in my dealings with a dimmer. Also, I keep this quote attributed to Plato in mind: "Be kind, for everyone you meet is fighting a hard battle." It is so true. Many (or all) of us have things that trouble us. Sometimes we know what's going on in someone's life, and sometimes we don't have a clue that there's anything wrong, although there may well be. That difficult person you're talking to may have a loved one with cancer, a child on drugs, an unemployed spouse and not enough income to pay the mortgage. Don't add to someone's burden. Be kind. Watch the words that come out of your mouth.
~ L.S., ASPIRING WRITER, DO-GOODER, AND ENTREPRENEUR - CURRENTLY WORKING ON A VENTURE THAT WILL ENCOMPASS ALL THREE, THINKS CHOCOLATE IS THE MOST IMPORTANT FOOD GROUP, HIP-HOP DANCER EXTRAORDINAIRE

Here are a few things I do: I repeat "cancel cancel cancel" when bad thoughts pop up, or simply command, "just stop it". On a more positive not, I ask for grounding, focus, clarity while imagining iridescent light and think of flowing water and focus on breathing... and saying this.... "May I be at peace; May my heart remain open; May I awaken to the light of my own true nature; May I be healed; May I be a source of healing for all beings."

~MARGARET MCELRATH, YOGINI, SPIRITUALIST, CONCERT WIDOW

I have to share how I deal with the dimmers of light in my life. (Love that phrase) I guess if I was to sum it up I would have to say that it's the mantra that I have had since my 20's that has helped me though life. "Everything happens for the best. Everything happens for a reason. Just Believe." Now it's easy to live that mantra when you find out that Nordstrom no longer has those fab Cole Haan shoes in your size, but it's really hard when you find that someone you love is no longer with you. I guess that's when my faith steps in. It's knowing that as hard as a situation is, somehow, the Universe will make something good out of it. We may find out 5 days, 5 weeks, 5 years or maybe we will never find out that something good came out of the tragedy, but it did. You just have to believe. My other belief is that everything is a blessing, the good and the bad. This past year, I have seen all my little hurdles as a blessing. When I asked God "why me?" the answer was "why not me?" Maybe I was suppose to have breast cancer so that I can raise enough funds for the Komen foundation so that some young woman, with beautiful young children will be diagnosed with breast cancer early enough to save her life and give her the opportunity to be there when her daughter buys her wedding gown. Who knows? I just believe! So that's my story, nothing special, just a way to meander through life with a smile on my face and love in my heart. It's all going to work out. I believe.

~DENISE VIDAL BENNETTE, SR. IT MANAGER, GADGET GIRL, LIFE DANCER

There are times when friendships run their course. And when they do, it doesn't mean you did anything wrong or they did... just time to move on

and celebrate those moments you did share. I'm trying to have more of a carefree attitude about the small stuff and again I ask myself, WWDND and the movie that runs through my mind is of you trying on Chanel glasses sipping champagne laughing and telling me chill as you smile and ask for more bubbly!

~ CATHERINE (CAT) TOLTON, FUNDRAISER, SUPER MOM, SPECIAL FRIEND, LITTLE SPARK PLUG

My Mamma always said, "Don't cry over anyone who's not crying over you!"

~WENDY ZOBERMAN, LAWYER, OPTIMIST, CHUCKLE INDUCER, SERENITY SEEKER

Here's how I get rid of the "positivity robbers" in my life: We owe it to ourselves to do as much as possible to make ourselves as happy as we possibly can for as long as we possibly can. For me, this means being around people who bring me joy. If someone doesn't fit into this category, I don't allow them in my space. This could be limiting my time with them or deciding that they are no longer allowed in my life. If I don't have a choice regarding whether or not I have to be in their company, I just decide that I'm going to be positive and not let them "dump" their negativity on me. Have you ever known someone, who, no matter what positive thing you say, they always counter with something negative? Well, I used to give up and let them have their "down and out, woe is me and woe is the world" party. Not anymore. I refuse to let them win the war of negativity when it comes to me. I might not change their minds, but I don't let them change mine or stop me from believing that everything has a good side-- sometimes we just have to wait for it or perhaps it's not clear that it's there, but it always is.

~ DAWN WYNN, ATTORNEY, WIFE, MOM, SALSA DANCER, BOXING OFFICIAL, MARATHONER AND THE BEST FRIEND YOU'LL EVER FIND IF YOU'RE LUCKY ENOUGH!

How do I deal with people who bring negative energy? I do give them a chance to tell their story but then slowly and very politely I try to see less and less of them. I'm not afraid to say I'm sorry. Negative energy is always a consequence of some unhappiness, some unfulfilled desire, some problems in the life of that person. A good reason /reasons are behind the negativism

and if the person gets to the bottom of it by eliminating or solving the problem, many times a new individual emerges out of it. I have witnessed it on numerous occasions. There are always the exceptions to the rule, those who no matter what, are the constant complainers. They never see the light at the end of the tunnel and simply love to live in the pit of their own misery. They enjoy everyone's pity and feel good when others feel sorry for them. In this case I just walk away. People like that always bring rain in my life, the wind blows too harsh and my hairdo gets too messy. I can't help but stop listening and just try politely to avoid them.
~NIKI NIKOLOVA, EDUCATOR, TENNIS MOM TO PRO-IN-THE-MAKING VANESSA, SEASHELL SEEKER, BEACH BABE

Dealing with dimmers of the light People – spend as little time as possible with the dimmers. Send them love and light from a distance and fulfill obligations (unless they are actually evil, in which case one must hit "delete"). When I'm actually in their presence I just try to have a sense of humor. Places/Things – when I find myself in a situation where the energy is not positive or that affects me in a weird way, I return to my breath and try to notice colors around me – whatever they are – and just try to recognize/focus on what's around me so that I can become more present (and find something to like/enjoy in the situation).
~JODIE EISENHART, PROJECT MANAGER, SARONG SISTA, DOG RESCUER, FOODIE BLOGGER, GRATEFUL OBSERVER

I picture negative or toxic people like a dose of the flu. They're almost unavoidable, and unfortunately they spread easily. They can make you really ill and depressed, but the only way to get over them is to keep doing what you know you need to, and rely on your own inner health to see you through. It really helps me to think of them as a virus that I can recover from. I also sometimes think of them as potholes in the road – if you can't avoid them, you have to get over them with as little damage to the karma (wink wink) as possible! And the older I get, the more determined I am not to waste my joy on people who don't have any themselves. It's a total shame that there are so many in the world, huh? Maybe heaping the love on the positive people will make the negative ones shrink?
~CLAIRE PRYOR, JEWELLERY DESIGNER, MOTHER, SISTER, FRIEND

I let my focus wonder off to something natural and beautiful...if I'm inside, it might be the curvature or coloring of a leaf on a plant, or the graining in a piece of wood. If I'm outside, I appreciate the sun on my face, the soft touch of a breeze, or the gracefulness of a bird in flight. "Life" is precious. I pause to see it, feel it, breathe it...and my mood lifts.
~Karen Steele, dedicated to family, friends, animals, and nature, world traveling, biking, dancing, laughing, and marketing consulting, a Gemini in every way - Hiking in Alaska or shopping in Paris, working all night or dancing 'til dawn

I seldom if ever, allow anyone to get to me. I know me, and I am only bothered when Jack is hurt or when I meet mean people. Then I can just talk to Jack, as we have no time for mean people. None. Life is too short. I think when you're walking around with cancer like I am, there's no time for being negative. I can't lie, because I'd never remember what I said, so I tell the truth, as kindly as possible, or just smile. So the only real answer to your question is to make sure very few have a reason for negative energy, and if they do, find the right person to solve their problems. The final answer is: You can't allow anyone to dim your lights. Turn on that inner generator and smile as you say bye-bye, great to meet you, hope you have a great an evening as I'm going to have...then, find a happy person. I find joy in helping others, no matter how small the joy may be at the time. It all adds up to a lot of happiness for me in the end. So, NO DIMS. I refuse to accept a dim! Carry an extra battery and no one would have a dim light for more than a minute. Love honestly and completely. Put the dims you don't want into the dim box, and keep them there. And, smile a lot. I smile when I really don't want to, then break out laughing all by myself at even thinking about dealing with any negative energy.
~Janet Boyle, retired elementary school teacher, philanthropist, mentor, music lover, Coca Cola in bottles only fanatic, interior decorator, flower fan, cat lover - feral cats to Persian cats - any cat, politics though no party in particular, as common sense is more important to our Country

You have two choices. If you can avoid them, do so and release them back into the universe through your compassion and understanding of their low self-esteem due most probably to painful events and experiences originating from their childhood. Secondly, ask why they came into your life and what lessons you can learn: such as maintaining healthy boundaries, by expressing the power of NO and whatever other feelings without blaming them. If the person is a big complainer and keeps dumping negativity on you, use this two step approach: first show understanding and compassion and then help them regain their self-control by asking this powerful question: "what do you intend to do about this situation?" Another thing that I mentioned in my book—seeing difficult people as wounded animals helps avoid anger and frustration, which are not healthy emotions for us.
~EDWIGE GILBERT, WELLNESS/LIFE COACH AND AUTHOR OF "THE FRESH START PROMISE, 28 DAYS TO TOTAL MIND, BODY, SPIRIT TRANSFORMATION", TRANSFORMS STRESS INTO STRENGTH, SPREADS JOIE DE VIVRE

Sometimes you just have to laugh and little ditties help. Here are my two favorites: "Oh my my, hell yes, it's time to put on that party dress because we are having a party and we are all so excited, especially because you are not invited!" and "May the toes that you step on today not be connected to the ass you have to kiss tomorrow." Also, "May you never have more money than manners."
~TERESA STODDARD, CORPORATE FLIGHT ATTENDANT, ENTHUSIASTIC GLOBETROTTER, AUTHOR OF THE ARRANGEMENT: THE NEW MARRIAGE, TRADEMARK HOLDER OF THE RING

Putting labels on people is not the lens through which I see life because we all have our daily uphill battles. I realize, though, that setting boundaries can prevent the negative energy of others from impacting my innately positive outlook. It's understood that friends want to help each other out, and certainly the people you care about need to be heard and supported when problems assail them. It's important to be honest with yourself and others in

relationships, to communicate when you can be truly helpful, and when you can't. Life is too short to be dimmed.
~**Lena Rivkin**, artist, graphologist + good friend

CONNECT: WHAT TO DO WITH THE TRUE + COOL

It's like your heart is made of chimes, and this person is the wind. You make beautiful music together.
~Gemini horoscope, *The Palm Beach Post*, date unknown (though timeless!)

Now that you've disconnected, it's time to connect. Being weed-free, you can now cultivate your garden so that you and others can fully bloom. Nurture real friendships, starting with all the nontoxic peeps you hitched a star to earlier. Who's in your entourage? Who are the members of your band? Who are your groupies? Your fans? The prez of your fan club? Who do you make beautiful music with?

Spend time with people who keep it real, who have a life, who care about you and your wishes, dreams, pains, sorrows, everything and anything about your life—the good, the bad, and the ugly. Birds of a feather really do flock together.

Who's on your dream team? In your support system? One of your trusted advisors? Do you have a mentor? Who do you mentor? It's all about connecting, teaching, supporting, growing, enhancing.

There are a number of ways to stay connected, to offer support, to show concern, to inspire and motivate each other, to celebrate others' joys, including the basic joy of being alive, and to be a thoughtful, caring carrier and giver of light. Many of my close friends live out of state and even out of the country. I truly have a global family. We stay connected through thoughtful e-mails and snail mail, texts, trips, lunches, happy hours, and Facebook posts, pokes, and peeks. We take the time to stay in touch. Sure, we're all busy and in vastly different time zones, but we find time for each other no matter what. We share our lives based not on what we can do for each other in terms of work titles and the like, but instead from the same plane of *joie de vivre*, happy dispositions, creative souls, a sense of humor, and primarily, authenticity and depth. I am incredibly blessed to have these women in my life, many of whom I recently met. Quality over quantity in all aspects of your life including relationships keeps your body+mind+heart+soul light.

CYBERSPACE CAN BE A HEART-SHARING + WARMING PLACE

Social networking is a funny/fun thing. I'm a huge Facebook fan. When people comment in a not-so-positive way that they don't have time for *that*, I explain that not everyone is into managing a farm—that you are in complete control of how much time you commit to it. I spend about thirty minutes a day, sending birthday greetings in the morning, and posting links, photos, and anything else of interest that I discovered that day before I go to bed. I'm not promoting sitting in front of your computer while your family is in the other room enjoying a home-cooked dinner for six minus one. Human contact is essential. Cyber hugs just don't cut it. But, the connections can be more real in many ways.

WRITE, MAKE RITE + SIMPLY RIGHT EXPRESSIONS

Acknowledging others is a gift that keeps on giving. A hug, a note, a "just checking in to say hey" text, listening and really hearing, all make a tremendous difference in someone's life.

I know we must save our environment one tree at a time, and the technology today is fascinating and allows us to connect like never before. I don't know what I'd do without my iPhone, MacBook, iPad, and Facebook page. But there's something special about finding an envelope in your mail box addressed to you in beautiful handwritten script, perhaps with colorful swirls and whirls sent by your creative chum, or neat blocks penned with a black Sharpie that you know comes from your brother.

When I was a teenager, I was assigned to make sure that then Miss Florida Nancy Stafford made her fashion show changes according to plan. She was a joy to work with. After the show, I received—on Miss Florida stationary, no less—a handwritten note thanking me for my help. I still have it. My first boss in the legal world would do the same. Win or lose, he'd pen a note filled with thanks for my help on a case. A successful lawyer and a community leader who was, and still is, a powerful presence in the political and legal arena, taking the time to write a sincere "thank you" to his law clerk is unheard of these days. So many people believe a paycheck shows more than enough appreciation. While money is important and is the primary reason many of us work, the personal thoughtfulness through the expression of gratitude is the equivalent of a million dollar bonus on some level. I saved his notes, too.

I love stationery, cards, stickers, and colorful pens, and I put all to good use often. I make my note jotting a ritual. I fill a basket with all the goods and retreat outdoors for some solar-powered connection inspiration. My trademark is to load notes with not only heartfelt words, but also sparkly metallic bits or magnets, Post-its, chicktail napkins, or buttons with cute sayings on them. Oh yeah, and BlueQ gum, if I'm feeling a little sassy (think eight bits of cinnamon gum enclosed in a box that reads "let's pretend I give a shit and leave it at that" or fruit flavored chew housed in a "does this gum make my ass look fat?" box—smile inducers, all of them!). I have dear friends that do this, too, and if like magic, when I'm having one of *those* days, I need not look beyond my mailbox for a pick-me-up. My pals *just know*. Freaky fabulous!

Just as rare as snail mail these days is a simple acknowledgment. I am stunned how little, if any, gratitude is expressed. Why do people sparingly dole out a "thank you," "great job," or "way to go"? Let yours out. All. Day. Long. It's free and takes less than a couple of seconds to say. People need to stop taking others for granted and to start letting people know that they matter.

A sparkly chick is a sparkly friend. She's a friend who thinks of her friends at random times like when she's shopping and sees something that is sooooo like her friend. She takes the time out of her busy day to send a friendly hello message just to let her friend know that she's thought of. Most importantly, a sparkly chick is honest with her mind and can say "I love you."

~TAMMY FIELDS, MOM, WIFE, ATTORNEY, SPARKLY FRIEND, CREATIVE THINKER, CANCER SURVIVOR + DO-GOODER EXTRAORDINAIRE

In the Noble Eightfold Path of Buddhism, there's a discipline called "Right Speech." This is a wonderful way to show up in and connect with the world. Essentially, it states that we should ask ourselves these five questions before we speak (I've given them a Concert Chick tweak): Is the timing right? Will what I say be of value to the other person? Am I speaking with kindness? Can I say it without complaint? Is it true? Commit to making it your practice, starting today.

You now have all the power tools you need to successfully cope with the "tools" you may have in your life. You've learned much about yourself and others. You know how to strengthen your power source, and the red rope is up and discerning well. You're connecting with like-minded, creative, loving souls. I am so proud of you. All that's left is your red carpet debut. Make sure to have a good night's sleep. You'll need your rest for the big celebration. *Bonne nuit et gros bisous.* See you at the party!

Chapter 9

Celebrate Yourself!

Live your life in such a way that when your feet hit the floor in the morning, the devil shudders and says, "Oh hell...she's awake!"

~UNKNOWN

You've reached Step 4 and are ready to head out the door. Two snaps and a twist and glitter showers galore. *Le tapis rouge roule pour vous aujourd'hui! Oui,* the red carpet is being rolled out for you today. Sashay, sashay, hooray! You're awesome! By now you should really know and embrace this fact.

You rocked the first week of rehab and rolled in the second. It's now time to join forces to rock *and* roll! Your body+mind+heart+soul have been turned inside out and upside down and otherwise scrambled and shined, and you are ready to walk into the real world on that red carpet that will always be under your feet from this day forward. It's the day to show 'em what you've got, which, by the way, is a lot! I hope you're as proud of yourself as I am of you. You are freer to do what it is that you were put on this planet to do, *ma belle,* which is mainly to *be you*. Did I mention how proud I am of you?

Today is sorta like a debutante's coming-out party, though it's all about you and only you (and there are no cookie-cutter rules to follow or curtsies to perform, but do go for the princess white gown and elbow-length gloves if you so desire). Whatever it is that you do, don't forget your tiara! It's truly your song, your dance, your stage. How are you going to rock (and roll) it?

CHICK CAVEAT

Happiness is when what you think, what you say, and what you do are in harmony.
~Mohandas Karamchand Gandhi

Attention partiers! Here are some important tips on how to not trip on the red carpet. I know you're excited about the champagne and the cupcakes that beckon, but let me tell you this: You will feel awful—perhaps the crappiest ever—if you go "too much, too soon." You can really screw things up and land yourself back in rehab. If your celebration includes some refreshing libations, adopt Virgin Wine's slogan: "drink it, love it, know when to stop." Cheers to that! Moderation, my little chickie, moderation.

As you've heard many times, your red carpet debut is all about you. What and who you want to do, eat, drink, say, think, be with, and be is your call, but please keep in mind that your system has shifted toward the light and it may be quite a shock to load it with booze, brownies, and bummer behavior such as bitchin' and bad-mouthing that can turn off your light quicker than you can pour a bag of Reese's Pieces down your throat. I'm the last person on the planet to tell you not to uncork the Veuve Clicquot and to toss the Almond Joys. But let me be the first to tell you that you must pay careful attention to how you feel before, during, and after. Sense the joy and bubbles well up inside of you, not only outside of you.

Don't go hog wild and order everything on the menu that makes you salivate. Pigging out will only make you pout later, and you know how important it is to smile. Jennifer "Gin" Sander's "be a food snob" tip from her book *The Martini Diet: The Self-Indulgent Way to a Thinner, More Fabulous You!* is genius: "...the higher your nose is in the air about what you eat, the smaller your butt will be." Chin-chin, Gin! Embrace food snobbiness from this day forward. It's the only acceptable form of snobbery permitted in the Concert Chick world. Hold your head high, nose up (but please do make sure your tiara is securely fastened for the duration of the flight!)

This is a great day to shine and put into action all you've learned in rehab. Practice celebrity eating. The paparazzi could snap your photo at any time. How would you want to show up on the cover of *People*? What would the tabloid headline mentioning your name say? For the same reason, think before you drink. I suggest no more than two chicktails and lots of water before, between, and after. And this isn't only about your eating and drinking behavior. It's about what comes out of your mouth, too. This alert isn't meant to be a humongous killjoy raindrop on your red carpet parade. I think it's only fair to give you a heads up, especially when the goal is to keep your head high, nose up, tiara on.

Go about your day with a renewed sense of "i rock!" and pay attention to all the details—walloping or not. See how it feels when you are mindful and moderate, or if you stray to the mindless and massive. Use today as a rehearsal of how you're going to show up in your life, on your stage, every day.

Here's an example of mindfulness in action. You want a Coca-Cola. You haven't had one in two weeks and feel that you've earned a can. If this beverage in all its carbonated and sugary glory is what your body+mind+heart+soul really wants, pop the top and enjoy. But maybe you're just thirsty. A bottle of water would be a better choice. Besides being much healthier for you, you save yourself a whopping 142 calories that you can put toward one of those fabulously delicious homemade snickerdoodles you also have your eye on. It's all about making conscious choices, moment by moment. OK, so there may be a time in Tijuana where the cheep tequila shots sorta make your decisions fuzzy and you will wish for one of those rickety buses to run over you because you feel like you've already been hit by a train, so "please put me out of my misery already" is teetering at the tip of your tongue. But that (hopefully) is a vacation-fueled blip in your self-respect plan. Besides, you don't want your cute butt dragged to a real rehab or hospital, do you? Especially in Tijuana. Not that there's anything wrong with this South of the Border paradise...just saying that there might be a better place to get you some medical assistance.

Ask yourself this very important question as you make decisions about what to eat, what to drink, what to wear, where to go, and with whom: Is what I'm about to do or say loving and respectful to my body+mind+heart+soul? If you know that you'll feel drained, zapped, bloated, anything less than your sparkly self, don't go there or do that. From this day forward, everything you do should support your best you. Does that sugar-coated, raspberry jam-oozing doughnut make your heart soar? Is it fresh from the *patisserie* to be savored with some mint chamomile tea served in a porcelain cup? Or is something just there, two days old, and what with all the starving children in China, it would be criminally wasteful if not consumed, so you polish it off, making your waist full instead? There is nothing "best you" about stale pastry and the resulting puffiness. There are healthier ways to do charity work, my little apple fritter.

SHOW DAY SURVEY

Before you launch into full-blown red carpet debut blissfulness, there are a few rehab exit assessments to do. Hop on the scale, measure up, and record the numbers in your journal like you did during intake (you know the drill—pee-poop-weigh-measure). Keep in mind that it is never about losing weight. It is always about gaining health. Please don't get discouraged if you didn't lose as many pounds as you hoped to. Remember, a pound is pound is a pound. I know it doesn't sound like much, as we've been conditioned to want everything right away in a big way, but if you lose, for example, a pound a week (which is very easy to do with just one tweak, such as cutting out soda), in a year you'll have dropped fifty-two big ones! Chances are that you do not need to lose that much weight to be healthy, but I offer this example to highlight the magnitude of what seems to be hardly worthwhile.

Now that the stats are in, open your journal. How do you feel about those numbers? Make note of how you feel, period, starting when you woke up this morning. In charge of your well-being? Strong? A sense of accomplishment? In what ways is your body+mind+heart+soul lighter? Did you create space? How many drawers did you empty? How many boxes and bags did you bring to Goodwill? What one brave thing did you do during rehab? What did you like the most about detoxing? The least? What are you most proud of? What's still left to try? What is your bliss? Who is your best self? What does she wear, do, say?

Set your intentions for the day. Where are you going and how do you want to show up? For fun, prepare an "acceptance speech." List your unique and terrific traits and talents that make you different from anyone else. Whom must you thank? Take a few moments to reflect on your words. Let the reality of the results of your hard work register. Bask in your glory. Take a deep breath. Slowly stand up and take a bow and then haul ass to your Swag Lounge and snag your celebration "i rock" Rox Detox graduation treat. Congratulations, chickstar! You did it! As *mon ame sœur*, Edwige, would say, "Victory to you!"

GO GLAM + GET GLOW FOR YOUR SHOW

It's now time to get all sparkly for the red carpet. After taking a special soak or shower, sprinkle, brush, swipe, and spray shimmer and glimmer on your face, body, lips, lids, and even your lash tips and in your hair. It's *your* day to show your glow. And *every* day following today is another day to shine, even brighter than the day before. You deserve the super-*etoile* treatment always.

Slip on your debut outfit. Decorate yourself with lots of external bling if that's your thing. Put on the shoes you bought especially for your red carpet strut. With each and every step you take today, punctuate your commitment to a Concert Chick life on the red carpet. As my friend Evie would so beautifully say as only she can while flashing her best beauty-queen-pageant-winner smile and wave (you know the one, hand up, palm facing forward, waving right to left with a simple wrist twist, not up and down like a standard bye-bye wave), "Love you, love your hair, hope you win." And win you did. The grandest prize of all—your sparkly self, who has always been there, just a little dusty. Always remember that fairy dust easily cancels toxic rust.

Holy Manolo! You are absolutely stunning! Your inner and outer light is illuminated brilliantly. Don't forget to capture this glorious day with some photos to place in your journal, wallet, day planner—any conspicuous oft-seen place as a reminder of the power you have—to create a *wow* life for yourself without outside interference and static, simply by tuning into what your body+mind+heart+soul needs and desires.

There's still one more pre-party to-do. Let's wrap up the *Rock 'n' Roll Rehab* ritual you started on rehab eve. With cape/bracelets on or off and hot shoes/invincible attitude definitely on, write "i rock!" on the large rock you set aside just for today and gently roll it around a bit. Oh, yeah! You are one rockin' and rollin' Concert Chick but we knew that from the start, didn't we? Now get out there and claim your place on the red carpet!

THINGS TO DO TO CELEBRATE YOU
LAISSEZ LES BONS TEMPS ROULER!

Let the good times roll indeed! A Concert Chick has many people to see, things to do, and places to be, so it isn't always easy to focus. Just in case you've been distracted by detox bliss, I've created some "red carpet debut" celebration ideas to get you thinking about how you can celebrate yourself. Some are outrageously silly, crazy even, but that's what it's all about, *non?* Embrace your *joie de vivre* and let it guide you all the way, now and every day.

Be A Lush + Get Bombed

You could definitely say I'm a big LUSH—fan that is! In addition to spas, shoes, costume jewelry, travel, and blow-dries, I'm addicted to bombs and bars—as in LUSH bath bombs and bubble bars. I find "Aura Suavis," a swirly yellow and pink bar with clary sage and spearmint oils, especially intoxicating, and "Pleasure Dough," a rose, lavender, and peppermint crumble-into-the-tub treat, gives me quite a buzz. If I'm going for an all-out blitz, I soak in water infused with a LUSH bomb. My favorites are "Waving Not Drowning" (lavender) and "Honey Bee" (honey and mud). After you've selected your LUSH fix, gather a trashy novel, a bottle of champagne, an assortment of Vosges Chocolat ("Wink of Rabbit" caramels and Barcelona candy bars are delish), and a plastic/acrylic flute (Please, no glass near the tub! A glass bath is not cool—this I know firsthand—and I suspect it could really hurt—fortunately, this I do not know firsthand), and take all into your *salle de bain*. Drop a bomb or bar in the tub and fill your flute. Place your book, bubbles, and bites within reach. Step in and soak. Sip and flip pages and savor decadent *chocolats*. Repeat, often. A bath boy to pour your bubbles, to rest a cold compress across your forehead when it gets a tad steamy in there, and to hand you a red carpet bath towel is optional, but remember, it is your day…lush it up large. *A votre santé*!

Be a Roadie

Play tourist without leaving your own backyard. Rent a car (in red?) of your dreams (Bentley!) with a driver (multitalented bath boy perhaps?). Stretch your limits and go limo. Hop on and off public transportation throughout the day. Take a cab. Watch *Driving Miss Daisy*. Be Miss Daisy. Pick daisies. Stop by your local chamber of commerce or convention and visitors bureau and score a guidebook. Go out for breakfast at a greasy-spoon diner and map out your day. Visit tourist traps for food, drink, and shopping. Buy a souvenir. Take photos. See where you live through the eyes of wonder and wonder how come it took you so damn long to notice all the beauty in the town you live in. It's time to really live there! A camera around your neck and black socks and sandals are optional. Don't forget sunscreen (red carpet, not red skin). Be really wild and check into a motel. When was the last time you did that? Or, be the most wild of all and really hit the road. Be daringly spontaneous and buy an airplane ticket to anywhere. Wake up in another town. You get the drift! Concert Chicks do get around!

Pack It, Park It

Fill a picnic basket or cooler with sumptuous treats and refreshing beverages. Pack a tote with a red blanket, a good book and/or a good man, and head to your favorite park or, better yet, to one you've never been to before. Delight in kids' play. Watch them, be one. Swing, slide, climb. Take a nap on your red carpet blanket. Eat Chunky Monkey ice cream while relaxing on a park bench. Trade monkey mind for monkey bars. Climb a tree. Bring some Band-Aids in case you get a boo-boo, and don't forget a corkscrew if your refreshment comes in a corked bottle.

From "C" to Shining + Tasty "C"

Take the signature Concert Chick challenge! Everything you do, wear, eat, and drink must begin with a *c* as in *celebration.* Think champagne, cookies, candy, cosmos, cupcakes, caviar, chili, and crab cakes. Cheese and crackers and coffee cake. *Chocolat*! Wear sexy capris, a flowing caftan, sassy culottes, a sporty cardigan, and/or a superhero cape. Create! Color with crayons. Color your hair. Cut and paste images—collage! Cut your hair. Play with clay. Curl your hair. Cozy up in a red comforter and watch cartoons and comedies. Be carefree, chuckle lots. Be courteous. Curtsy. Make it a cool chic chick celebration day!

Biker Chic Chick

Ride a bike with a motor or without. Rent a Harley. Borrow a bright red beach cruiser (extra chickie if it has a wicker basket on the front to hold biker bites and bevs, streamers dangling from the handlebars score extra points). Wear a temporary tattoo—or go for the real thing! (My butterfly memento from Vegas is really cute and didn't hurt at all—after a glass of pinot noir). Leather, boots, jackets, pants. Wear red socks with those hot boots. Helmet up! Do Billy Idol proud and give a rebel yell. Go to a biker bar (be careful—be ready to yell again). Ride on, babe!

Create Some *Ooh La La*

Are you like *moi*, a right-brain chick dreaming of Left Bank bistros? This solo gala is for you! Create savory moments through culinary experiences and collage. Pretend you're in Provence. Wear a bejeweled beret. Sip Ruinart or Sancerre. Splurge on *chocolat noir, croissants aux amandé, macarons aux pistaché*, fresh baguettes and herb-encrusted brie. Gather all your supplies—scissors, glue, glitter, magazine images and words, red paper, sparkly bits and pieces, old and new photos, a rainbow of pens and markers, and anything else from the arts and crafts store that invites your inner *artiste* to come out and play. Art journal your rehab experience and your debut—using the red carpet paper, of course. Assemble a new vision board. Whatever you do, get lost in it. Paint the town red before you go to bed. *Bonsoir, gros bisous et doux rêves.*

Chic Chickulture

Appreciate and be inspired by other creative souls' works. Visit a museum, an art gallery, a photographic exhibition, an art show, a sculpture garden, or an antique fair. Attend a book signing, a lecture, a class. Watch a film, a ballet. Listen to a symphony, an opera, a concert. Many cultural centers offer tea, lunch, and chicktails. Browse venue gift shops. Wear a ladies-who-lunch hat. Noses and pinkies up, darling crumpet!

Be a Bird Brain

Every smart chick knows she needs a total brain-dead day full of blond moments,[32] one where we walk around shrugging our shoulders and saying "I dunno" and "duh" a lot. Be silly. Be cuckoo for Cocoa Puffs, right from the box. Go quackers, right off your rocker. Just roll with it. Read Dr. Seuss books to your dogs.

> *I like nonsense, it wakes up the brain cells. Fantasy is a necessary ingredient in living.*
> ~Dr. Seuss

Tell lame jokes. Laugh out loud. Cluck like a chicken. Talk in Pig Latin. Watch *Sesame Street* Big Bird reruns or Alfred Hitchcock's *The Birds*. Eat candy all day. Drink soda pop (with or without the Captain, as in Morgan, as in Spiced Rum). Wear jammies all day. Carry around a lucky red blankie. Bird watch. Summon the bluebird of happiness. Share bread with the birds in a park. Soar!

Pitch A Tent, Not A Fit

Convert your backyard into Camp Concert Chick. Invite your peeps to pitch tents. Roll out sleeping bags (preferably red), spray on skeeter repellant, gather 'round a campfire, roast marshmallows and weenies, make s'mores, drink Stellas, tell scary ghost stories, have a séance, write a book or read a book by lantern light or moonlight. Star count and gaze. Wish upon a star. Count your blessings. Concert Chicks are happy campers!

Mermaid Madness

This one is for you beach babes out there—a mermaid chick-of-the-sea soirée. Don a curly, super-long wig to wear all day if you don't already rock mermaid locks. Adorn yourself with seashell jewelry and a daring bathing suit (topless or not, depending on where you are) and a sarong (optional). Perhaps one of those clamshell bikini

---

32 Wear a blond wig if you're not already there, or follow me to the salon.

tops if you must wear something up there? Build a sandcastle, go for a refreshing ocean swim, hunt treasure, frolic with dolphins, nap on a red carpet beach towel, walk along the shoreline, look for starfish, collect shells, flip your tail. Experiment with seaweed and sea salt-based body and face treatments, scrubs, suds, masques. Whet your appetite and wet your whistle with mango margaritas and assorted munchies. Grouper cheeks and clam chowder, washed down with Clamato Bloody Marys anyone?

No matter how you celebrate you, be true to you!

SPARKLES FOR BUBBLY YOU!

Voila! Finally, the bubbles I offered during our meet and greet. (Since you had to wait so long, it's only right for me to present to you the entire bottle!) With champagne flute in hand and raised, I offer this toast in your honor:

May champagne corks always pop,
May there always be a tiara atop,
May you always find the perfect shoe,
And, most important of all,
May you always be true to you!

Sparkle on, Concert Chick! The red carpet beckons.

Now what? Bask in the bliss, beauty, and bounty of your red carpet debut and then join me at the after-party.

Chapter 10

After-Party Afterthoughts

When a butterfly has emerged, it can never turn back into a caterpillar.
~Colin Wilson

You did it! You've been through rehab and your red carpet performance on debut day was Academy Award material. Your mission now is to keep your Betsey Johnson peep-toe boots firmly planted on that magic red carpet.

The typical after-party follows the show, but since your debut appearance was *the* party, the Rox Detox after-*fête* is a bit different, just like much in this book has been (consistency is a good thing). The party we're hosting here takes place when you return to soulitude to regroup, reflect, and recharge your sparkle.

Your motivation and confidence are at an all-time high. You've proven to yourself that you can take control of the things you *can* control—who you spend your free time with, what stuff surrounds you, what you put in your mouth, what comes out of your mouth, and much more. You've detoxed, purged, scrubbed, scoured, waxed, plucked, sucked, dumped, and hopefully chucked all the stuff that weighed you down and dimmed your light.

You created space for miracles to happen. The past two weeks have been an introduction to a lifestyle that you can sustain for the rest of your life. What are your takeaways? Have a little chat with yourself to find out.

POST DEBUT INTERVIEW OF YOU BY YOU

As you open a new chapter in your life today, break in a new you journal with a little post-debut Q&A:

- How do you feel right now?
- How do you feel compared to this time yesterday?
- Was your debut everything you hoped it would be? More? Less?
- Did you overdo it?
- What would you have done differently?
- What changes do you still want to make?
- How do you want to show up on the red carpet of life every day?
- What are you willing to do to make it happen?

Are you beating yourself up for something you did or didn't do? Clobbering yourself for over gobbling? Thinking there was too much drinking? Second-guessing aspects of your debut? STOP THAT! No matter what's next, you must drop perfectionism as you move forward if you want a lifetime of happy living. Choose reflection and intention instead.

> *Usefulness is not impaired by imperfection; you can drink from a chipped cup.*
> ~Greta K. Nagel

Good intentions, like good eggs, soon spoil unless they've hatched. Keep cracking! It's all about the big picture and making adjustments as needed with the gift of a new day. Consciousness is the key to ongoing Concert Chick success.

WHAT'S NEXT?

You may very well decide to adopt the Concert Chick way of life because you feel the best you have ever felt—you have more energy, your skin is glowing, your eyes sparkling. You are surrounded by supportive, like-minded souls. You're not only nontoxic, you're nonreactive to others' toxicity. You know who you are and where you want to go. And your new shoes (a third pair perhaps—life's that good!) will take you down that path. Life is an exciting odyssey!

On the other hand, you may decide to never, ever drink water again without Kool-Aid crystals or a splash of vodka with a twist of lime. You can insist that desserts-only give you all the energy you need to conquer the world, or that playing around the detox way does not make you feel better at all. Or perhaps you'd rather hang out with vampires because the view from upside down is interesting and batty is OK. Maybe you delight in overstuffed closets and need a protective coat wrapped around your heart for the time being. Tis the beauty of free will. You can do whatever you want to do. And that includes sabotaging your health with toxic people, places, beliefs, behaviors, and things. It's your call who gets behind your red velvet rope, after all.

But seriously, I know it's easier said than done. It took me over a decade to sever a relationship that was toxic and I'm still working on some that have run their course, so I get it. Go with the flow with awareness and consciousness and everything will fall into place, as it should, and as it will. The biggest and greatest gift we possess is the gift of choice. Choose well. Embrace everything and everyone that brings you peace, harmony, happiness, and health, with the occasional Milly something-something thrown in for good treasure.

And please, don't be hard on yourself. Do you want to fit into those awesome, sexy size 6 low-slung slacks? Well, that Krispy Kreme glazed you're thinking about shoving down your throat ain't gonna get you in them. What means more to you? What will make you feel better? Maybe a juicy peach while you wear your True Religions? And if you do choose that doughnut, it's OK. Wipe the powdered sugar from your lips and say "wow, that was delish!" followed by a lip gloss reapplication, and then move on. Dismiss any notion that you've screwed up and thus deserve self-inflicted punishment by eating the entire baker's dozen. The naturally sweet life you desire is being served now.

KEEPING THE LIGHT SWITCH ON

While this book has given you one helluva start, I know there's much more out there for you to explore. Rehab injected some strong doses of self-care, so now you know what resonates with you. Your Rox Detox experience wasn't intended to be another quick fix. It's time to take your life to the next level. There are hundreds of resources on health, relationships, career planning, closet organizing, and other lifestyle topics. Hang out in the Swag Lounge for a while and poke around for anything and everything that resonates with you. But always know that you are ultimately the best expert in, for, and of you.

Continue the harmonious relationship you have with your body+mind+heart+soul. Faithfully check in and see how you feel, what you need, what you want. Treat yourself with great love and deep respect. Check into rehab at least a couple of times a year. Spring and autumn are the best seasons for body+mind+heart+soul detoxing and purging on all levels. You will learn something new each time. Guaranteed. You are a work in progress and process that by design will take a lifetime to complete.

Loyally tune in to sense if someone or something is enhancing or draining your energy, dimming or brightening your light. I know these questions have been repeated often throughout the pages of this book, but the intention is to keep practicing until they pop up automatically as you gracefully flow through your day, your life. Checking in with your best self will soon be second nature, similar in magnitude to your uncanny ability to spot a shoe sale two states away.

Here are some questions to keep in mind as you continue your red carpet sashay and play through life:

- Will what I am about to eat, drink, or do keep me stuck in muumuus or twirling in tutus?
- Will the choice I make bring me long-term fulfillment or short-term gratification?
- Am I doing something for myself or because someone else wants me to?
- Will my choice add zip to my life force or zap my energy?
- Will this choice empower or disempower me?
- Am I coming from my higher self or ego?
- Does it enhance or dim my light?
- Does it weigh me down or beam me up?
- Is this an act of self-love and respect or hate and neglect?
- Am I being authentic or am I trying to win someone's approval?
- If what I am about to do or say makes the evening news or the morning's headline, will I be proud or red-faced?
- Is what I am about to say kind, true, necessary or is it nasty gossip?

It's very important to keep in mind that the food and thoughts you feed your body+mind+heart+soul will become you. Your body is constantly replacing cells, and what you allow to enter your temple is transformed into those cells. Is your soul's home a junkyard? A toxic wasteland? A nuclear reactor plant? Being aware of this as you chow down on that Quarter-Pounder with cheese or freak out after seeing psycho chick playing with her voodoo dolls again may cause you to pause, take a deep breath, and make a healthier choice next time.

Whenever you're tempted to toss aside your tiara for a Twinkie, remember that you are a star and can find life's sweetness outside a little *crème*-filled cake thingie. But sometimes only a Twinkie will do, so savor it, sweetheart. The only requirement besides taking off the plastic wrapper is to wear your twinkly tiara while Twinkie-ing. Always show up authentic, expressing your desires and doing what you want to do that's true to you without guilt or shame.

It's OK to stand tall, tiara on top, Twinkie in hand (both hands if that's what your body+mind+heart+soul desires), not worrying about what others think. The treats of life come in many shapes and forms, some more sparkly than others, so if your goal is to glow gloriously, which I hope it is, make sure you go for the inner twinkle more than you reach for the outer Twinkie.

Incorporate all you've learned in rehab into your daily life. Imagine that you are always on the red carpet. Stay aware and be conscious. Let the Concert Chick Credo found in Chapter 11 be your guiding light.

WRITE YOUR OWN SCRIPT + SONG

Let's have a little fun organizing what's left to be done, shall we? You are a work in progress, a masterpiece undergoing constant refinement, your essence being fine-tuned everyday until your last day if you are truly living and not merely existing. Just like the seasons of the year, you follow the natural order of things—growing, opening, expanding, contracting, releasing, shedding, hibernating, emerging over and over and over again.

Open your journal and write these headings at the top of separate blank pages: F@$k it!, Dream it! Do it! Be it! See it! Create it! A super-charged, fine-tuned bucket list of sorts. Scribble sky's the limit entries under each. Write down whatever comes to mind no matter how impossible you may think something is. If there's a time to be untethered and undeterred, it's now. Remember, your words are prayers to the universe. Your unseen yet definitely there support system will conspire and co-create with you. There's no better collaborator than the whole freakin' universe. Where do you think the expression "the sky is the limit" comes from? *They* know.

A comprehensive review of your entire journal will help you zero in on what's important to you. Look for themes that pop up more than once. What did you write about most? Who occupied some serious space on your pages? Who, what, where, when do you still need to address, visit, release, embrace?

You are embarking on the next leg of your journey. You are penning your own script, the lyrics to your own song. Use your lists as your map that will lead you to your destination. Just know that paths may change. Go with the flow. Have a plan, but be flexible. Just when you think a sundress is enough, it snows out of the blue. Such is life—a magnificent, ever-changing adventure.

Keep in mind as you soar forward that how you feel and yes, even how you look (because your outers are a reflection of your inners) is more important than anything else in the world. If you find your house on fire and grab a giant bag of peanut M&Ms to douse your inner turmoil, it won't work. Your house will burn down just the same. So dial 911, pull out a fire extinguisher, and take care of the matter at hand. Adding poundage to your frame won't save your house or your ass; nor will screaming at the top of your soon-to-be-smoke-filled lungs and scurrying around tossing cups of water into the flames do you or your soul's home any good. Breathe in calm and give the M&Ms to the cute firefighters after they put away their hoses. Your body is the temple for your soul and all the other miraculous bits and parts that make you *you* and keep you ticking, twinkling, sparkling, and *oui*, even shoe shopping! Do not destroy the home you live in every day.

Your Rox Detox debut celebration of you wasn't a one-time gig. You are booked for life now. Every day you make a grand entrance, because with every sunrise, a new you emerges. You must incorporate more "yay for me!" days. Start with each season, then once a month. Be daring and go for every other week. Be really bold and pen in weeklies, or be Concert Chick crazy outrageous and celebrate your life every day, always. By carrying on the daily practices you learned and experienced in rehab, you'll maintain body+mind+heart+soul harmony, which is cause for celebration, every day, forever.

Your life is your show. The world is your stage. How will you show up? What kind of act will you put on? How will you perform? The credo in Chapter 11 can help you decide.

Let's pass through the gateway for some parting wisdom, shall we?

Chapter 11

Your All-Access Vip Pass To Magic Red Carpet Rides For Life

Live your life as an exclamation, not an explanation!
~Rox, the original Concert Chick

Congratulations on successfully completing the *Rock the World Rehab* adventure. You've purged and surged through the Rox Detox, celebrated yourself on the red carpet, and had a contemplative after-party of one where you pondered your next move. But there's still some unfinished business. In order to graduate from rehab, you must commit to certain addictions. You read right. You must leave detox a full-blown addict.

BE A SPARKLE JUNKIE

Recall how we forced you to adopt something before you could leave the VIP area? Well, it's something like that. You'll be a rehab success story only if you leave hooked on being yourself, doing what's right, and following your bliss. We're talking daily overdoses of awareness, consciousness, grace, presence, bling, play, attitude, gratitude, abundance, kindness, brilliance, and smiles. In essence, you must be a sparkle junkie before you officially check out of rehab and into your spectacular life.

It's time to bring it all full circle during these last moments together. The Rox Detox introduced you to specific disciplines, actions (nonreactions!), and behaviors to create space and lightness in your body+mind+heart+soul. Your mission, if you choose to accept it—great! I knew you would!—is to continue walking the red carpet while strewing gobs of glitter along the way for others to enjoy. Consider this chapter your glitter bag, filled with small flashes of brilliant light to gather and sprinkle on every person, place, and thing you encounter. To litter with glitter is not against any law,[33] especially of the karmic kind.

You do this through the Concert Chick Credo[34]. Each of the eleven rays of light that form the Credo bring you right back from where you began in Chapter 2. The Credo is more of a stream of consciousness than anything else because each of us is a unique being who approaches life in a different way. I've woven words that you've seen in other chapters throughout the Credo musings after every dose. Take from it what you will. Pick up your prescription below. The eleven powerful doses will last a lifetime if administered daily. They were created to spark your imagination and to further your intentions and commitments to the Concert Chick way of living.

Allow your body+mind+heart+soul to be your interpretation team. Keep your journal nearby as you read the words so you can jot down those that speak to you, those that leave you scratching your head, those you think are downright trite or poppycock, and so on. Everything that stirs something inside of you is worth exploring. You'll

---

[33] This is an unverified statement. I suspect it's a felony somewhere in the world because God only knows there are crazy ass laws on the books, so please do check before strewing because there will be no suing. In the meantime, don't be jittery...get glittery! And if you do get caught, beg for forgiveness. It's often easier than asking for permission. Go, glitter girl, go!

[34] Shameless plug *deux*. This credo sprays out of a champagne bottle on Concert Chick's inaugural "Celebrate Yourself" tee that can be found in the boutique at www.concertchick.com Rox thinks the tee rocks and would command you to order one ASAP, but Concert Chicks aren't pushy.

see that there is some overlap. That's because of the deep connection between your body+mind+heart+soul that cannot be severed. Ever.

CONCERT CHICK CREDO

1. *let music inspire, motivate, move you. go with the flow. dream. believe. receive. lighten up. live your light.*

   You're the conductor of your life. Collaborate with the universe to make sweet music. It's your symphony. How do you want it orchestrated? What instrument do you play? Who's playing by your side, on your side, with you, against you? Do you pull on heartstrings? Do you nourish and nurture the most exquisite instruments on this planet: your body+mind+heart+soul? Embrace all channels on your station. Tune into the continuous stream of your body+mind+heart+soul. Keep your antenna up. Receive and emit good vibrations. Live in harmony with the rhythm of your body+mind+heart+soul. Follow your bliss. What's on your playlist? Diversify it. Dream list? The sky is the limit. Bucket list? Anything is possible. F@$k it! list? Let go, without guilt.

2. *perform with grace + gratitude. abundance. blessings. you have enough, right now. say "please" + "thank you". buy yourself flowers. wear a tiara. bravo!*

   Acknowledge and share your unique gifts. Be grateful from the moment you wake up, even before you open your eyes, until the fullness of the day reunites your eyelids. Curiously look through the windows of your soul and really see, as if for the first time, with the innocence of a child. Know that there is enough to go around. If you dream of releasing the artist that resides in you yet think that no one will buy your creations because there are so many other artists out there that you think are better than you and every other flippin' limited thought you can muster, you need to pluck that silly notion from your head pronto! There is an audience for what you were born to do. You must share your talents. Accept bouquets graciously. If you have a passion for something, the universe always provides a fan club. The tiara on your head is an antenna that picks up vibes and signals constantly. Pay attention. The universe can't resist a passionate soul with an earth halo. When you ask, say "please," and that will please the universe so much that it will deliver abundantly. Don't forget to say "thank you" upon receipt.

3. *be an original you, not a cheep imitation of some other chick. you are enough, as you are, at this moment. rock + roll the world with your upbeat energy + good vibrations.*

Don't be a copycat. Chicks and cats don't mix well. There's a natural order to things and you play a divine part. Develop your own signature style. What is your brand? Brush on that sky blue nail polish and position that zebra print cowgirl hat on your gorgeous head. Energize through what you wear, say, do, how you show up. Don't try to prove anything to anyone except yourself, and be compassionate and imperfect while doing so. You are perfectly divine by design at this very moment.

4. *i rock. you rock. we all rock. rock on. be you. let others be. embrace differences. stay connected. make sweet music. text, hugs + rock 'n' roll.*

Accept everyone as he or she is, starting with yourself. Cultivate connections with like-minded souls and stay connected. It's also OK to disconnect; in fact, it's essential. Be generous with hugs and smiles. Support others' dreams. Tweet and text "thinking about you" messages, e-mail "have an awesome day," dial up an "I love you" just because. Share photos, journeys, your life with family and friends, old and new. Pray for everyone known and unknown. Call that 800 number on the back of the truck in front of you and report how wonderfully the driver is handling his vehicle. Send congratulations, happy birthdays, hope you feel betters, thank yous, and woohoo for yous. Expand your horizons. Get out of your comfort zone and your time zone. Embrace other cultures. Be a citizen of the globe.

5. *march to your own drummer. enjoy life one step at a time. do what's right. wear fabulous shoes. leave your mark. get your groove on. be groovy.*

Walk fast, walk slow, haul ass! Cruise at a pace that feels right for you, but stay mindfully in each step. Carry yourself on your journey in the manner that will get you where you want to go. Get lost in the space you created in rehab. Go with the flow. Tittup, sashay, get out of your way. Don't run others over. Stand tall. Don't fear heights. How do you want to be remembered? What will your legacy be?

6. *sing your own song. speak up! shut up! be heard. listen. giggle. don't chirp about others. no cuckoo chick stuff. brush, floss + apply sparkly lip gloss after meals.*

Even if you can't carry a tune, open your beak. Speak your truth, in your own voice. Know when to keep your beak shut. Treat words like rare gems to be shared carefully to enhance, not to be a smarty-pants. Say more with less. Tweet! Lighten up. Laugh at yourself and with others. Clean out your ears. Listen. Dangle sparkly chandelier earrings from your lobes not only because they look stunning, but because they remind you with every jingle to not only listen but to hear. Give others the floor. Flash a brilliant smile, framed in glitter.

7. *honor + respect yourself + all peeps. ignore the cluckers. what goes around, comes around. mean what you say, say what you mean. never, ever be mean. be nice. play nice with others.*

Treasure and nourish your body+mind+heart+soul. When you do, you are treasuring and nourishing others. You're setting an example, inspiring and motivating other peeps to take care of themselves. This is what you are here to do. With give and take in balance, with an even flow and exchange of energy, problems will be resolved. "Nice" isn't a nasty four-letter word. It is…well…er… duh…*nice*. It's not a sign of weakness. It shows tremendous strength. Be strong all day long to do what's right, not to be right. Be nonreactive. Keep promises.

8. *dance to your own music. keep moving, evolving, growing. slow but sure. shake your tail feathers, often. wear glittery, snazzy, jazzy dancin' shoes, during the day.*

Do all this without one shred of concern about what anyone may think. Give yourself permission and approval to be who you are. Ignore the rules that society makes about how you should show up. Keep moving forward and spiraling upward, bravely climbing one step at a time, taking care not to catch your stiletto in any ingrate of the day. Boas are badass. Silver-sequined boots are kickass. Work it, shake it, all day long, to your song.

9. *let your heart sing. spread your wings + soar. follow your bliss. be blissful.*

What song is your heart singing? The Concert Chick's version of Helen Reddy's "I Am Woman, Hear Me Roar" is "I Am a Concert Chick, See Me Soar!" ("I Am!" for short). *Sing it out loud.* Keep your ♥ harmonized with your body, mind, and soul. This ensures fuel for takeoffs, smooth flights, and safe landings even during turbulent times. Bliss juice indeed! It's quite all right, necessary even, to rest your wings every day. Counter wing zaps with regular naps. Concert Chicks are followers only when bliss is involved. Lead with your heart and wings. Kiss your bliss often.

10. *the world is your stage. stand tall with confidence, front + center. sparkle! twinkle, twinkle you're a star. share your brilliance. wear a feather boa. no fears. no worries. take a bow.*

Hang a disco ball in your office. Dance the happy dance in your party pants or pinstripe suit—you're the same person inside the different wrappings. Hang a feather boa where all can see. Wrap it around you before you enter a serious meeting. Did I already mention that boas are badass? Oh yes, I did and, oh yes, they are. Wear sparkles during the day so the sunlight can dance on and off the little crystals. Perform under the moonlight. Count all the stars in the sky. Keep that twinkle in your eye, and a tiara and a tutu nearby.

11. *live your life as an exclamation!, not an explanation. less whine. more wine. everything in moderation, except for shoes. celebrate your bubbly, sparkly self. light up (the world) + get high(on life). cheers to you!*

No explanation required. It's easily summed up in three words:

joie de

vivre

Oui, the joy of living. What more is there?

The Swag Lounge contains a copy of the Concert Chick Credo to print, carry, and refer to often. Consider it your diploma, your all-access VIP pass. Please share the Credo with other chicks. That's what Concert Chicks do: they shine their light brightly on others to help guide them to their best self, too.

It's time to get high on life and keep your body + mind + heart + soul lit, as in up—brightly— shining your magnificent light wherever you are. As a sparkle junkie and Rox Detox alum, you must commit to never ever fearfully drink the Kool-aid to the point of numbness. Instead, you must fiercely slurp up sparkles to the point of joyous intoxication. Be a glitter glutton and gobble up as much of the sparkly stuff as you can, with grace. Do not be a quitter—share the glitter! The Concert Chicks of the world must fearlessly, radiantly, and brilliantly unite! Let the Concert Chick revolution begin!

As they say, we write the book we need to read, and this surely has been just that for me. I am forever grateful and blessed to be able to share my journey with you, and doubly thankful from the bottom of my heart that you allowed me to join you on your journey. The world can and *will* shift and expand brilliantly one sparkly Concert Chick at a time.

I wish you all the best as you sing your own song, dance to your own music, and march to your own drummer as you be yourself, do what's right, and follow your bliss. You truly do rock!

Bonne chance, you magnificent, sparkly Concert Chick!

VIP (Very Important Peep) Swag Lounge

Welcome to your very own VIP Swag Lounge! This area is stocked with loads of information and treats to encourage, inspire, and support you. As you step into this special place, you will discover all the resources you need for a successful rehab and life experience. The first section contains the documents referenced in the various chapters, including your commitment agreement and daily prescriptions. As you continue to browse through the lounge, you'll see that each chapter has its own swag (books, Web sites, products, tunes, and more!) related to that chapter's subject. Happy swag strolling and shopping!

THE FINE + OH-SO-FINE PRINT
THE "ROCK THE WORLD REHAB" COMMITMENT

I, _____, will check into rehab for two weeks starting on the _____ day of _____, 20__ for a complete body+mind+soul+heart detox adventure.

Upon completion of rehab, I, with a sparkly and light body+mind+heart+soul, will walk that red carpet on my debut day, confidently, while wearing the most amazing shoes that have ever touched my feet (you go girl!).

My rehab commitments are as follows:

I promise to focus on me me me *moi* and only *moi* without guilt.
I promise to clean out (or at least take a peek at) my closets, drawers, files, friendships, car, refrigerator, cabinets, nooks and crannies, and every other space that may contain people, places and things that dim my light.
I promise to buy two pairs of fabulous shoes, with the highest heels I can manage without teetering and toppling.
I promise to visit the Swag Lounge every day to claim my reward for a gig well done.
I promise to say, "yes, *merci*" to me by saying "no, thanks" to people, places, and things demanding my attention and/or dimming my light while I'm detoxing and for the rest of my life.
I promise to memorize and live the Concert Chick Credo.
I promise to fill the daily prescriptions (or at least read every word contained therein).
I promise to forgive myself if I don't do everything as prescribed, because, most of all, I promise to be myself, follow my bliss, and do what's right.
Amen + pinkie swear with glitter on top,

_____
Red Carpet Celebrity Autograph (that be you!)
Date:_____

CONCERT CHICK CREDO

let music inspire, motivate, move you. go with the flow. dream. believe. receive. lighten up. live your light. **perform with grace + gratitude. abundance. blessings. you have enough, right now.** say "please" + "thank you". buy yourself flowers. wear a tiara. bravo! be an original you, not a cheep imitation of some other chick. you are enough, as you are, at this moment. rock + roll the world with your upbeat energy + good vibrations. i rock. you rock. we all rock. rock on. be you. let others be. embrace differences. stay connected. make sweet music. text, hugs, + rock 'n' roll. march to your own drummer. enjoy life one step at a time. do what's right. wear fabulous shoes. leave your mark. get your groove on. be groovy. sing your own song. speak up! shut up! be heard. listen. giggle. don't chirp about others. no cuckoo chick stuff. brush, floss + apply sparkly lip gloss after meals. honor + respect yourself + all peeps. ignore the cluckers. what goes around, comes around. mean what you say, say what you mean. never, ever be mean. be nice. play nice with others. **dance to your own music. keep moving, evolving, growing.** slow but sure. shake your tail feathers, often. wear glittery, snazzy, jazzy dancin' shoes, during the day. let your heart sing. spread your wings + soar. follow your bliss. **be blissful. the world is your stage. stand tall with confidence, front + center. sparkle!** twinkle, twinkle you're a star. share your brilliance. wear a feather boa. no fears. no worries. take a bow. live your life as an exclamation!, not an explanation. less whine. more wine. everything in moderation, except for shoes. celebrate your bubbly, sparkly self. light up (the world) and get high (on life). cheers to you!

YOUR DAILY PRESCRIPTIONS, A.K.A. YOUR DAILY SCRIPTS

This area of the Swag Lounge is where you pick up your daily scripts to support you through all four steps—instructions, directions, suggestions, genuflections (us to you), gyrations, salutations, elations, congratulations, and celebrations all on one handy dandy form per day. The scripts can be copied if you don't want to mark up your book, or go ahead and scribble all over the pages. It's your book to with as you please. Just make sure you color outside the lines!

Before we review your scripts, heads up that you've been prescribed the heavy-duty, extra-strength dose because we know you can handle it. If administered regularly, you could find yourself highly and smiley addicted to taking care of yourself. This is a very good life-altering, mood-enhancing thing.

Every day holds the promise of something new and exciting, and it's no different just because you're in rehab. While you have free will to pick and choose what you want to do—for you are the one who knows best what you need most—there are some highly recommended "dailies" that are noted on your scripts for step three detoxification. Each is described below, so when you see the reference on your script, you'll know the drill. Tiny square boxes are placed next to some activities, mostly on prep day pages, and near water consumption on detox days. These are spaces for checkmarks as you complete each activity. To-dos without a box can simply be crossed off. With each tick and swipe of a pen, you create a visual record of your progress that builds momentum throughout the day. You'll also find references to pertinent chapters in case you need a refresher. One last general note—the only segment of day specific activities are pills, eats, and drinks. Everything else can be done whenever you are so moved to do so. Rehab is your special time as defined by you.

ROCK! ROLL! ROCK+ROLL!: The upper left-hand corner of your script holds one of these exclamations that you may have embraced during the rehab eve ritual. The first week focus is on "rock", reminding you to stay grounded, stand strong and tall, be centered, firm in your beliefs, and solid in your commitment to becoming the best you ever. ROCK! prompts this focus, either through pulling one of the rocks from your basket or simply setting the intention to do all the rock represents. The second week is all about the roll—from your solid center, you go with the flow of whatever, whomever life puts on your path. Keep this in mind when you see ROLL! and/or grab a ball from your basket. Finally, you reach ROCK+ROLL! on your red carpet, debut day—you have it all going on, sister!

Pills To Pop: You'll start drinking and popping pills as soon as you wake up, and you'll wrap up your day with a final swig and fabulous swag (see "drinks to down" below). Obviously, this is unlike no other rehab program! Here's your daily pill-pop script:

>200 mg milk thistle 3x day
>200 mcg of chromium
>500–700 mg of magnesium, one dose late morning, another in the afternoon
>one multivitamin[35]

Drinks To Down : As mentioned above, you'll be drinking in rehab. Here's what to fill your glass with (and remember, energetically it's always half full):

Morning: You'll start every day with a cup of deep-cleansing Concert Chick "lemonaid." Squeeze the juice from a thick slice of lemon into a mug. Drop the slice in so that it rests flat on the bottom (keeps things juicy). Top with hot water (tea temperature),

---

[35] I recommend Flintstones Complete. I have been chewing these tablets daily for over a year thanks to the suggestion of the amazing NYC dermatologist Dr. Amy Weschler, author of *The Mind-Beauty Connection: 9 Days to Reverse Stress Aging and Reveal More Youthful, Beautiful Skin*. Merci, Amy! I also recommend reading her book and consulting with this gorgeous, smart, stylish derm the next time you're in the Big Apple.

and allow to cool a bit before sipping. Lemon promotes intestinal contractions that speed the elimination of waste excreted by your liver, making it an excellent liver toner. This helps with regulation, and who doesn't want that? For the record, this is the only kind of regulation a Concert Chick wants.

Time in between: Stay juiced up during the day by adding lemon to your beverages. Not only does it continue the waste removal kick-started by the lemonaid, it's refreshing and acts as a natural diuretic, which helps eliminate that awful bloated feeling. Lemon removes, soothes, and invigorates at the same time. *Ooh la la* lemon!

Evening: You'll end your day with a cup of "special" tea, a.k.a. "poop" tea. Yogi "Get Regular" and Traditional Medicinals "Organic Smooth Move" are my favorites. The Rox Detox menu will keep things moving, but if you didn't consume much fiber and fresh food prior to rehab you may find yourself a tad clogged, if you know what I mean. If you prefer pills, Perdiem is a natural vegetable laxative. Pop one to two a night and *voila*! Poop! It just ain't a detox if a major clean-out *there* isn't happening. Cheers!

Get Happy Hour: While we're on the subject of drinking, you'll be thrilled to know that happy hour is mandatory in rehab. Visions of smooth martinis and salty nuts most likely come to mind when you think "happy hour" (yay!—booze and bar snacks!). But in rehab, alcohol is taboo with the exception of a teensy bit on your grape days. The purpose of rehab happy hour is to…well…be happy. Profound, *non*? The Rox Detox happy hour commands you to do things that make you smile. And if only a real happy hour as you know it makes you light up, keep your debut day in mind, the day you can drink yourself silly if that's what you really want to do (which I doubt). All sorts of "get happy" ideas can be found in the Chapter 3 "how to avoid a relapse" section and in Chapter 6 if more private "happy" is desired.

Bon appétit!: This is your daily detox menu box, along with a reference to supping + sipping tips to check out in case you want to check out of rehab.

Play: No need to figure out how you're going to move it, move it to lose it, lose it. All you have to do is show up with that attitude we chatted about in Chapter 5 and we'll tell you what the game plan is.

Daily Dump: This box is a reminder to purge so you can surge. We're not talking tossing your cookies in a barf bag, though too much stuff can make you sick. Your daily purge can be as simple as emptying out a junk drawer to completely overhauling your closet. That kind of tossing—the space maker, not the face puker.

Ask yourself what you need to weed (retire) and what you want to seed (desire). Don't forget your kitchen. How many mushroom slicers do you really need? And sorry, that isn't vintage. It's a mug with a broken handle. Wrap your hand around it one last time and then deep six it! Drop at least two items a day in any bag or box, so by the end of rehab, you'll have released (purge!) no less than twenty-eight things that have weighed you down and kept you from soaring (surge!). Getting rid of things gives your life wings!

There's much you can do with the stuff that is no longer true to you, including donating to very worthy causes. The Chapter 3 area of the Swag Lounge contains the scoop. Your clutter may very well be someone else's bread and butter.

And remember, the Rox Detox is about more than your physical stuff. While it's easier to dump that very expired bottle of Advil than that very wired boyfriend of yours, your daily purge could be a decision to not see the boy tonight or at least not jump to respond to his text message. Teeny baby steps such as tossing a toothbrush or taking a Twitter timeout adds up.

Mope + Dope Alert!: This nice box comes to the rescue if you encounter the not-so-nice person. Simply and calmly open your Chapter 8 "tool" box to cope with that mope or dope.

Thank Bank: This is the place where you deposit three "thanks" a day—for the flowers in your garden, the challenges of your job, a particular friend, even that jerk of a co-worker who frays your nerves (because he or she is your best teacher), the food on your plate, the water in your tub, the gas in your car, the sun on your face, the pair of stunning shoes you found at a ridiculously low price, and the outrageously sparkly chicktail ring to add to your collection. Every. Single. Person. Place. Thing. Shoe. Ring. Even though you're only recording three, don't stop counting. Express your gratitude out loud, too, as you go about your day.

Bling: This sparkly box reminds you to pay attention to your body+mind+heart+soul, and not just one part of you, but all four essences that make you *you*. Tending to your inner and outer bling is a surefire way to do just that. The words "tiara on" is there to remind you to don your ultimate headdress every day, physically or virtually. It's mandatory—we are not joking when it comes to this bling! So, tiara on it is! *Always.*

Rox "Rah-Rah + Hurrah" Box: "Woohoo for you!" treats and tips from the original Concert Chick.

Swag: You know what it is and what to do—just don't forget to snag it!

Your Little Corner of the World: A huge part of rehab is creating space, which we have done just for you on your script. You'll find two empty boxes where you can doodle swirls and whirls or the mope's mug, affix images, pen dreams or the next big idea, sprinkle with sparkles, dust with glitter, scribble a fave quote, make notes to self (to-dos/not-to-dos), jot down lessons learned and aha! moments, and otherwise claim it as yours. You could also leave the area blank to remind you to create space in your life for the light to shine through.

Rock the World Rehab Daily Script

℞ Step 1: Intervention: You do need this!

Date:_____

Bonjour!

Review + do Chapter 3, Step 1 activities:

Admit it! ☐
Intake Assessment ☐
Calendar stint in rehab ☐
Book your date to celebrate ☐
Plan your "Red Carpet Debut" day ☐
Make reservations and appointments as necessary ☐
Autograph "i rock" pledge and post all over (Chapter 1) ☐
Autograph *"Rock the World Rehab* Commitment" (Swag Lounge) ☐

Rock the World Rehab Daily Script

℞ Step 2: Preparation: Get ready to do it!

Prep Day 1: Friday the _____ day of _____, 20__.

Bonjour!

Today's focus: Pay attention to how you show up in this world. Awareness is key.

What to eat + drink: Anything + everything your body+mind+heart+soul desires; the only mandate is to drink 8 glasses of water. Tick these boxes off as you drink up:
☐☐☐☐☐☐☐☐

Review + do Chapter 3, Step 2 activities (general + Friday specific):

DO THIS 1st! Play the numbers game ☐:
Weight_____lbs., Bust_____", Waist_____", Hips_____",
Thighs _____" (r)_____" (l), Calves_____" (r)_____" (l)
Photo shoot: Full body front, back, side + head shot (smile!) ☐
Journal exercises ☐
Practice daily dump ☐
Decide on one brave thing you will do while in rehab ☐ What is it?
_____
Place purge bags around your nest ☐
Host kitchen "pitchin' + ditchin'" party of one ☐

Go shopping for: Chicktail ingredients (Grade B maple syrup, a dozen lemons, cayenne pepper, cinnamon), pills to pop (milk thistle, chromium, magnesium, multivitamin,), a tiara, sparkly lip gloss, Saturday ritual supplies, and two pairs of shoes (one to wear as you walk into rehab, the other, when you step onto the red carpet) ☐

Set up Swag Lounge ☐
Put all your eggs in one basket (Chapter 6) ☐
Create collage (Chapter 6, egg #5) ☐
Chapter 8 activities:
    Create "disconnect" list ☐
    Create "connect" list ☐
    Assemble "tool" box ☐
    Conduct circumcision ☐
    Execute exorcism ☐
    Order red velvet rope (optional) ☐
    Order red carpet (optional) ☐
    Tie red velvet cord around wrist (optional) ☐
Set intentions for rehab ☐ What do you want from your detox adventure (don't be shy)?

_____
_____
_____
_____
_____
_____

Rock the World Rehab Daily Script

℞ Step 2: Preparation: Get ready to do it!
Prep Day 2: Saturday the ____ day of _____, 20__.

Bonjour!

Today's focus: Continue being aware of how you show up—do you dim or brighten?

What to eat + drink: Another day of anything + everything your body+mind+heart+soul desires; the only mandate is to drink 8 glasses of water. Tick these boxes off as you drink up:
☐☐☐☐☐☐☐☐

Wrap up anything you didn't get around to yesterday + Chapter 3, Step 2 Saturday specifics ☐
Review + do any Chapter 3, Step 3 activities today that will help you jump into rehab easily ☐
"Rock 'n' Roll Rehab Eve" Ritual ☐
Don't forget to swing by your Swag Lounge to score your Step 2 Prep swag! ☐

> **Rox "rah-rah + hurrah" Box**
> You are about to embark on a special journey. We are so proud of you for taking this first step towards total body+mind+heart+soul harmony. You rock!

Rock the World Rehab Daily Script

℞ Step 3: Detoxification: You are doing it!

Day 1: Sunday the ___ day of _____, 20__.

Welcome to rehab! It's time to step into detox with those awesome shoes you bought just for the adventure.

Let's get things rockin' by pulling your focus rock from your stash (if you did the ritual last night). Keep this reminder in plain sight.

ROCK!	drinks to down	pills to pop	bon appétit!	play
morning *bonjour!*	hot water with lemon slice	200 mg milk thistle 200 mcg chromium multivitamin	**bottoms up!** enjoy chicktails all day long... at least 6, no more than 10 sipping + supping tips (chapter 4)	it's sunday! lounge, nap, or otherwise laze around. yay! (chapter 5)
mid-morn **late morn**	water with lemon all day long ☐☐☐☐☐☐☐☐	 500–700 mg magnesium	**daily dump** (chapters 3, 7, 8): let go of two somethings/someones that dim your light + weigh you down: 1. 2. remember: purge to surge!	**inner bling: sparkle therapy** (chapter 6) ★ take an egg from your basket + crack it ★ journal **outer bling:** keep your sparkle + tiara on! (chapter 7) ★ visit chez moi spa ★ dress rehearsal
noon	enjoy unlimited "rehab red carpet concert chick bar" visits, where every hour is happy hour!	200 mg milk thistle	**thank bank** i'm grateful for: 1. 2. 3.	**mope + dope alert!** visit your tool box ASAP for some cope, if necessary (chapter 8)
midday **late afternoon**	keep chugging! 	 500–700 mg magnesium	**get happy hour!** things to do instead of stuffing your body+mind+heart+soul with crap: read chapter 6 + "relapse prevention" in chapter 3 + pick three: 1. 2. 3.	**rox "rah-rah + hurrah" box** have faith in yourself. know that you can do this, that you are supported. believe in miracles + sparkles, because you are both. we have faith in + are here for you!
evening don't forget your **swag!** *sweet dreams!*	poop tea	200 mg milk thistle	*your little corner...*	*...of the world*

Rock the World Rehab Daily Script

℞ Step 3: Detoxification: You are doing it!

Day 2: Monday the ___ day of _____, 20__.

ROCK!	drinks to down	pills to pop	*bon appétit!*	play
morning *bonjour!*	hot water with lemon slice	200 mg milk thistle 200 mcg chromium multivitamin	bottoms up! enjoy chicktails all day long... at least 6, no more than 10 sipping + supping tips (chapter 4) **shop:** juice for 2 days	upper body cardio warm up/cool down stretch (chapter 5)
mid-morn **late morn**	water with lemon all day long ☐☐☐☐☐☐☐☐	 500–700 mg magnesium	**daily dump** (chapters 3, 7, 8): let go of two somethings/someones that dim your light + weigh you down: 1. 2. remember: purge to surge!	**inner bling: sparkle therapy** (chapter 6) ★ take an egg from your basket + crack it ★ journal **outer bling:** keep your sparkle + tiara on! (chapter 7) ★ visit chez moi spa ★ dress rehearsal
noon	enjoy unlimited "rehab red carpet concert chick bar" visits, where every hour is happy hour!	200 mg milk thistle	**thank bank** i'm grateful for: 1. 2. 3.	**mope + dope alert!** visit your tool box ASAP for some cope, if necessary (chapter 8)
midday **late afternoon**	keep chugging! 500–700 mg magnesium		**get happy hour!** things to do instead of stuffing your body+mind+heart+soul with crap: read chapter 6 + "relapse prevention" in chapter 3 + pick three: 1. 2. 3.	**rox "rah-rah + hurrah" box** if you feel yucky on day 2 like i usually do, hang in there! as you let go of crap, it's only natural that you'll probably feel like crap. in a day or two, you'll be soaring through to a new you. you can do it! woohoo!
evening don't forget your **swag**! *sweet dreams!*	poop tea	200 mg milk thistle	*your own little corner ...*	*...of the world*

Rock the World Rehab Daily Script

R **Step 3: Detoxification: You are doing it!**
Day 3: Tuesday the ___ day of _____, 20__.

ROCK!	drinks to down	pills to pop	*bon appétit!*	play
morning *bonjour!*	hot water with lemon slice	200 mg milk thistle 200 mcg chromium multivitamin	get juiced + juicy all day long! 64 ounces of veggie/fruit juice. sipping + supping tips (chapter 4)	yoga cardio warm up/cool down stretch (chapter 5)
mid-morn **late morn**	water with lemon all day long ☐☐☐☐☐☐☐☐	500–700 mg magnesium	**daily dump** (chapters 3, 7, 8): let go of two somethings/someones that dim your light + weigh you down: 1. 2. remember: purge to surge!	**inner bling: sparkle therapy** (chapter 6) ★ take an egg from your basket + crack it ★ journal **outer bling:** keep your sparkle + tiara on! (chapter 7) ★ visit chez moi spa ★ dress rehearsal
noon	enjoy unlimited "rehab red carpet concert chick bar" visits, where every hour is happy hour!	200 mg milk thistle	**thank bank** i'm grateful for: 1. 2. 3.	**mope + dope alert!** visit your tool box ASAP for some cope, if necessary (chapter 8)
midday **late afternoon**	keep chugging!	500–700 mg magnesium	**get happy hour!** things to do instead of stuffing your body+mind+heart+soul with crap: read chapter 6 + "relapse prevention" in chapter 3 + pick three: 1. 2. 3.	**rox "rah-rah + hurrah" box** how about playing in nature today? sashay around a park; strut along a shoreline; skip into a sunrise/sunset. you are nature. nature is you. yahoo!
evening don't forget your **swag!** *sweet dreams!*	poop tea	200 mg milk thistle	**your little corner...**	**...of the world**

Rock the World Rehab Daily Script

℞ Step 3: Detoxification: You are doing it!
Day 4: Wednesday the ___ day of _____, 20__.

ROCK!	drinks to down	pills to pop	bon appétit!	play
morning *bonjour!*	hot water with lemon slice	200 mg milk thistle 200 mcg chromium multivitamin	**get juiced + juicy all day long!** 64 ounces of veggie/fruit juice. sipping + supping tips (chapter 4) **shop:** grapes for 2 days + wine!	**lower body cardio** warm up/cool down stretch (chapter 5)
mid-morn **late morn**	water with lemon all day long ☐☐☐☐☐☐☐☐	 500–700 mg magnesium	**daily dump** (chapters 3, 7, 8): let go of two somethings/someones that dim your light + weigh you down: 1. 2. remember: purge to surge!	**inner bling: sparkle therapy** (chapter 6) ★ take an egg from your basket + crack it ★ journal **outer bling:** keep your sparkle + tiara on! (chapter 7) ★ visit chez moi spa ★ dress rehearsal
noon	enjoy unlimited "rehab red carpet concert chick bar" visits, where every hour is happy hour!	200 mg milk thistle	**thank bank** i'm grateful for: 1. 2. 3.	**mope + dope alert!** visit your tool box ASAP for some cope, if necessary (chapter 8)
midday **late afternoon**	 keep chugging!	 500–700 mg magnesium	**get happy hour!** things to do instead of stuffing your body+mind+heart+soul with crap: read chapter 6 + "relapse prevention" in chapter 3 + pick three: 1. 2. 3.	**rox "rah-rah + hurrah" rox** always be true to yourself. express yourself authentically + bliss is yours. you matter. you are appreciated. thank you for being you—the real you. you are loved just as you are today.
evening don't forget your **swag**! sweet dreams!	poop tea	200 mg milk thistle	**your little corner...**	**...of the world**

Rock the World Rehab Daily Script

℞ Step 3: Detoxification: You are doing it!
Day 5: Thursday the ___ day of _____, 20__.

ROCK!	drinks to down	pills to pop	*bon appétit!*	play
morning *bonjour!*	hot water with lemon slice	200 mg milk thistle 200 mcg chromium multivitamin	solid wine with a splash grapes all day long, no more than 3 bags, preferably red + 4 oz. glass of wine (optional) *à votre santé!* sipping + supping tips (chapter 4)	cardio yoga warm up/cool down stretch (chapter 5)
mid-morn late morn	water with lemon all day long ☐☐☐☐☐☐☐☐	 500–700 mg magnesium	daily dump (chapters 3, 7, 8): let go of two somethings/someones that dim your light + weigh you down: 1. 2. remember: purge to surge!	inner bling: sparkle therapy (chapter 6) ★ take an egg from your basket + crack it ★ journal outer bling: keep your sparkle + tiara on! (chapter 7) ★ visit chez moi spa ★ dress rehearsal
noon	enjoy unlimited "rehab red carpet concert chick bar" visits, where every hour is happy hour!	200 mg milk thistle	thank bank i'm grateful for: 1. 2. 3.	mope + dope alert! visit your tool box ASAP for some cope, if necessary (chapter 8)
midday late afternoon	keep chugging!	 500–700 mg magnesium	get happy hour! things to do instead of stuffing your body+mind+heart+soul with crap: read chapter 6 + "relapse prevention" in chapter 3 + pick three: 1. 2. 3.	rox "rah-rah + hurrah" box repeat throughout the day: "i am free to be me authentically—yippee!" you can have it all where it truly matters—a harmonious body+mind+heart+soul.
evening don't forget your **swag!** sweet dreams!	poop tea	200 mg milk thistle	your little corner...	...of the world

Rock the World Rehab Daily Script

℞ Step 3: Detoxification: You are doing it!
Day 6: Friday the ___ day of _____, 20__.

ROCK!	drinks to down	pills to pop	*bon appétit!*	play
morning *bonjour!*	hot water with lemon slice	200 mg milk thistle 200 mcg chromium multivitamin	solid wine with a splash grapes all day long, no more than 3 bags, preferably red + 4 oz. glass of wine (optional) cheers! sipping + supping tips (chapter 4) **shop:** fruit for two days	cardio yoga warm up/cool down stretch (chapter 5)
mid-morn **late morn**	water with lemon all day long ☐☐☐☐☐☐☐☐	 500–700 mg magnesium	**daily dump** (chapters 3, 7, 8): let go of two somethings/someones that dim your light + weigh you down: 1. 2. remember: purge to surge!	**inner bling:** sparkle therapy (chapter 6) ★ take an egg from your basket + crack it ★ journal **outer bling:** keep your sparkle + tiara on! (chapter 7) ★ visit chez moi spa ★ dress rehearsal
noon	enjoy unlimited "rehab red carpet concert chick bar" visits, where every hour is happy hour!	200 mg milk thistle	**thank bank** i'm grateful for: 1. 2. 3.	**mope + dope alert!** visit your tool box ASAP for some cope, if necessary (chapter 8)
midday **late afternoon**	 keep chugging!	 500–700 mg magnesium	**get happy hour!** things to do instead of stuffing your body+mind+heart+soul with crap: read chapter 6 + "relapse prevention" in chapter 3 + pick three: 1. 2. 3.	rox "rah-rah + hurrah" box it's okay to change your course. follow your instincts. you have a VIP all access pass that entitles you to take a pass on what doesn't resonate with you. if you decide to ditch the menu, explore why and if still not to yes, focus on other areas that dim your light.
evening don't forget your **swag!** sweet dreams!	poop tea	200 mg milk thistle	*your little corner...*	*... of the world*

Rock the World Rehab Daily Script

℞ Step 3: Detoxification: You are doing it!
Day 7: Saturday the ___ day of _____, 20__.

ROCK!	drinks to down	pills to pop	bon appétit!	play
morning *bonjour!*	hot water with lemon slice	200 mg milk thistle 200 mcg chromium multivitamin	**get fruit loopy today!** enjoy fruit all day long; freeze your fruit for a refreshing treat sipping + supping tips (chapter 4)	cardio warm up/cool down stretch (chapter 5)
mid-morn **late morn**	water with lemon all day long ☐☐☐☐☐☐☐☐	 500–700 mg magnesium	**daily dump** (chapters 3, 7, 8): let go of two somethings/someones that dim your light + weigh you down: 1. 2. remember: purge to surge!	**inner bling: sparkle therapy** (chapter 6) ★ take an egg from your basket + crack it ★ journal **outer bling: keep your sparkle + tiara on!** (chapter 7) ★ visit chez moi spa ★ dress rehearsal
noon	enjoy unlimited "rehab red carpet concert chick bar" visits, where every hour is happy hour!	200 mg milk thistle	**thank bank** I'm grateful for: 1. 2. 3.	**mope + dope alert!** visit your tool box ASAP for some cope, if necessary (chapter 8)
midday **late afternoon**	keep chugging!	 500–700 mg magnesium	**get happy hour!** things to do instead of stuffing your body+mind+heart+soul with crap: read chapter 6 + "relapse prevention" in chapter 3 + pick three: 1. 2. 3.	**rox "rah-rah + hurrah" box** congratulations! one week down, one week to go. we're so proud of you!
evening don't forget your **swag!** *sweet dreams!*	poop tea	200 mg milk thistle	**your little corner...**	**... of the world**

Rock the World Rehab Daily Script

℞ Step 3: Detoxification: You are doing it!

Day 8: Sunday the ___ day of _____, 20__.
Now that you've rocked for a week, it's time to roll. Pull a ball to squash!

ROLL!	drinks to down	pills to pop	bon appétit!	play
morning *bonjour!*	hot water with lemon slice	200 mg milk thistle 200 mcg chromium multivitamin	**get fruit loopy today!** enjoy fruit all day long; freeze your fruit for a refreshing treat sipping + supping tips (chapter 4) **shop:** veggies for 2 days	it's sunday! lounge, nap + otherwise laze today (chapter 5)
mid-morn **late morn**	water with lemon all day long ☐☐☐☐☐☐☐☐	 500–700 mg magnesium	**daily dump** (chapters 3, 7, 8): let go of two somethings/someones that dim your light + weigh you down: 1. 2. remember: purge to surge!	**inner bling: sparkle therapy** (chapter 6) ★ take an egg from your basket + crack it ★ journal **outer bling: keep your sparkle + tiara on!** (chapter 7) ★ visit chez moi spa ★ dress rehearsal
noon	enjoy unlimited "rehab red carpet concert chick bar" visits, where every hour is happy hour!	200 mg milk thistle	**thank bank** i'm grateful for: 1. 2. 3.	**mope + dope alert!** visit your tool box ASAP for some cope, if necessary (chapter 8)
midday **late afternoon**	keep chugging!	 500–700 mg magnesium	**get happy hour!** things to do instead of stuffing your body+mind+heart+soul with crap: read chapter 6 + "relapse prevention" in chapter 3 + pick three: 1. 2. 3.	**rox "rah-rah + hurrah" box** pay no attention to what others say about your stint in rehab. they simply wish they had the courage to take care of themselves. you are brave + amazing. You are admired + adored.
evening don't forget your **swag!** *sweet dreams!*	poop tea	200 mg milk thistle	your little corner…	… of the world

Rock the World Rehab Daily Script

℞ Step 3: Detoxification: You are doing it!

Day 9: Monday the ___ day of _____, 20__.

ROLL!	drinks to down	pills to pop	bon appétit!	play
morning *bonjour!*	hot water with lemon slice	200 mg milk thistle 200 mcg chromium multivitamin	**veg out + about!** all sorts of veggies all day long sipping + supping tips in (chapter 4)	upper body cardio warm up/cool down stretch (chapter 5)
mid-morn **late morn**	water with lemon all day long ☐☐☐☐☐☐☐☐	 500–700 mg magnesium	**daily dump** (chapters 3, 7, 8): let go of two somethings/someones that dim your light + weigh you down: 1. 2. remember: purge to surge!	**inner bling: sparkle therapy** (chapter 6) ★ take an egg from your basket + crack it ★ journal **outer bling: keep your sparkle + tiara on!** (chapter 7) ★ visit chez moi spa ★ dress rehearsal
noon	enjoy unlimited "rehab red carpet concert chick bar" visits, where every hour is happy hour!	200 mg milk thistle	**thank bank** i'm grateful for: 1. 2. 3.	**mope + dope alert!** visit your tool box ASAP for some cope, if necessary (chapter 8)
midday **late afternoon**	 keep chugging! 	 500–700 mg magnesium	**get happy hour!** things to do instead of stuffing your body+mind+heart+soul with crap: read chapter 6 + "relapse prevention" in chapter 3 + pick three: 1. 2. 3.	**rox "rah-rah + hurrah" box** mondays can be blah days so how about booking an after work massage? you'll have something to look forward to all day as you get back into the work groove.
evening don't forget your **swag!** sweet dreams!	poop tea	200 mg milk thistle	**your little corner...**	**... of the world**

Rock the World Rehab Daily Script

℞ Step 3: Detoxification: You are doing it!
Day 10: Tuesday the ___ day of _____, 20__.

ROLL!	drinks to down	pills to pop	bon appétit!	play
morning *bonjour!*	hot water with lemon slice	200 mg milk thistle 200 mcg chromium multivitamin	**Veg out + about!** All sorts of veggies all day long sipping + supping tips in (chapter 4) **shop:** fruit + veggies for the next 2 days	yoga cardio warm up/cool down stretch (chapter 5)
mid-morn **late morn**	water with lemon all day long ☐☐☐☐☐☐☐☐	 500–700 mg magnesium	**daily dump** (chapters 3, 7, 8): let go of two somethings/someones that dim your light + weigh you down: 1. 2. remember: purge to surge!	**inner bling: sparkle therapy** (chapter 6) ★ take an egg from your basket + crack it ★ journal **outer bling:** keep your sparkle + tiara on! (chapter 7) ★ visit chez moi spa ★ dress rehearsal
noon	enjoy unlimited "rehab red carpet concert chick bar" visits, where every hour is happy hour!	200 mg milk thistle	**thank bank** i'm grateful for: 1. 2. 3.	**mope + dope alert!** visit your tool box ASAP for some cope, if necessary (chapter 8)
midday **late afternoon**	keep chugging!	 500–700 mg magnesium	**get happy hour!** things to do instead of stuffing your body+mind+heart+soul with crap: read chapter 6 + "relapse prevention" in chapter 3 + pick three: 1. 2. 3.	**rox "rah-rah + hurrah" box** day 10 is the perfect day to explore your wild side...wear something outrageous, swipe on bright red lipstick, be positively fierce. speak up. you have something to say. we're listening. purrrr + grrrrr...
evening	poop tea	200 mg milk thistle	**your little corner...**	**... of the world**

don't forget your **swag**!

sweet dreams!

Rock the World Rehab Daily Script

R̶x̶ Step 3: Detoxification: You are doing it!

Day 11: Wednesday the ___ day of _____, 20__.

ROLL!	drinks to down	pills to pop	bon appétit!	play
morning *bonjour!*	hot water with lemon slice	200 mg milk thistle 200 mcg chromium multivitamin	today starts the combo happy meal: veggies + fruit all day long sipping + supping tips in (chapter 4)	lower body cardio warm up/cool down stretch (chapter 5)
mid-morn **late morn**	water with lemon all day long ☐☐☐☐☐☐☐☐	 500–700 mg magnesium	**daily dump** (chapters 3, 7, 8): let go of two somethings/someones that dim your light + weigh you down: 1. 2. remember: purge to surge!	**inner bling: sparkle therapy** (chapter 6) ★ take an egg from your basket + crack it ★ journal **outer bling: keep your sparkle + tiara on!** (chapter 7) ★ visit chez moi spa ★ dress rehearsal
noon	enjoy unlimited "rehab red carpet concert chick bar" visits, where every hour is happy hour!	200 mg milk thistle	**thank bank** i'm grateful for: 1. 2. 3.	**mope + dope alert!** visit your tool box ASAP for some cope, if necessary (chapter 8)
midday **late afternoon**	 keep chugging!	 500–700 mg magnesium	**get happy hour!** things to do instead of stuffing your body+mind+heart+soul with crap: read chapter 6 + "relapse prevention" in chapter 3 + pick three: 1. 2. 3.	**rox "rah-rah + hurrah" box** sneak out for a matinee and sneak in your fruit/veggie snacks. while you're in sneaky mode, do some undercover play while watching the movie. ooh la la.
evening *don't forget your* **swag!** *sweet dreams!*	poop tea	200 mg milk thistle	**your little corner...**	**... of the world**

Rock the World Rehab Daily Script

℞ Step 3: Detoxification: You are doing it!
Day 12: Thursday the ___ day of _____, 20__.

ROLL!	drinks to down	pills to pop	bon appétit!	play
morning *bonjour!*	hot water with lemon slice	200 mg milk thistle 200 mcg chromium multivitamin	still enjoying the combo happy meal: veggies + fruit all day long sipping + supping tips (chapter 4) **shop:** enough souper you soup stuff to last for two days	yoga cardio warm up/cool down stretch (chapter 5)
mid-morn **late morn**	water with lemon all day long ☐☐☐☐☐☐☐☐	500–700 mg magnesium	**daily dump** (chapters 3, 7, 8): let go of two somethings/someones that dim your light + weigh you down: 1. 2. remember: purge to surge!	**inner bling:** sparkle therapy (chapter 6) ★ take an egg from your basket + crack it ★ journal **outer bling:** keep your sparkle + tiara on! (chapter 7) ★ visit chez moi spa ★ dress rehearsal
noon	enjoy unlimited "rehab red carpet concert chick bar" visits, where every hour is happy hour!	200 mg milk thistle	**thank bank** i'm grateful for: 1. 2. 3.	**mope + dope alert!** visit your tool box ASAP for some cope, if necessary (chapter 8)
midday **late afternoon**	keep chugging!	500–700 mg magnesium	**get happy hour!** things to do instead of stuffing your body+mind+heart+soul with crap: read chapter 6 + "relapse prevention" in chapter 3 + pick three: 1. 2. 3.	rox "rah-rah + hurrah" box always remember this factoid: even when it's dark + stormy, the sun is still there shining brightly. nothing extinguishes its light or yours. shine on!
evening **don't forget your swag!** **sweet dreams!**	poop tea	200 mg milk thistle	your little corner...	... of the world

Rock the World Rehab Daily Script

℞ Step 3: Detoxification: You are doing it!
Day 13: Friday the ___ day of _____, 20__.

ROLL!	drinks to down	pills to pop	bon appétit!	play
morning bonjour!	hot water with lemon slice	200 mg milk thistle 200 mcg chromium multivitamin	souper you! sip soup all day long sipping + supping tips in (chapter 4)	cardio warm-up/cool down stretch (chapter 5)
mid-morn late morn	water with lemon all day long ☐☐☐☐☐☐☐☐	 500–700 mg magnesium	daily dump (chapters 3, 7, 8): let go of two somethings/someones that dim your light + weigh you down: 1. 2. remember: purge to surge!	inner bling: sparkle therapy (chapter 6) ★ take an egg from your basket + crack it ★ journal outer bling: keep your sparkle + tiara on! (chapter 7) ★ visit chez moi spa ★ dress rehearsal
noon	enjoy unlimited "rehab red carpet concert chick bar" visits, where every hour is happy hour!	200 mg milk thistle	thank bank i'm grateful for: 1. 2. 3.	mope + dope alert! visit your tool box ASAP for some cope, if necessary (chapter 8)
midday late afternoon	 keep chugging!	 500–700 mg magnesium	get happy hour! things to do instead of stuffing your body+mind+heart+soul with crap: read chapter 6 + "relapse prevention" in chapter 3 + pick three: 1. 2. 3.	rox "rah-rah + hurrah" box did you notice that it's friday the 13th day? be fearless! do one scary thing today: bungee jump, bikini wax, streak. Let go of superstitions. believe in magic! we believe in you!
evening don't forget your swag! sweet dreams!	poop tea	200 mg milk thistle	your little corner...	... of the world

Rock the World Rehab Daily Script

℞ Step 3: Detoxification: You are doing it!

Day 14: Saturday the ___ day of _____, 20__.

ROLL!	drinks to down	pills to pop	*bon appétit!!*	play
morning *bonjour!*	hot water with lemon slice	200 mg milk thistle 200 mcg chromium multivitamin	souper you! sip soup all day long sipping + supping tips in (chapter 4) **shop:** celebration bubbles + bites	cardio warm up/cool down stretch (chapter 5)
mid-morn **late morn**	water with lemon all day long ☐☐☐☐☐☐☐☐	 500–700 mg magnesium	daily dump (chapters 3, 7, 8): let go of two somethings/someones that dim your light + weigh you down: 1. 2. remember: purge to surge!	**inner bling: sparkle therapy** (chapter 6) ★ take an egg from your basket + crack it ★ journal **outer bling: keep your sparkle + tiara on!** (chapter 7) ★ visit chez moi spa ★ dress rehearsal
noon	enjoy unlimited "rehab red carpet concert chick bar" visits, where every hour is happy hour!	200 mg milk thistle	**thank bank** i'm grateful for: 1. 2. 3.	**mope + dope alert!** visit your tool box ASAP for some cope, if necessary (chapter 8)
midday **late afternoon**	 keep chugging! 500–700 mg magnesium		**get happy hour!** things to do instead of stuffing your body+mind+heart+soul with crap: read chapter 6 + "relapse prevention" in chapter 3 + pick three: 1. 2. 3.	**rox "rah-rah + hurrah" box** by now you should be feeling peacefully blissy + optimistic about your future. today is your last day in rehab. you are fabulous + awesome!
evening don't forget your **swag!** sweet dreams!	poop tea	200 mg milk thistle	*your little corner...*	*... of the world*

Rock the World Rehab Daily Script

℞ Step 4: Celebration: You did it!
Red Carpet Debut: This day is all about you!
Sunday the ____ day of _____, 20__.

Bonjour!

You rocked the first week, you rolled the second—it's now time to ROCK + ROLL!

Play the numbers game again ☐:
Weight_____lbs., Bust_____", Waist_____", Hips_____",
Thighs _____" (r)_____" (l), Calves_____" (r)_____" (l)

Set today's intentions ☐
Open your journal and do your show day survey ☐
Prepare + practice your "acceptance speech" ☐
Pen "i rock" on the larger stone you set aside from your pre-rehab ritual + roll it around a bit ☐
Photo of rock star you ☐

Continue the wonderful, healthy actions that you took in rehab including:

Drinks to down (plus champagne, wine, and/or whatever your body+mind+heart+soul desires) ☐
Pills to pop ☐
Daily dump ☐
Non-reactivity to mopes + dopes ☐
Inner bling time (your intention setting + survey count!) ☐
Outer bling: super-sized today for your red carpet debut! ☐

Bon appétit! Enjoy whatever your body+mind+heart+soul desires with awareness, appreciation + grace. Cheers to you! ☐
Here are some other to-do's you learned in rehab to embrace on this special day + all days thereafter:

Go slow ☐
Moderation in all things ☐
Be a "food snob" ☐
Practice mindfulness in all you do ☐
Conscious living—eating, drinking, showing up on your red carpet, the stage of your life ☐
Step onto the red carpet in those amazing shoes + shine your light while you celebrate yourself! ☐

We're very proud of you! You truly do ROCK + ROLL!

Cool Stuff For Hot Chicks

SOURCES OF INSPIRATION, MOTIVATION, FASCINATION, RELAXATION, EDUCATION, PERSPIRATION (GLISTEN!), CELEBRATION, CREATION, APPLICATION, SPARKLELATION, MEDITATION, DIVINATION+ SO MUCH MORE FOR REALIZATION OF BODY + MIND + HEART + SOUL HARMONIZATION!

This is the chapter-by-chapter area of the Swag Lounge where you'll find some of our favorites for sparkly living, doing + being. If a direct link isn't provided, you know what to do: be a glittery Google girl! I hope you find at least one something something that speaks to, and then through, you.

Meet + Greet

playlist
Strength of a Woman, by Shaggy
My Vision, by Seal
Lost My Faith, by Seal

Chapter 1: The "Rock The World Rehab" Tour

playlist
Just the Way You Are, by Bruno Mars
You're Unbelievable, by EMF
Born This Way, by Lady Gaga
F**kin' Perfect, by Pink

Chapter 2: Get Your Attitude Adjustment Here

Sail Into Your Dreams: 8 Steps To Living A More Purposeful Life, by Karen Mehringer
The Art of Growing Up: Simple Ways To Be Yourself At Last, by Veronique Vienne and Jeanne Lipsey
The Red Book: A Deliciously Unorthodox Approach To Igniting Your Divine Spark, by Sera Beak www.serabeak.com
The Life You Were Born To Live: A Guide For Finding Your Life Purpose, by Dan Millman
This Time I Dance!: Creating The Work You Love, by Tama J. Kieves www.awakeningartistry.com
The Four Agreements: A Practical Guide to Personal Freedom, A Toltec Wisdom Book, by Don Miguel Ruiz
Different Like Coco, by Elizabeth Matthews

playlist
Own It, by The Black Eyed Peas
Dream On, by Aerosmith
True Colors, by Cyndi Lauper
Shining Star, by Earth Wind & Fire
Gratitude, by Earth Wind & Fire
Do Your Thing, by Edwin McCain
It's In the Way That You Use It, by Eric Clapton
What You Want, by Evanescence
I Am What I Am, by Gloria Gaynor
Shine the Light On, by Illumine
Star, by Illumine
Thank You for This Day, by Karen Drucker
I Give Myself Permission, by Karen Drucker
Firework, Katy Perry
What the Fuck Are We Saying?, by Lenny Kravitz
You Get What You Give, by New Radicals
If Everyone Cared, by Nickelback
Something to Be, by Rob Thomas

Free, by Seal
Second Chance, by Shinedown
Thank You, by Sly & The Family Stone
Take Me As I Am, by Sugarland
Live Your Life, by T.I.

Chapter 3: It's Time To Rock 'n' Roll

Step 1: Intervention

write
Pick up amazing journals here:
www.moleskine.com
www.papayaart.com

If you're an electronic journaler, this keyboard will make you smile:
http://www.keyboardforblondes.com/

Step 2: Preparation

nest
www.etsy.com/shop/sugarcookiedolls for the most adorable, feathery, sparkly pixies
www.nestfragrances.com for wow candles; the "Beeswax & Whipped Cream" candle is awesome
www.yourspaceforsuccess.com for a great feng shui resource
www.containerstore.com for stuff to organize your stuff
www.redcarpetrunway.com for red heart-shaped solo + other carpets
www.expogoods.com for your own red velvet rope (every chick should have one!)

European-like market totes
www.ebags.com/brand/medina
www.frenchselections.com

shoes

My friend Lanell had a dream: sparkly flip-flops for sparkly girls. She went from her kitchen table "factory" to a full-blown, international success story biz and I'm happy to share that the perfect "Get Red Carpet Ready" flip-flops can be found at www.ladylanells.com. Shop the Classic Collection ("classic red with red + clear crystals") and the Flower Collection ("red with clear flower & red center") and strut the red carpet every day with your sparkles on!

If you can't always wear sparkly flip-flops (dreary day job dress code), you can always insert a red liner into any pair of your fabulous shoes for an instant secret but you know it's there red carpet. The passed-our-test insole can be found at www.summersoles.com. The Ultra-Absorbent (in red, of course) rocks! You can also paint your soles red or touch up your Christian Louboutins by picking up some "Save Your Sole" red touch-up paint or red rubber soles at www.redsoles.co.uk

Here are some of our fave sources for shoes, shoes + more shoes:
www.zappos.com
www.nordstrom.com
www.beverlyfeldmanshoes.com
www.betseyjohnson.com
www.stevemadden.com
www.jessicasimpsoncollections.com
www.bluefly.com
www.naughty-monkey.com

play the numbers game

www.bathroomscaleart.com for the coolest *art de toilette* scales on the planet! The "work it" is the official Concert Chick weigh-in station, of course.

places to donate your stuff
www.clothingdonations.org Vietnam Veterans of America makes it easy with pick up service!
www.stuffedanimalsforemergencies.org donates gently used stuffed animals to homeless shelters, hospitals + emergency aid workers... it may be time to say goodbye to all your animals.
www.cleantheworld.org now you know what to do with all those hotel shampoos + soaps you've collected!
www.bridesagainstbreastcancer.org do you really need that wedding gown?
www.greenphone.com donate your old phone to keep it out of trash + a tree will be planted for every phone recycled...hello!!
www.soles4souls.org sole recycling is good for your soul!
www.mustcreate.org make sweet music karmically by passing along the musical instruments you haven't picked up in years. Let someone else with talent make some happy noise!
www.iloveschools.com do the right thing by sending some things to write with + other office supplies to be used in our nation's classrooms.
www.habitat.org/carsforhomes let your vehicle drive some good vibes your way while you make someone else's day!
www.greendisk.com safely recycles all those mystery cables, old mice, CDs, DVDs, VHS tapes, and more technotrash...you know you have 'em...now donate 'em!
www.cottonfrombluetogreen.org warm your heart + others' hearts (+more!) by donating your jeans to be recycled into insulation for communities in need.

playlist
Let's Get It Started, by The Black Eyed Peas
People Get Ready, by Eva Cassidy
Higher, by Creed
Learn to Fly, by the Foo Fighters
Change the Game, by Jay-Z
One Step at a Time, by Jordin Sparks

Fly Away, by Lenny Kravitz
Take Time, by Lenny Kravitz
Jump, by Madonna
Pocketful of Sunshine, by Natasha Bedingfield
Unwritten, by Natasha Bedingfield
Save Your Life, by Newsboys
Maybe, by Sick Puppies

Chapter 4: Feeding Your Body+Mind+Heart+Soul

The Yoga of Eating: Transcending Diets and Dogma to Nourish the Natural Self, by Charles Eisenstein
Women Food and God: An Unexpected Path to Almost Everything, by Geneen Roth

juicers + juicing
www.vitamix.com
www.consumersearch.com/juicers
www.crazysexydiet.com
The Big Book of Juices: More Than 400 Natural Blends for Health and Vitality Every Day, by Natalie Savona, Duncan Baird, 2010
www.orientaltrading.com for little cocktail umbrellas

tea
www.numitea.com Bushman's Brew Honeybush Herbal Teasan rocks!
www.teagarden.com for Dr. Tea's Mint Chocolate Chip Ice Cream, Pina Colada, Candy Bar + more!
www.aveda.com Aveda Comforting tea is beyond comforting
www.tripleleaf-tea.com for tasty green and ginger teas
www.yogiproducts.com the Egyptian Licorice in regular + mint is my fave!
www.bonjourproducts.com/c_FrenchPresses.html for the perfect French press
www.kusmitea.com

playlist
Pour Some Sugar On Me, by Def Leppard
Happy Hour, by Eumir Deodato
Drive, by Incubus

Chapter 5: You Gotta Move It, Move It To Lose It, Lose It

general
Pooh's Little Fitness Book inspired by A.A. Milne with Decorations by Ernest H. Shepard

secret weapon of ass destruction
www.brazilian-lift-workouts.info order your Brazilian Butt Lift stuff here!

cardio
www.drums-alive.com your online beat it! resource…march to your own drummer girls!
www.zumba.com find your cha cha cha for some ooh la la here
www.chiwalking.com the natural way of walking that does your body more than good
www.chirunning.com ditto but for the runners out there
www.sfactor.com for all your pole dancing needs
www.badkittyexoticwear.com for all your stripper attire needs
The S Factor: Strip Workouts for Every Woman by Sheila Kelley

chick power
www.valeofit.com for Neoprine coated, colorful light hand weights

yoga
www.yogafinder.com to find yoga classes in your area
www.kristinmcgee.com for fabulous instructional DVDs + an informative daily blog

www.yogajournal.com for general yoga information + free instruction downloads
www.yogatuneup.com you'll never look at balls the same after experiencing one of Jill Miller's sessions!
www.blissology.com for the Blissology Project

40 Days to Personal Revolution: A Breakthrough Program to Radically Change Your Body and Awaken the Sacred Within Your Soul, by Baron Baptiste
Slim Calm Sexy Yoga: 210 Proven Yoga Moves for Mind/Body Bliss, by Tara Stiles
Yoga From the Inside Out: Making Peace With Your Body Through Yoga, by Christina Sells
My Body is a Temple: Yoga as a Path to Wholeness, by Christina Sell
The Seven Spiritual Laws Of Yoga: A Practical Guide to Healing Body, Mind, and Spirit + companion Guidebook, by Deepak Chopra + David Simon
The Yoga Sutras of Patanjali translated + introduced by Alistair Shearer
Yin Yoga, by Paul Grilley
Walking Yoga: Incorporate Yoga Principles into Dynamic Walking Routines for Physical Health, Mental Peace, and Spiritual Enrichment, by Ila Sarley + Garrett Sarley
The Yoga Body Diet: Slim and Sexy in 4 Weeks (Without the Stress), by Kristen Schultz Dollard + John Douillard

for yoga mats + props, check out
www.yogamatic.com Rox has her own custom mat from this place...claim your own!
www.stick-e.com for my pal Libby's yoga + Pilates accessories

for sassy yoga togs
www.lululemon.com
www.balidog.com

www.prana.com
www.bepresent.com
www.victoriassecret.com

security
walking.about.com/od/beginners/a/safewalkingrule.htm for safe walking tips
www.pepperface.com for Concert Chick get-the-hell-away spray (of course, we like the crystal iced ones the best)

play shoes to tone your butt + thighs
www.us.mbt.com for the original MBT (Masai Barefoot Technology) shoes to rock your roll
www.fitflop.com for the scoop on these stylish sandals; at the time this book went to print, online orders from this site in the UK only, but they can be found at Macy's + online at www.zappos.com
www.reebok.com/US for Reebok EasyTones
www.skechers.com for Skechers Shape-Ups

playlist
My Hump, by The Black Eyed Peas
Rock That Body, by the Black Eyed Peas
Bamboogie, by Bamboo
You Should Be Dancing, by the Bee Gees
Shake a Tail Feather, by The Cheetah Girls
Tiny Dancer, by Elton John
'Till I Collapse, by Eminem & Nate Dogg
Drumming Song, by Florence & The Machine
Danse Avec Moi, by French Affair
Fired Up, by Funky Green Dogs
Pink Panther Theme, by Henry Mancini & His Orchestra (stealth health theme song)
Boogie Shoes, by K.C. & The Sunshine Band
Just Dance, by Lady Gaga

The Chase, by Manafest
Strip For You, by R. Kelly
Don't Cha, by Pussycat Dolls
I Like to Move It, by Reel 2 Real
Fire Burning, by Sean Kingston
Dancin' on a Pole, by Three 6 Mafia
Play that Funky Music, by Wild Cherry
Gettin' Jiggy Wit It, by Will Smith

Chapter 6: Sparkles In: That Inner Bling Thing

www.toyconnection.com for red plastic eggs

inspirational reads
The Persistence of Yellow: A Book of Recipes for Life, by Monique Duval
Hope for the Flowers, by Trina Paulus
To Bee or Not to Bee: A Book for Beeings Who Feel There's More to Life Than Just Making Honey, by John Penberthy
The Little Prince, by Antoine de Saint-Exupéry
Gift from the Sea, by Anne Morrow Lindbergh
My Beautiful Broken Shell: Words of Hope to Refresh the Soul, by Carol Hamblet Adams
The Princess Who Believed in Fairy Tales: A Story for Modern Times, by Marcia Grad
Spilling Open: The Art of Becoming Yourself, by Sabrina Ward Harrison
Ordinary Sparkling Moments: Reflections on Success and Contentment, by Christine Mason Miller
The Alchemist, by Paulo Coelho (and any other book by this incredible man)
Eat, Pray, Love: One Woman's Search for Everything Across Italy, India and Indonesia, by Elizabeth Gilbert
Story of a Soul: The Autobiography of St. Therese of Lisieux, by St. Therese Lisieux
Ocean Star: A Memoir, by Christina DiMari

The Prayer of Jabez: Breaking Through to the Blessed Life, by Bruce Wilkinson

egg #1: pray
www.etsy.com/shop/meditation for beautiful mala beads
www.etsy.com/shop/GracefulRosaries for precious rosaries
Illuminata: A Return to Prayer, by Marianne Williamson
Blessings: Prayers and Declarations for a Heartful Life, by Julia Cameron
Coloring Your Prayers: An Inspirational Coloring Book for Making Dreams Come True, by Carolyn Manzi
The Energy of Prayer: How to Deepen Your Spiritual Practice, by Thich Nhat Hanh
Give Me Grace: A Child's Daybook of Prayers, by Cynthia Rylant

egg #2: meditate
www.chopra.com for the 21-day meditation challenge + downloads (anything by Davidji is especially outstanding…he has *the* best voice)
www.gabbyb.tv for all spirit junkies
www.labyrinthsociety.org for walking meditation sites
The Miracle of Mindfulness: An Introduction to the Practice of Meditation, by Thich Nhat Hanh
Mantra Meditation, by Thomas Ashley-Farrand

egg #3: be present
www.mindful.org for chime reminders to upload to your computer
Stillness Speaks, by Eckhart Tolle
The Power of Now: A Guide to Spiritual Enlightenment, by Eckhart Tolle
A New Earth: Awakening to Your Life's Purpose, by Eckhart Tolle
Peace Is Every Step: The Path of Mindfulness in Everyday Life, by Thich Nhat Hanh

egg #4: speak up + be heard
See Chapter 3 swag for journal sources
Journal Bliss: Creative Prompts to Unleash Your Inner Eccentric, by Violette
You Can Heal Your Life Affirmations Kit, by Louise Hay
What to Say When you Talk To Yourself, by Shad Helmstetter

egg #5: create
www.artjournaling.blogspot.com for mind + heart embracing art journal prompts
www.makeavisionboard.com for dream board how-tos
www.theartistsway.com for Julia Cameron's treasures
www.violette.ca for Violette's Creative Juice
www.artellaland.com for lots of fantastic bits + pieces of creative everything
www.SARK.com anything + everything from + by SARK will sparklelize your life!
www.wishstudio.com a beautiful, peaceful spot for e-camps + more
1,000 Artist Journal Pages: Personal Pages and Inspirations, by Dawn DeVries Sokol
True Vision: Authentic Art Journaling, by L.K. Lidwig
Creative Awakenings: Envisioning the Life of Your Dreams Through Art, by Sheri Gaynor

egg #6: seek wisdom from others
www.goddessguidebook.com you must join the goddess circle!
www.yeahdave.com the discoverer of wine+chocolate+yoga. Need I say more?
www.kimberlywilson.com kimberly's seasonal teleclasses + tranquilista e-course are wow!
www.marianne.com a course in miracles + so much more
www.soundstrue.com for access to many life masters
www.kripalu.org for life-changing workshops
www.eomega.org for more life-altering workshops

plus the talent mentioned in egg #5
The Answer is Simple Oracle Cards, by Sonia Choquette

egg #7: get lit + inhale
Let It Go: Burn, Bury, Rip, Repeat: And Make Way for What Makes You Healthier, Happier, Wealthier, Wiser, by Joanna Arettam
The Burn Your Anger Book: 80 Tear-Out Pages to Reduce Your Anger to Ashes!, by Karen Salmansohn

candles
www.capecodsoycandle.com oh, joy! the best soy!
www.madelineislandcandlecompany.com for all sorts of candles
www.beeswaxcandleco.com mind your beeswax over here
www.essexcandle.com for crystal journey candles

incense
www.spiritualscents.com any kind of incense imaginable
www.nagchampa.com my personal fave

aromatherapy
www.youngliving.com it should be a crime to not have some Thieves in your nest!
www.wisdomoftheearth.com a magical place in Sedona for essential oils

crystals
Healing With Stones And Crystals by Gregory Branson-Trent

twinkly lights
www.partylights.com

egg #8: pop natural sedatives
Wild Comfort: The Solace of Nature, by Kathleen Dean Moore

egg #9: give yourself a break
www.hammockcompany.com swinging in a hammock doing nothing = pure bliss
365 Ways to Get a Good Night's Sleep, by Ronald L. Kotler + Maryann Karinch
The Art of Doing Nothing: Simple Ways to Make Time for Yourself, by Veronique Vienne

egg #10: hallucinate
Creative Visualization: Use the Power of Your Imagination to Create What You Want in Your Life by Shakti Gawain
Mirroring People: The Science of Empathy and How We Connect with Others, by Marco Iacoboni

egg #11: make some noise!
www.bettyroimusic.com *La Lumiere du Sol*, by Betty Roi, a yoga instructor/chanteuse
www.sing-like-a-rockstar.com to learn to sing like a rock star
www.sankofasong.com for "sacred sound" therapy
Chanting from the Heart: Buddhist Ceremonies and Daily Practices, by Thich Nhat Hanh + the Monks + Nuns of Plum Village
Chanting: Discovering Spirit in Sound, by Robert Gass + Kathleen A. Brehony

egg #12: wear a tiara
www.rhinestonejewelry.com for the twinkliest tiaras
www.erinsmithart.com for hysterical "Holy Crap" tiaras
Crowns & Tiaras: Add a Little Sparkle, Glitter & Glamour to Every Day, by Kerri Judd + Danyel Montecinos

playlist
Deep Channel, by Afro Celt Sound System
Money Can't Buy It, by Annie Lenox
New World, by Attaboy

Spirit, by Atman
Benedictine Monks Chant
Mombassa, by Big Bud
The Lazy Song, by Bruno Mars
Sing, by The Carpenters
Spirit of Water, by Dean Evenson
Buddha's Dream, by Dean Evenson
Sacred Alchemy, by Devaa Haley
Ordinary World, by Duran Duran
Sing a Song, by Earth Wind & Fire
Zenlicious, by Fabeku Fatunmise
Relax, by Frankie Goes to Hollywood
Believe, by Lenny Kravitz
Morning Prayer: I Will Surrender, by Karen Drucker
Kuan Yin's Mantra, by Lisa Thiel
Om Mani Padme Om, by Sacred Earth
If It's In My Mind, It's On My Face, by Seal
The Healing Room, by Sinéad O'Connor
Pure, by Superchick
I Wanna Talk About Me, by Toby Keith

Chapter 7: Sparkles Out: That Outer Bling Thing

for frocks that rock
www.carynanina.com for ooh la la custom-made kimonos
www.tranquilitee.com for the perfect travel attire
www.betseyjohnson.com for art you wear
www.etsy.com/shop/princessdoodlebeans for tutus in all colors, sizes + lengths (you know you want one!)
www.anniefink.com for the sweetest knitted sleeves, leggings + headbands made for you to wear your heart on your sleeve + to honor your chakra points

meet your stylist
www.instyle.com/instyle/makeover/ to play with different hairstyles + looks

www.gotryiton.com to upload your photo + get instant feedback on your look
www.stylefind.com for great outfit ideas brought to you by InStyle
www.itunes.com for the great apps *My Style Fashion Assistant* (organize your wardrobe department) + *Stylish Girl* (plan what to wear)
Beauty by the Book: Seeing Yourself as God Sees You, by Nancy Stafford
Like I Give a Frock: Fashion Forecasts and Meaningless Misguidance, by Michi Girl
Parisian Chic: A Style Guide by Ines de la Fressange, by Ines de la Fressange + Sophie Gachet
Style A to Zoe: The Art of Fashion, Beauty, & Everything Glamour, by Rachel Zoe

peeper keepers
www.ray-ban.com the Wayfarer is *the* classic movie star shade
www.vintagesunglassesshop.com shades from the 40s to the 90s are yours with one click
www.shopsueyboutique.com cheep sunglasses!

Here's where to donate used eyewear:
www.donateglasses.org Lions Clubs International volunteers collect old sunglasses, reading glasses + eyeglasses. so if your prescription no longer works or the style just isn't you anymore, donate your shades to this wonderful eye-opening cause
www.onesight.org/na/get_inspired/path_of_recycled_glassses for another eyeglass recycling option

sparkly accessories
www.etsy.com/shop/angels9 for amazing vintage Paris flea market religious + vintage rosary creations with bling
www.swarovski.com for super-blingy thingies
www.dogeared.com for make-a-wish bracelets—they'll come true if you do!

Cool Stuff For Hot Chicks || 281

www.alexandani.com for the coolest, positivity enhancing charm bangles on the planet

http://www.shop4sparkles.com/ for celebrity looks for less—lots less

shoes
we covered these treats in Chapter 3 swag

secret assists
www.hollywoodfashionsecrets.com for all sorts of extenders, lifts, cushions, tape, straps, enhancers + more to build the foundation for rockin' that slinky red carpet look

www.spanx.com for all your slimming for slinky needs

www.barenecessities.com for Commando takeouts + cupcakes (silicone breast enhancers) + top hats + low beams (nipple concealer adhesives)

the Swag Lounge makeup counter
General sources for all your makeup needs/wants/wishes:
www.sephora.com
www.beauty.com
www.stila.com
www.nars.com
www.maccosmetics.com
www.brushoff.com for cosmetic brush cleaning

peepers
www.Revitalash.com for the best lash-lengthening serum
www.blincinc.com for eyelash + eyebrow magic
DiorShow Mascara
L'Oreal Extra-Volume Collagen Mascara
d.j.v beautinizer 3D & Fiber-In Film-Coating Lash Kit
Hourglass Film Noir Lash Lacquer
www.frenchblueeyedrops.com for Innoxa drops that will pop your eyes (in a good way)

face

www.miracleskintransformer.com an amazing line disappearing act for under your eyes

The Mind-Beauty Connection: 9 Days to Reverse Stress Aging and Reveal More Youthful, Beautiful Skin, by Amy Wechsler, M.D.

lips

www.purplelabnyc.com This company's tagline is "double duty beauty for multi-tasking mavens". With "huge lips skinny hips" lip plumpers called "no panty lines," "kitty poledancer," + "red sole" + little lip "luvah" compacts with a stain + a pearly gloss in "rich jerk," can you see why we're entranced?

www.lipstickqueen.com for luscious, fun lipsticks + glosses produced by Poppy the Lipstick Queen—check out "Jean Queen Lip Gloss- It's Jeanius" + lipstick of the same name

www.katespade.com for Superfragilipstick created with the aforementioned Poppy

www.chanel.com for Rouge Coco Shine Hydrating Lipshine in any + every color

hair

www.sallybeauty.com for Euronext clip-on, human hair extensions

www.hairuwear.com for Jessica Simpson + Ken Paves hair pieces

www.dreamcatchers.com for hair extensions Paris Hilton wears

www.cottoncandysugarrush.com for Lady Gaga Hair Bows in many colors + fab hair accessories

www.franceluxe.com for hair treats galore

www.etsy.com/shop/FeatherMagic for hair feathers (every chick needs a few)

www.bangobeauty.com for an at-home bang trimming kit that even Rox can use

www.masonpearson.com for the best brushes you will use forever—pricey but you're worth it

Monroe Teasing U brush for some serious pouffiness

Tigi Rockaholic dry shampoo for those days you just don't wanna get wet
See egg #12 above for tiara 411

ooh la la spaaaaahhhhh
Pleasure Healing: Mindful Practices & Sacred Spa Rituals for Self-Nurturing, by Mary Beth Janssen + Horst M. Rechelbacher

body bare + care
Soap + Glory *Slimwear* "amazing butt-draining peptide balm that trims, contours, smoothes and reduces the appearance of cellulite." You have to love a product that states: "Slimwear was safety/efficacy tested in the UK on a plethora of slightly-padded people." Soap & Glory *Feel the Knead* is also a fabulous product. It's a super invigorating spa massage soap with exfoliating bamboo beads, seaweed suds + essential oils of cacao + carouba. Both can be found here: www.shopbootsusa.com
Tarina Tarantino's Sparklicity Shimmer Dust
www.laroche-posay.us for Anthelios sun protection
Neutrogena Light Sesame Oil
www.alkalineandloseweight.itworks.net the body contouring herbal wraps really work!
www.spacenk.com for White Gold Detoxifying Crystal Salt INA (Inner Nutritional Alchemy) Crystals
www.fresh.com for Rice Sake Bath + Rice Oil
www.lushusa.com for bath bombs, bubble bars + tub loads more
www.honeycatcosmetics.com Chick Of The Sea Foaming Bath Crystals, Chocolate Bath Melt Treats, + Honeycat Warm Milk Martini will make you purrrrrrrrrr
www.loccitane.com for treats from Provence—the Almond Shower Oil is amazingly aromatic, sudsy + extraordinarily skin softeny

www.notsoapradio.com for "I'm not here, I'm really walking the red carpet" body soufflé, sugared body polish, dry oil spray + foaming body & hand wash. According to the package, the sense is this: "dressed in couture, on the arm of my fabulous date. Throngs of people call my name as I glide effortlessly past the flashing lights of paparazzi that capture my every glance, every nuance. Turn, smile and wave at the crowd, I am sparkling, glamorous, invincible. The night is mine. Reality is simply what you make of it." Oh yeah! So perfect for your red carpet debut day!
www.Knieppus.com for powerful natural baths
www.kiehls.com for icon products
www.caudalie-usa.com for wine-based products for your outer body
www.kinaraspa.com for the Red Carpet Facial Kit

get nailed
www.Essie.com *j'adore*: "rock star skinny," "a-list," "steel-ing the scene" + "topless & barefoot"
www.OPI.com especially in "bubble bath," "in the spotlight pink," "Paris Couture for Sure glitter topcoat," "I Only Drink Champagne" + "Stars in My Eyes"
www.minxnails.com for fancy nail stickers in an array of colors + patterns
www.sallyhansen.com Salon Effects DIY nail stickers ("misbehaved" + "fly with me" are woohoo!)
www.sephora.com for nail patch art DIY nail stickers (French Dentelle is amazing + Pink Zebra + Gold Cheetah are amusing!)
www.diamancel.com for the best foot file in the world

playlist
Glamorous, by Fergie
These Boots are Made for Walkin', by Jessica Simpson
How to Stuff a Wild Bikini, by The Kingsmen
The Most Wonderful Girl, by Lords of Acid
Vogue, by Madonna
Diamond Girl, by Seals & Crofts

How Could Anyone, by Shaina Noll
Barbie Girl, by The Starlite Singers
She's a Beauty, by The Tubes

Chapter 8: How To Cope With The Dope + The Mope

One Soul, One Heart: The Scared Path to Healing All Relationships, by John E. Welshons
Rules of Engagement, by Yehuda Berg
The Law of the Garbage Truck: How to Respond to People Who Dump on You, and How to Stop Dumping on Others, by David J. Pollay
The Untethered Soul: The Journey Beyond Yourself, by Micheal Singer
Since Strangling Isn't An Option... Dealing with Difficult People—Common Problems and Uncommon Solutions, by Sandra A. Crowe
See Chapter 3 swag for red carpet + red velvet rope ordering info

for awesome greeting cards
www.curlygirldesign.com
www.erinsmithart.com
www.papayaart.com

playlist
Peace of Mind, by Boston
F**k You, by Cee Lo Green
The Beautiful People, by Christina Aguilera
I Don't Need Anymore Friends, by Collective Soul
Let It Be, by The Beatles
I Just Wanna Live, by Good Charlotte
With a Little Help From My Friends, by Joe Cocker
What Goes Around Comes Around, by Justin Timberlake
We Are All Angels, by Karen Drucker
Walk Away, by Kelly Clarkson
Reasons to Forgive, by Kirsty Hawkshaw Meets Tenishia

Live, by Lenny Kravitz
Express Yourself, by Madonna
No More Drama, by Mary J. Blige
Cooler Than Me, by Mike Posner
What Do You Think About That, by Montgomery Gentry
Broken Wings, by Mr. Mister
Let Us Love, Needtobreathe
Gotta Be Somebody, by Nickelback
When We Stand Together, by Nickelback
Respect, by Otis Redding
I Don't Care Anymore, by Phil Collins
We are Family, by Sister Sledge
Lies of the Beautiful People, by Sixx:A.M.
Mean Girls, by Sugarland
Apologize, by Timbaland

Chapter 9: Celebrate Yourself!

The Martini Diet: The Self-Indulgent Way to a Thinner, More Fabulous You!, by Jennifer "Gin" Sander
Celebrate Yourself and Other Inspirational Essays, by Eric Butterworth

for bites + sips
www.barefootwine.com cheep + delish!
www.rockandrollwine.com our sparkly chick experts' biz
www.vosgeschocolate.com the toffees, truffles + marshmallows are to fly for
www.veuve-clicquot.com what chick doesn't cherish the yellow label bottle's bubbles?
www.ruinart.com form + substance (*magnifique* caged bottles!)
www.moet.com try Moët Ice in the white bottle
www.franciscoppolawinery.com the Sofia Wine Minis (think pink can of bubbles with a straw)
www.pommery.fr for Pommery Pop single serves with a straw attached to the bottle

for party bits

www.mermaidcostumesonly.com for an outfit for "mermaid madness"

www.temptu.com for "biker chic chick" temporary tattoos

www.ehow.com/how_632_make-smores.html how to make s'mores for "pitch a tent, not a fit"

www.southpacificberets.com/beret-nu-de-france.php for *magnifique* berets

www.sephora.com for bling bandages

www.wikihow.com/Speak-Pig-Latin for lessons on how to speak pig latin

playlist

This Is Your Night, by Amber
I Gotta Feeling, by The Black Eyed Peas
Party Out of Bounds, by B-52's
Rock Lobster, by B-52's
Rebel Yell, by Billy Idol
Girls Just Want to Have Fun, by Cyndi Lauper
Free to Be Me, by Francesca Battistelli
Free, by Illumine
Private Party, by India.Arie
Who Wouldn't Want To Be Me?, by Keith Urban
Welcome to the Party, by Kid Rock
Supermodel (Work It), by RuPaul
Holiday, by Madonna
And the Crowd Goes Wild, by Mark Willis
Rockstar, by Nickelback
Raise Your Glass, by Pink
I Just Want to Celebrate, by Rare Earth
This is My Time, by Raven-Symon
Cheers (Drink to That), by Rihanna
New Tatoo, by Saving Abel
Amazing, by Seal
Celebrate, by Three Dog Night

Chapter 10: After-Party Afterthoughts

The Fresh Start Promise: 28 Days to Total Mind, Body, Spirit Transformation, by Edwige Gilbert www.newlifedirections.com

Yeah Dave's Guide to Livin' the Moment: Getting to Ecstasy Through Wine, Chocolate and Your iPod Playlist, by David Romanelli www.yeahdave.com

Eating the Moment: 141 Mindful Practices to Overcome Overeating One Meal At a Time, by Pavel G. Somer, Ph.D

Pooh's Little Instruction Book inspired by A.A. Milne with Decorations by Ernest H. Shepard

The Official Booty Parlor Mojo Makeover, by Dana B. Myers

Girl Seeks Bliss: Zen and the Art of Modern Life Maintenance, by Nicole Beland

The Skinny: How To Fit Into Your Little Black Dress Forever, by Melissa Clark + Robin Aronson

Seven Sacred Pauses, by Macrina Wiederkehr

Love Your Body, Love your Life: 5 Steps To End Negative Body Obsession and Start Living Happily and Confidently, by Sara Maria

The IntenSati Method: The Seven Secret Principles to Thinner Peace, by Patricia Moreno www.satilife.com

Hip Tranquil Chick: A Guide to Life On and Off the Yoga Mat, by Kimberly Wilson

Tranquilista: Mastering the Art of Enlightened Work and Mindful Play, by Kimberly Wilson

Happy Yoga: 7 Reasons Why There's Nothing to Worry About, by Steve Ross

A Course in Weight Loss: 21 Spiritual Lessons for Surrendering Your Weight Forever, by Marianne Williamson

The Age of Miracles: Embracing the New Midlife, by Marianne Williamson

Spirit Junkie: A Radical Road to Self-Love and Miracles, by Gabrielle Bernstein

Woman's Retreat Book: A Guide to Restoring, Rediscovering and Reawakening Your True Self—In a Moment, An Hour, Or a Weekend, by Jennifer Louden

Woman's Comfort Book: A Self-Nurturing Guide for Restoring Balance in Your Life, by Jennifer Louden

Starring in Your Own Life: Reveal Your Hidden Star Quality and Make Your Life a Blockbuster Hit, by Lena Nozizwe

Quantum Wellness Cleanse: The 21-Day Essential Guide to Healing Your Mind, Body and Spirit, by Kathy Freston

Life Beyond Your Eating Disorder: Reclaim Yourself, Regain Your Health, Recover for Good, by Johanna S. Kandel

The Way of the Fertile Soul: Ten Ancient Chinese Secrets to Tap into a Woman's Creative Potential, by Randine Lewis

Women, Work & the Art of Savoir Faire: Business Sense & Sensibility, by Mireille Guiliano

French Women for All Seasons: A Year of Secrets, Recipes, & Pleasure, by Mireille Guiliano

French Women Don't Get Fat, by Mireille Guiliano www.frenchwomendontgetfat.com

The EveryGirl's Guide to Life, by Maria Menounos

A Survival Guide for Landlocked Mermaids, by Margot Datz

Body Brilliance: Mastering Your Five Vital Intelligences, by Alan Davidson

Learn, chickie, learn

In addition to eggs #5 + #6 wise peeps, go here:

www.mrsgraham.com for tell it like it is karma clearing by a gifted psychic

www.JanaFleming.com to experience healing peace in all areas of your life

www.feelgoodexpress.com if you want to "live longer, feel better, look younger, and attract abundance" you must hop on this express!

www.abouthandwriting.com to learn about yourself + others through graphology

www.mayamalay.com for spiritual support based on Buddhism

www.newlifedirections.com for conscious life-changing empowerment
www.astrologyzone.com for amazingly accurate monthly insights... for free!
www.destinytarot.com for tarot + astrological-based forecasts
www.mylifetime.com for freebie weekly "what's in the stars" for your sign messages
www.dailyom.com for awesome lessons + daily doses of om

playlist
Keep Your Head Up, by Andy Grammer
The Time of My Life, by David Cook
All I Know, by David Rhodes
Shine, Depeche Mode
Alive, by Dirty Vegas
I'm Letting Go, by Francesca Battistelli
Proud, by Heather Small
Suddenly I See, by KT Tunstall
Don't Stop 'Til You Get Enough, by Michael Jackson
Born Again, by Newsboys
If Today Was Your Last Day, by Nickelback
Something to Believe In, by Parachute
Alive, by Pearl Jam
You Are More, by Tenth Avenue North
You Can't Always Get What You Want, by The Rolling Stones
Bittersweet Symphony, by The Verve

Chapter 11: Your All-Access Pass to Magic Red Carpet Rides For Life

No Regrets: 101 Fabulous Things To Do Before You're Too Old, Married, or Pregnant by Sarah Ivens, (#1 suggestion? Learn to love champagne. That's my girl!)
Cowgirl Smarts: Hope to Rope a Kick-ass life by Ellen Reid Smith
www.partyfeathers.com for boas
www.prosounddepot.com for disco balls

www.rhinestonejewelry.com for tiaras (already mentioned but worth repeating)

playlist
Beautiful Life, by Ace of Base
Don't Look Back, by Boston
Brand New, by Icharus
Gifts of The Goddess, by Karen Drucker
Live Like We're Dying, by Kris Allen
Butterfly, by Lenny Kravitz
Free Bird, by Lynyrd Skynyrd
Twinkle Twinkle Little Star, by Mary Stahl
Peace, by Sabrina Johnson
Crazy, by Seal
Life is Beautiful, by Sixx:A.M.
Brand New Day, by Sting
Life is a Highway, by Tom Cochrane

La Gratitude

> *At times our own light goes out and is rekindled by a spark from another person. Each of us has cause to think with deep gratitude of those who have lighted the flame within us.*
> ~ ALBERT SCHWEITZER

There are no words known to humankind that can fittingly express the colossal appreciation that is nestled in my heart for the many supportive souls, near and afar, known and unknown, who sent supportive sparks to me from this book's conception to its birth. My global tribe, many of whom are busier than any bee, found a few seconds here and there often to send "happy writing" wishes, "how's the book going?" queries, and "can I help?" invitations. My strong belief that this book could, should, must come to be was affirmed repeatedly with each thoughtful outreach. A round of applause for everyone who lighted the flame within me in his or her own special way, with an extra whoop and *merci beaucoup* to…

…my dear husband Joe, who never once freaked out and packed up after seeing me wear the same jammies four days in a row while I was cocooning to create this book. Your belief in me on all levels is the most splendid gift of all. You are the rock that keeps me grounded, yet untethered. I love, respect, admire, and learn from you so much.

...the other special guy in my life, my father Mel, whose daily morning phone pep chats sprinkled with the occasional "I am very proud of you, Willie" made me beam ear-to-ear and sit a bit taller in my desk chair as I hit the keys. If anyone should be writing a book on how to live life, it's you, Dad. I love you with all my heart.

...my "kids" Roxi and Oliver who spent many a day and night motivating me with their tail wags and *bises* even when I wasn't tossing them treats. I could always count on you two to eagerly join me in a happy dance whenever a chapter was wrapped. Oliver, I can now say that your shredding of my Chapter 4 edits was adorable. Barrels of Beggin' Strips coming your way, kiddies.

...my beloved Nana who will always be my super-stylish role model for fierce independence. You taught me how to embrace and enjoy life, and you are solely responsible for my obsession with sparkly costume jewelry and the beach and all that comes with it—suntan, seashells, sleeves of saltines, and sips of sugar-free tea. I miss you so much.

...my Aunt Delores whom I've admired from afar since I was a little girl. Your beauty, grace, love of travel and adventure, worldly knowledge, and many Golden Door visits (including two with me!) has played a big part in who I have become and what I believe I can do—anything!

...Catherine for being my tireless cheerleader. The continuous flow of your rah-rah, sis boom bah uplifting texts (even when I pulled all nighters—chime—there you were!), email messages, snail mail care packages, and chapter reviews/comments boosted me every step of the way. We may not be fluent in French (yet), but we did walk away from class with a lifelong sister-like bond that I will treasure dearly eternally. You are my forever partner in wine, anti-whine, and all things divine. Clink, clink to you, sweetie.

...*mon ame souer*, Edwige, for helping me transform stress into strength and for permanently installing *joie de vivre* into my essence. You are a gifted healer and teacher whose beauty runs deep on all levels. Your belief in my creative endeavors and me played a huge part in the manifestation of this book. In your name I proclaim, "Victory to *moi*!" *Gros bisous*.

...my dear eternal soul sister Jane—the light you transmitted and all the "you go girl!" messages from Hong Kong kept me energized—what would I have done without your positive vibes and belief in me from the first day we met in Bali? You are a gifted, connected, and deeply appreciated spirit.

...Claire, my fun-loving Aussie sissy—you continuously entertained and inspired me with your über creative written words praising mine and the occasional bit of *bijoux* that you produced with your own two hands and thoughtfully sent my way made me squeal with delight! You always make me smile. We WILL be successful in our recruitment efforts for Versailles soirée table dancers the next time we meet in Paris. But we will NOT order champagne mojitos ever again. *Ever*.

...Kathleen, my twinkly, purple-loving, spa girlie-girlfriend, thank you for listening to all my sparkly thoughts without chuckling, for encouraging me to tell the Rox story to anyone within earshot, and for sharing your moments of synchronicity with me. You are an angel. May your tiara never tarnish and may all your dream board wishes come true!

...Tammy, Janet, and two other dear friends (who will go unnamed because there are mean people out there who can and will twist anything), for taking a peek at a couple of verses and/or chapters with my day job in mind. If anyone thinks a County Attorney and a tiara and a tutu don't mix, I'm sending 'em your way!

...Drew who patiently listened to my biz and book ideas, which were inevitably the topic of my ramble whenever he responded in the affirmative to my "I'm thirsty" emails. I could always count on you to tell me what you thought about where I was heading—the good, the bad, and the ugly. Many a good idea was borne (and fortunately, many a bad one died) at the YC and Roxy's. The next round of fruity drinks is on me!

...Anna, the youngest member of Team Denise + Rox, who refers to me as "her main human mentor". As I always tell you, you are very knowing and wise beyond your years, but I must correct you (aha! finally!). It is *you* who mentored me in many ways. The thoughtful message you sent when I was pulling out my hair—the one that included these so true words: "...there are no shortcuts to places worth going...you can't expect it to be absolutely wonderful and easy...you get one or the other, my friend"—was printed and placed in each and every draft of my manuscript. I chose wonderful with you in mind. I am very proud of you! Keep singing your song!

...Linda, my cherished, respected literary agent who graciously granted me permission to soar solo here, to collaborate with only the universe. Your belief in my work has propelled me for many moons. See you in the Big Apple one day soon to celebrate our big deal!

...all the sparkle experts who shared their tips and thoughts for this book—your words greatly enhanced THE message—a round of virtual bubbles for Aavo, Anna, Barbara, Byron, Catherine T., Catherine W., Chris, Claire, Dawn, Denise D., Denise V.-B., Drew, Edwige, Erin, Greg, Halle, Herb, Jane, Janet, Jennifer, Jimmy, Jodie, Joe, John a.k.a. Bodyguard, Karen, Kathleen, Kathryn, Krista, Kristen, L.S., Lena, Lenny, Marcelle, Margaret, Niki, Rod, Sonny, Suzanne, Tammy, Teresa, and Wendy.

...my "carrot at the end of the stick" team (as in—chapter done, I deserve a treat!): Janice, Toni and her precious daughter Reagan, and Linda who not only created, supplied and/or stowed the merch in their own special and sparkly way, they took the time to send sweet treats, added bonuses, and thoughtful notes of encouragement. We're all here to support each other and I can't thank each of you enough for doing just that for me!

...the gurus who transformed, inspired, and empowered me to explore and explode my creative side through their books, blogs, posts, workshops, retreats, videos, teleclasses, online courses, art, right brain business savvy, and more— Kristin McGee, David

Romanelli, Goddess Leonie, Gala Darling, Kimberly Wilson, Maya Malay, Edwige Gilbert, Randine Lewis, Jodie Eisenhardt (sarong sista!), and Susan Ariel Rainbow Kennedy, a.k.a. SARK. You all fearlessly rock *and* roll!

…my awesome Createspace project team. *Wow*! I sensed a genuine interest in my work from the get go and it never waned. The constructive, instructive, supportive, and creative guidance and assistance provided no matter what stage the book was in is greatly appreciated. You all gave me the space to create and translate my ideas from heart to paper. What more can a writer desire?

…my Facebook friends and Rox's fans who joined me every step of the way—your comments, support, interest, and encouragement added to the fun of the creative process.

…and last, but certainly not least and truly always first in the big scheme of things, God, my angels, and the entire universe who constantly co-create and recreate my life with and for me. There's no better creative partnership, and with no contract required! The divine plan and flow is always binding, with both parties walking away happy. Imagine that. *Amen*!

About The Author

Denise Marie Nieman is a writer, globetrotter, big-time government lawyer, yogini, Francophile, entrepreneur, creative old soul, natural health Ph.D'er, and an ex-ballerina who still wears a tiara and tutu. She's also Rox's handler and chief wineglass washer and the Chick-in-Charge of Concert Chick Productions, LLC, a biz she created to inspire the girls of this world to enjoy a sparkly, balanced life. Denise's first book, *Christmas Party Celebrations: 71 New and Exciting Party Plans for Holiday Fun*, was published in 1997. Stay tuned for a reprint of this party book as part of the Concert Chick brand's series dedicated to living a life filled with discovery, fun, well-being, and adventure. Denise lives by the beach in Jupiter, Florida, with her amazing husband, Joe, and their two hairy, precious kids, Roxi and Oliver.

✪ ✪ ✪ ✪

We'd love to hear about your Rox Detox experience. What worked, what didn't, your fave part, the most dreaded? Don't be shy! There are a few ways to connect to tell us what's on your mind and to otherwise keep in touch because we are family now:

Supersonic electronic: denise@concertchick.com
Tweet on Twitter: @theconcertchick
Like on Facebook: www.facebook.com/concertchick
Send care packages to: P.O. Box 504, Palm Beach, FL 33480
(Rox adores Peeps + Prada)

And please visit us at www.concertchick.com, a global virtual community devoted to brightening your journey's path with encouraging words, lifestyle resources, and fun stuff (with a bit of fluff because sometimes you just have to go there!)

Sparkle on, Concert Chick extraordinaire! The world needs your magnificence, brilliance, and radiance.

Made in the USA
Lexington, KY
28 March 2012